IMPROVING INCENTIVES

Improving Incentives for the Low-Paid

Edited by
Alex Bowen
Head of Policy Analysis and Statistics
National Economic Development Office

and

Ken Mayhew
Economic Director
National Economic Development Office

Foreword by Walter Eltis
Director General
National Economic Development Office

in association with the
NATIONAL ECONOMIC
DEVELOPMENT OFFICE

First published 1990

Published by
MACMILLAN ACADEMIC AND PROFESSIONAL LIMITED
Houndmills, Basingstoke, Hampshire RG21 2XS
and London
Companies and representatives
throughout the world

Typeset by Footnote Graphics,
Warminster, Wiltshire

Printed in Great Britain by

WBC Print Ltd., Bridgend, Mid Glam.

British Library Cataloguing in Publication Data
Improving incentives for the low-paid.
1. Great Britain. Personnel. Remuneration. Incentive
schemes
I. Bowen, Alex   II. Mayhew, Ken   III. National Economic
Development Office
331.21640941
ISBN 0–333–52544–2 (hardcover)
ISBN 0–333–52545–0 (paperback)

Contents

v

List of Illustrations

List of Tables

Foreword

Walter Eltis

When I became Director General of the National Economic Development Office (NEDO) in November 1988, it was agreed that the *National Economic Development Office* would organize two conferences a year in which important economic or industrial policy issues would be discussed by an expert group of academic economists and representatives of the CBI and the TUC. Representatives of government departments would be present at the conferences to listen but they would not introduce policy papers. The issues for such conferences are ideally areas where governments are interested, where the precise policies they will adopt are still undecided, and where advice will therefore be helpful.

The enhancement of incentives for the low-paid is such an issue, and the National Economic Development Office organized its first policy seminar to discuss this in September 1989. The present book contains revised versions of the papers presented then, together with a concluding chapter (Chapter 9) which highlights some of the main themes which emerged.

In the last ten years, incentives have been improved at all income levels, but they have been enhanced far more for the high- than the low-paid. Until 1979 the highest earners kept 17 per cent of their marginal earnings but they now retain 60 per cent. In 1979 a good many of the lowest-paid were in fiscal and social security traps where they actually became worse off if they obtained a pay increase or took on extra part-time work that the authorities were aware of. Effective tax rates of over 100 per cent (including money lost from the withdrawal of benefits) are now far rarer than in 1979 but it is by no means uncommon for low earners to gain only 20p when they earn an extra £. Figure F.1 shows the extent to which effective tax rates have been reduced at different income levels between 1978 and 1989 and it demonstrates how there are still low earners who in effect face marginal tax rates that are comparable to those that the highest earners had to pay in 1979. They cannot arrange to be paid through corporations registered only in the Cayman Islands but the very poor will be no less anxious than the wealthy to avoid paying effective tax rates of 80 per cent. Like the highest earners they react to such rates

Figure F.1   Marginal tax rates including the withdrawal of benefits (married man, two children)*

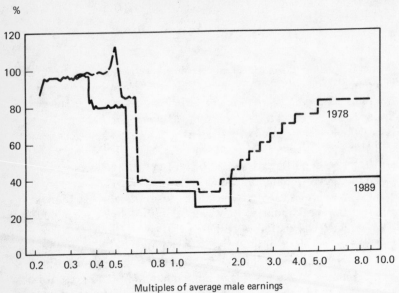

Multiples of average male earnings

* Wife not working and two children aged 4 and 6.

Source: DSS, NEDO estimates and smoothing.

by attempting to hide income, by going through tortuous processes to minimize what they must pay to the state (and maximize what they receive from it), and by simply not taking on extra work.

It is very damaging socially that there are known to be more than 200,000 families who are subject to such pressures because they face marginal tax rates of over 80 per cent. We know of 200,000 such families because they have legally known incomes which are subject to marginal deductions of 80 per cent or more. It is likely that there are many more who have reacted to such potential marginal tax rates by arranging with the cooperation of those who employ them to be paid in a manner where the surveillance of the state is evaded.

It is a matter of concern that families are subject to this degree of temptation to break laws. It is equally damaging that because the poorest stand to gain least from extra work, citizens are persuaded to acquiesce in breaches of the law by being willing to pay for work in cash without written receipts.

Marginal tax rates of 80 per cent or more have an economic cost. Where the low-paid react by not taking on work that is on offer, society loses potential production that could add to the national income and it also loses because of labour shortages which would be relieved if more worked. The functioning of the labour market is damaged because there are jobs on offer in parts of the United Kingdom which cannot be filled and there are workers available to do these jobs who prefer to stay at home because they stand to gain nothing financially from collecting fares on buses, sorting or delivering letters, or helping to clean a school. Hermione Parker reminds us that in 1985 only three-fifths of the fathers of four or more children were employed, and that they have to earn more than £150 a week to receive significantly more from paid work than the benefits to which they are entitled. The wives of unemployed workers are another group of United Kingdom citizens who stand to benefit only slightly if they work legally at modest rates of pay. Their declared earnings are deducted pound for pound from the income support their husbands receive, so they stand to gain nothing from ordinarily paid part-time work. A high fraction of women who work take only part-time jobs for obvious family reasons, but they cannot do the work which comes naturally to them if their husbands are unemployed. These are just two major examples out of many in Britain where family members cannot readily better their economic condition through legally paid work of a kind that is compatible with their talents and qualifications. West Germany does not deduct the incomes of wives from the unemployment benefits of husbands in this way.

The two examples illustrate the two principal traps. The unemployment trap sets a barrier which dissuades the unemployed and the wives of the unemployed from taking low paid work. The poverty trap makes it difficult for those with many dependants and modest technical qualifications to increase their incomes by working harder or longer. The wives of the unemployed whose families will gain nothing if they work are in the unemployment trap: the low-paid fathers of four or more children are in the poverty trap.

The National Economic Development Office serves the National Economic Development Council which includes 6 members of the Cabinet, 6 representatives of the CBI and 6 representatives of the TUC, so it is incumbent on us to seek policy changes which will have the support of all of these. We are also invited to 'give independent advice on ways of improving the economic performance, competitive power and efficiency of the nation' and such advice need not necessarily expect to receive tripartite support, but we can certainly anticipate the support of the Government, the CBI and the TUC for the furtherance of policies which will reduce the numbers caught in the unemployment and poverty traps. The government will welcome cost-effective measures which place onside families which are now caught offside because they cannot improve their financial circumstances through legally paid work, and it will welcome the improved economic performance that will ensue if more who are only qualified to do part-time or low paid work enter the labour market.

The industrialists whom the CBI represents will welcome any increased willingness by men and women to seek work. Average United Kingdom unemployment has now fallen to 5.7 per cent and there are many areas, especially in the South where unemployment rates are down to under 3 per cent. Companies and public employers in such areas now have many vacancies they are unable to fill. Anything that enhances the supply of labour to fill these will be helpful.

The trade unions will especially welcome any changes which enhance the incomes of the low paid. Almost all the measures that would lessen the numbers caught in the unemployment and the poverty traps would involve higher family incomes for the unemployed and the poor and for others besides, and especially those with below average incomes. There is therefore a good deal of potential support from the government, the CBI and the TUC for any developments which significantly reduce the numbers caught in the various traps.

There is, however, one way of reducing the numbers caught in the unemployment trap which would not receive universal support. If benefits are only receivable by those genuinely unable to find work, and they are withdrawn from those who refuse low-paid jobs, then the unemployed could be obliged to take work at rates of pay below current benefit levels. But such moves towards workfare involve the use of officials to force families towards work which could produce less money than they would receive from the state in the absence of such pressures. That could involve a degree of coercion and interference by officials in the detailed lives of individuals that used to be more commonly observed in the East than the West. It would certainly lack the support of the unions and it is likely that members of the government would far prefer a situation where the unemployed sought work because it paid them to do so, than because officials bullied them to work when this reduced their families' incomes at the same time.

Unfortunately the market approach to reducing the numbers in the various traps is extremely expensive. Those caught in the unemployment trap tend to be those with large families who are entitled to receive from income support between £11.75 and £20.80 depending on age for each child from the state (averaging perhaps £14.50) if they do not work. If all families with young children were allowed to receive £14.50 a week, that is, if child benefits were doubled from £7.25 to £14.50 a week, there would be no work disincentives to families with many children because they would receive £14.50 a child from the state whether they worked or not. But increasing child benefits to £14.50 a child for all children would cost about £4.5 billion a year, so easing the unemployment trap by ceasing to withdraw £7.25 a week of support per child from poor families when a parent takes officially paid work would have a budgetary cost equivalent to approximately 1 per cent of the national income.

If benefits are targeted at the poor, the unfortunate families involved will at the margin pay 25 per cent income tax plus a social security contribution of up to 9 per cent and in addition suffer a withdrawal of benefits which can cost them in total 80 per cent to 96 per cent of any extra income earned. If benefits such as child benefits are universally available, the poor will pay income tax and social security like almost everyone else when they earn more, but they will not be subject to a withdrawal of benefits in addition, so they will not face higher marginal taxation than the wealthy.

In the case of child support, extending the £14.50 a week benefit that the poor receive universally to the parents of all children will cut the effective marginal tax rates of the poor at an exchequer cost of perhaps £4.5 billion. The same analysis applies to other targeted benefits. If these are universalized, the low-paid will face lower effective taxation when they work so their incentives to take legally paid work will be enhanced, but at a heavy overall budgetary cost.

If over the medium term the British economy continues to grow at 2.5 per cent, approximately the average rate achieved since 1979, and real government expenditure continues to be allowed to grow about half as fast as the national income, taxes can be remitted to the extent of perhaps 1.25 per cent of total public expenditure each year, or by perhaps £2 billion. This means that over a five-year parliament a government that pursues these broad policies can remit taxation by a total of perhaps £10 billion.

Insofar as such remissions can be directed at the various poverty traps, incentives for the low-paid can be enhanced and the various difficulties referred to ameliorated. £10 billion over five years could be used to cut the standard rate of tax, and each percentage point cut (at an annual budgetary cost of about £2 billion) would enhance by 1 percentage point the fraction of marginal income that a low-paid worker who earned enough to pay tax could retain. Thresholds could be raised and this would increase the proportion of the low-paid who had no income tax obligation and who would therefore gain 25 per cent of any extra they earned at the margin. Some of the £10 billion which could become available to enhance incentives for the low-paid over five years could also be deployed to universalize some benefits and so reduce the extent to which these have to be withdrawn as the low paid take work. Any such movements towards the universalization of benefits would technically raise public expenditure instead of cutting taxation but the object would be to enhance incentives.

Several of the chapters in this volume are directed at the question of which of these courses of action would do most to improve incentives and take families out of the various traps which all deplore. Incentives, however, relate not only to the tax-benefit system. The incentives for those on the margins of economic activity to improve their skills matter too, and this volume is therefore also concerned with how the skills of those who can now command only low pay can best be enhanced, and how their prospects may be improved by other changes in the structure and working of the labour market.

In conclusion I would wish to emphasize that tax cuts are often spoken of as if they help only the better off and that it is extra public expenditure that is helpful to the whole community. In fact, if tax cuts are aimed especially at the lowest-paid members of the community in some of the ways which have been outlined, they will enhance the degree to which the poor can join the legal economy and at the same time contribute to the incomes of their own families. Extra public expenditure on social services can also benefit the whole community in various important ways, and it is for elected governments to decide whether those who need help most are best assisted via extra public expenditure or by reductions in taxation which are targeted especially at the various traps in which so many of the low-paid languish. It is therefore a great oversimplification to see extra public expenditure as assisting mainly the poor, and lower taxation as assisting mainly the better off. The low paid can be helped greatly by extra public expenditure, and by lower taxation that is targeted especially at their detailed financial circumstances.

The National Economic Development Office organized this first policy seminar to improve the level of understanding of some of these ssues, and we are grateful for the very great trouble that the authors of the chapters have taken to offer such interesting analyses of the questions. Their articles are of course entirely personal and it should not be assumed that any part of this book reflects the opinions or judgements of the National Economic Development Council or any of its members.

The detailed administration of the seminar and the presentation of the articles for publication has been handled by Maggie Hobbs, Liza McKinney and Michelle Shemming. The papers have been edited by Ken Mayhew, the Economic Director, and Alex Bowen, the Head of Policy Analysis and Statistics, who were responsible for the overall organisation of the conference.

I hope the book will receive close attention from those concerned with economic policy, that it will help to bring the low-paid into more effective competition in the labour market, and that it will gradually lead to improvements in the conditions in which they participate in our society.

WALTER ELTIS
Director General
National Economic Development Office

Notes on the Contributors

Tony Atkinson is Tooke Professor of Economic Science and Statistics at the London School of Economics.

Alex Bowen is Head of Policy Analysis and Statistics of the National Economic Development Office.

Dominic Brewer is a member of the Department of Economics at the University of Wisconsin–Milwaukee.

Walter Eltis is Director General of the National Economic Development Office.

Ewart Keep is a Research Fellow at the Industrial Relations Research Unit, University of Warwick.

Ken Mayhew is a Fellow of Pembroke College, Oxford, and Economic Director at the National Economic Development Office.

Patrick Minford is Edward Gonner Professor of Applied Economics at the University of Liverpool.

Hermione Parker is Secretary of the Basic Income Research Group and works at the House of Commons.

Paul Ryan is a Fellow of King's College, Cambridge.

Holly Sutherland is a Research Officer at the London School of Economics' Suntory–Toyota International Centre for Economics and Related Disciplines.

1 Incentives for the Low-Paid: Setting the Scene[1]

Alex Bowen, Dominic Brewer and
Ken Mayhew

Improving incentives for the low-paid is an important objective for the low-paid themselves and for the economy as a whole. Providing a constructive means for people to enhance their well-being by their own efforts is an appropriate social goal. The route may be working longer hours, or seeking out a better-paid job, or acquiring more marketable skills. Improving incentives is a matter of making the extra effort or investment entailed appear worthwhile. This also applies to people not currently receiving a wage, who might be discouraged from labour market participation because they do not regard the expected benefit from working as sufficient (this expected benefit depends not only on gross wage rates attached to particular jobs and on the tax–benefit system but also on the probability of acquiring particular jobs). Thus we should not restrict ourselves to consideration of the currently low-paid, but should also bear in mind the circumstances of groups with a marginal attachment to the labour market, including the unemployed. The economy as a whole can benefit through the extra output produced when the quality and quantity of labour input is increased. This is particularly important when demographic trends point to a fall in the number of young people entering the labour market in the next few years (NEDO, 1988).

The design of appropriate incentives for individuals who are low-paid or who have marginal attachment to the labour market depends on how they are likely to react to changes in their net income from employment and from other sources. For this reason, we survey in section 1 some of the academic work on labour supply responses. Given the complexity of much of this literature, this section contains some technical material which some readers may wish to skip. Section 2 briefly discusses the possible definitions of low pay and reviews some data about its incidence in the UK, as well the participation of marginal groups.

1

We then proceed, in section 3, to look at the role of the tax and
social security systems and the way they interact. Specifically we
attempt to evaluate the UK's record on incentives with regard to the
working poor and the unemployed. However, it is also important to
consider various aspects of the labour market, since it is there that
gross wages are determined. We look at a number of these in section
4: the 'good' jobs/'bad' jobs debate; direct administrative intervention in wage setting via Wages Councils; some recent developments
in collective bargaining; the impact of employment protection legislation; and an evaluation of policies designed to facilitate the participation of women in the labour force, such as maternity benefits and
childcare provisions. We present our conclusion in section 5, stressing
the importance of the labour market for incentives, and suggesting a
number of areas in which further research is needed.

1 LABOUR SUPPLY: WOULD CHANGES IN INCENTIVES MATTER?

The decision whether or not an individual should participate in the
labour market, and the extent of his or her participation, is a supply
side decision. In this section, we look at how this has been modelled
by economists and some of the problems encountered. We seek to set
this analysis within the context of other supply side influences, and
possible constraints placed on the participation decision by demand
side variables such as the structure of jobs, the restrictions placed by
employers on hours worked by their employees, and the overall availability of jobs. We provide a summary of the prevailing consensus,
such as it is, on supply responsiveness for the UK.

Some Theoretical and Methodological Issues

Traditionally labour supply has been analysed within the framework
of static neoclassical consumer theory: individuals maximize utility
subject to a budget constraint, by choosing an appropriate combination of goods (or income) and hours of leisure (work). In the simplest
model, indifference curves are continuous and convex and the budget
constraint consists of two linear segments determined by the net wage
rate and non-labour income. Labour force participants will work
extra hours and take less leisure the lower is the income they obtain
whether they work or not. If the wage rate is increased, the

substitution effect tends to increase labour supply but the income effect tends to reduce it. Some individuals will choose not to work at all. Social security benefits contribute to income obtained without work. The problem that people not in employment do not know what wage they would be paid with certainty is finessed. The demand for labour is simply assumed to establish a going rate for a particular type of labour. The vast literature on the subject has been devoted largely to the empirical task of measuring the substitution and income effects generated by wage change, within various specifications of labour supply. As Pencavel (1986) has pointed out, very few have actually questioned the validity of this basic model: it has been treated as a maintained hypothesis even though some empirical studies have produced results which would appear to be at odds with the predictions of the theory (see estimates reported in Table 1.1). On a more general level there is some unease about the use of such a simple model to analyse a complex, multidimensional decision, and there have been a variety of attempts to move beyond it.

In the very simplest model, the budget constraint facing individuals who work is linear, implying a constant wage rate for each hour worked. In reality, however, there are likely to be fixed costs (such as transportation) and benefits (such as health insurance) associated with working that are independent of the number of hours worked, and some employees receive pay on a piece rate or commission basis. As Hausman (1980) has shown, inclusion of these factors adds to the complexity of the budget constraint. For the UK, Brown *et al.* (1986, 1987), have stressed the impact of different types of payments systems on the shape of the budget constraint. Many workers have a basic wage rate with additional rates for certain hours, others are paid via a basic rate plus commission, yet others a salary that applies to a variable number of hours. Bonus systems of various sorts are common, and numerous types of merit pay and profit related pay have spread in recent years. A Treasury survey found that around 53 per cent of workers faced a non-linear system of pay, although the figure was considerably lower for women in general (39 per cent) and married women (32 per cent) in particular. Since women are more likely to be low-paid than men this feature of jobs, whilst potentially important, may not be so critical for our purposes.

Of course the major cause of non-linearities is the impact of the tax and benefit systems and their interaction. These arise because of the progressive tax system, with discrete rises in rates resulting in kinks. In the UK, means tested benefits like Family Credit (formerly Family

Income Supplement) and Housing Benefit, and the system of National
Insurance contributions also lead to discontinuities in budget constraints for some individuals (see, for example, Beenstock *et al.*,
1987). These alterations to the simple framework pose difficulties for
the measurement of labour supply responses, but given that the
relevant variable for an individual making a participation decision is
the *net* wage rate, their effects cannot be ignored. In some cases it is
possible to approximate the budget constraint by a linear segment
and identify an individual's optimal labour supply; in others it is
necessary to evaluate utility over each particular segment of the
budget constraint and determine the globally optimal point. In
empirical work early studies tended to ignore taxation and benefits or
confine themselves to a particular linear segment of the budget
constraint (as in Atkinson and Stern, 1980, for example). A number
of techniques have been used in an attempt to approximate the
behaviour of an individual faced by a complex constraint.

As attention has focused on the increasing participation of women
in the labour force, further alterations have been made to labour
supply models. An early extension was to move away from models
with just 'leisure' as one of the variables and towards a more general
model of the allocation of time (originally based on the work of
Becker, 1965). More recently a number of studies have attempted to
develop a more general theoretical framework for the analysis of
integrated life-cycle models of consumption and family labour supply
(for the UK, see for example, Atkinson and Stern, 1980; Blundell
and Walker, 1982; and Browning, Deaton and Irish, 1985). This
pioneering work greatly enriches the basic model by permitting the
explicit incorporation of demographic factors such as the number of
children in a household, and is especially apt for the analysis of
female labour supply.

Although we noted at the outset that the participation/hours
decision was a supply side one, it is clear that the budget constraint
faced is determined on the demand side of the labour market. Yet the
role of the demand side is often understated in both theoretical and
empirical work. Rigidities in the labour market may prohibit or limit
changes in hours of work within any particular job (see for example,
Blundell *et al.*, 1984; Brown *et al.*, 1986). Taking account of such
phenomena may alter supply side estimates. One of the most obvious
limitations on free choice of hours is that employers generally insist
that their employees work a standard schedule of hours per week,
and weeks per year. In the short run there is an 'all or nothing' choice

facing those contemplating entering the labour market. If the employer places an upper limit on the number of hours available to existing employees, then the effective marginal wage rate beyond this number will be zero unless a second job is acquired. Over the past few decades, hours per week have declined, whilst holidays have lengthened. These changes have been less pronounced for women, however, reflecting greater numbers in part-time work. Indeed, with a quarter of all employment now part-time, there may be more flexibility in choosing the number of hours to be worked. Nevertheless there is a sense in which hours are *collectively*, rather than individually, determined by employers, often in consultation with the trade unions (this point is made in the discussion following Blundell and Walker's 1988 paper). Most obviously, though, the number of hours that an employer is prepared to offer will depend on the overall level of demand in the economy, and it is on this which we focus below. In the longer run it may be that a worker is able to choose an occupation with hours that best suit his or her preferences. In a competitive world wage rates will respond to the variations in supply to different occupations, with compensating differentials arising.

It is not too unrealistic, however, to believe that the labour market, with all its institutional rigidities, does not function perfectly. All but the most ardent neoclassical economist would accept that the labour market may not always clear, and that there might be involuntary unemployment due to deficient aggregate demand. If this is the case, then any incentive/disincentive effects that operate will depend partly on the level of demand (Micklewright, 1986). Individuals will be faced with a restricted choice of job opportunities (dependent on regional variations, level of education and so forth) and have to undertake longer job search. Those in work may see overtime hours cut back. For the UK, a survey conducted for the Treasury among 3300 households revealed considerable evidence of demand constraints (Brown *et al.*, 1986, 1987). Only 19 per cent could work more paid hours in their main job, whilst 79 per cent could not (2 per cent did not answer). The possibility that this constraint could be overcome by acquiring an additional part-time job was found to apply to only 3 per cent of the constrained group. Taking into account this second job, and the *possibility* of another job, an absolute minimum of 55 per cent were constrained. The pattern was similar for both men and women. This evidence is revealing in indicating the extent to which the demand side may be important in restricting labour supply responses. This survey was conducted during the autumn of 1980, a period when the demand for labour was undoubtedly low, so the constraint may have been particularly severe. Further evidence on the extent of hours constraints is provided by Dex (1988) using the 'Women and Employment' survey data.

An issue related to the level of demand, and one that has received rather less attention, is the *nature* of jobs. Not only will the number of job opportunities facing an individual have an important influence on his or her supply decision, but so will the type of jobs on offer. Much of the labour economics literature in the 1970s focused on this idea, with the development of the concepts of 'job competition' (Thurow, 1975), internal labour markets and segmentation (Doeringer and Piore, 1971), but little has been said on its importance for labour supply decisions. Considering the qualitative nature of trends in labour force participation (such as the shift to white collar jobs, or towards part-time work) this is, perhaps, somewhat surprising. It would appear to be an area in which research is warranted.

In empirical work there have been a number of attempts to capture the effects of the demand side on labour supply but in general it is captured via the determination of the net wage. The possibility that prime age males may not be free to choose their hours of work is explicitly modelled in Blundell and Walker (1982) who estimate both a 'rationed' and 'unrationed' leisure-goods model, whilst Minford and Ashton (1989) include a number of proxies for demand in their regression equations (such as employment and unemployment over a decade, and industry group dummies).

Thus economists have generated a vast literature on labour supply with considerable developments in both theoretical and empirical work. In fact three generations have been identified in empirical estimation of labour supply (Heckman *et al.*, 1981). The first generation studies tended to adopt the direct labour supply specification approach, made no distinction between participation/non-participation and intensity of labour supply (hours of work), and made no allowance for non-linearities in budget constraints. Second generation studies increasingly focused on the latter (due to taxation and fixed costs of working). To this we may add third generation, namely the development of dynamic and life-cycle models. This third generation has developed alongside the continuing use and extension of second generation models. The literature has reached an impressive degree of sophistication. Within the narrow confines of the basic two-dimensional model (money versus leisure) a whole host of variables can now be captured, including demographic influences.

Elasticity Estimates for the UK: A Summary of the Evidence

In the preceding section we have attempted to provide some feel for the difficulties of modelling labour supply. Given the large number of possible specifications of utility and labour supply functions it will not come as a surprise to readers that there exists a wide range of elasticity estimates. Here we do not attempt to make detailed comparison of these (such an exercise is fraught with problems), but rather provide a brief overview of the prevailing consensus, to the extent that it exists. We concentrate on results from cross-sectional data, which are widely regarded as more useful than earlier time-series studies. More technical surveys with an emphasis on US literature may be found in Pencavel (1986) for men, and Killingsworth and Heckman (1986) for women.

One might ask *why* labour supply estimates are important for incentives, especially as the estimates reported are for a particular sample of individuals at one point in time. These cannot be independent of the incentives then prevailing. Thus it may be that married women are more responsive precisely *because* of the tax–benefit system, and that other incentives also work in this way. LSE's TAXMOD model for simulating reform proposals thus takes no account of behavioural responses and reports only 'first round' effects. Atkinson and Sutherland (1988) note that it would be misleading to present results as though the responses were known with much certainty. We would argue, however, that policy proposals cannot be considered without some background knowledge of the likely responses (and particularly here since our main interest is specifically that of improving incentives). A reform may change marginal tax rates but this is not especially important if labour supply decisions (participation or the supply of more or fewer hours) are unaffected (Dilnot *et al.*, 1988). The Institute for Fiscal Studies has attempted to incorporate supply elasticity estimates into simulations of reform proposals (see for example, Blundell *et al.*, 1986, 1988).

Table 1.1 shows the situation for British men. The results we report give estimates for some or all (where estimated) of the following: the uncompensated elasticity of hours of work with respect to wages (i.e. the combined income and substitution effects); the income elasticity (or as Pencavel, 1986, terms it, the 'marginal propensity to earn'), measuring the effect of changes in non-wage income on hours worked (i.e. the income effect); and the income compensated elasticity of hours with respect to wages (i.e. the substitution effect).

Table 1.1　Elasticity estimates for men[1]

	Own-wage elasticity[2]		Income elasticity
	Uncompensated	*Compensated*	
Brown *et al.* (1973)[3]	−0.131	0.223	−0.35
Layard (1978)[4]	0.13	−0.09	−0.04
Atkinson and Stern (1980)[5]	−0.16	−0.09	−0.07
Ashworth and Ulph (1981a)[6]	−0.13	0.23	−0.36
Blundell and Walker (1982)[7]	−0.23	0.13	−0.36
Brown *et al.* (1982–3)[8] (a)	−0.33	0.17	−0.50
(b)	−0.14	0.30	−0.44
Blundell and Walker (1983)[9]	−0.004	0.20	−0.20
Brown *et al.* (1987)[10]	0.00	0.10	−0.10
Minford and Ashton (1989)[11]	−0.07	0.13	−0.20

Sources: Greenhalgh and Mayhew (1981) Table 3; Pencavel (1986) Table 1.2; original studies.

Notes:
1. We report a representative estimate from each study on British married men. Footnotes below provide some details of each study but readers are strongly urged to refer to the original sources for completeness, since there is considerable variation in methodology and data sources. Life-cycle estimates are reported in the text.
2. Elasticities are own-wage elasticities on hours worked evaluated at sample means and total income elasticities evaluated at sample means.
3. 1971 British Market Research Bureau sample of 284 married men; we report estimates where husband only works (col. 4B, Table 1, p. 274 and Pencavel, 1986). Non-linear budget constraint. Ordinary Least Squares (OLS) estimation. Uncompensated own-wage elasticity becomes less negative as wage rate rises and eventually becomes positive.
4. 1974 General Household Survey (GHS) sample of 2700 married men. Linear specification. OLS estimates.
5. 1973 Family Expenditure Survey (FES) sample of 1617 households with male head. Stone–Geary utility function; linear portion of budget constraint was used (i.e. households outside particular earnings range were excluded). Maximum Likelihood Estimation (MLE). Uncompensated own-wage elasticity becomes less negative as wage rate rises and eventually becomes positive. Note that the uncompensated elasticity is reported (p. 214) but compensated and income elasticities are *not* directly reported by Atkinson and Stern but calculated by Pencavel (1986).
6. 1971 British Market Research Bureau sample of 335 married men. We report estimates from estimation of generalized Constant Elasticity of Substitution (CES) indirect utility function with non-endogenous non-linear budget constraint. (Summarized in Table 10.2, p. 136 and in Pencavel, 1986).
7. 1974 FES sample of 103 households with working husband *and* wife.

MLE. Joint labour supply and commodity demand system. Stone–Geary indirect utility function with linear budget constraint. Figures for elasticities are those reported by Pencavel (1986) as *implied* by parameter estimates. Blundell and Walker report a 'labour supply' elasticity of −0.2863 (Table 3, p. 326).

8. 1980 Treasury sample of 810 (a) one- and (b) two-worker households. Estimates reported are for families with 2 children. Applied methodology as in Ashworth and Ulph (1981a), see note 6.

9. As Blundell and Walker (1982), see note 7, except 1971 FES sample of 308.

10. Treasury sample. Estimates reported in Minford and Ashton (1989).

11. 1980 GHS sample of 7119. Direct estimation of labour supply function using a sample grouped according to appropriate budget constraint segment. Estimates reported are from revised paper, Chapter 4 in this volume. Note that the reported figures are direct coefficient estimates on net marginal wage and income, rather than calculations of elasticities at sample means.

It would appear that men are relatively unresponsive to changes in wage rates. The mean compensated wage elasticity is 0.13, with all but two of the studies reporting a positive coefficient. Income elasticities are, without exception, negative and rather larger in absolute terms. Of course a summary table by its very nature conceals a great deal of information; these studies use various specifications, and different data sets. Recent estimates which make use of models of labour supply over a person's life-cycle report similar findings to those in Table 1.1. In these models, the wage elasticity of labour supply refers to the increase in labour which a person would plan to supply in periods when he expected his real wage to be higher. For supply in terms of hours, Browning *et al.* (1985) report an intertemporal substitution elasticity of this sort of 0.4. Blundell and Walker (1986), using a number of specifications, put compensated elasticities in the range 0.013 to 0.041 and income elasticities between −0.227 and −0.315 depending on household composition. In general it is found that younger men tend to be more responsive to wage changes, and that the addition of children to the family unit also increases responsiveness.

Table 1.2 shows a selection of estimates for married women: we report the responsiveness of labour supply to the own-wage, the husband's wage and unearned income with respect to both participation and hours of work. The results are rather less consistent than those produced for men, although certainly they indicate a far greater responsiveness to wage changes than those for men.

Table 1.2   Elasticity of hours and elasticity of participation estimates for women[1]

	Own wage[2]	Husband's wage	Unearned income
(a) *Participation*			
Layard *et al.* (1980)[3]	0.49	−0.28	−0.04
Greenhalgh (1980)[4]	0.355	−0.452[5]	
Zabalza (1983)[6]	0.41	−0.09	0.00
Arrufat and Zabalza (1986)[7]	1.41	−0.93	−0.14
(b) *Elasticity of hours*[8]			
Layard *et al.* (1980)	0.08	−0.10	−0.003
Greenhalgh (1980)	0.637	−0.235	
Zabalza (1983)	1.59	−1.12	−0.18
Arrufat and Zabalza (1986)	0.62	−0.34	−0.06
(c) *Overall elasticity*			
Layard *et al.* (1980)	0.49	−0.32	−0.04
Greenhalgh (1980)	0.992	−0.687	
Zabalza (1983)	2.00	−1.21	−0.18
Arrufat and Zabalza (1986)	2.03	−1.27	−0.20

Notes:
1. We report estimates from studies of *married* women using British data. There are a number of additional studies such as those of Ruffell (1981) and Ashworth and Ulph (1981b), using small samples and producing results which the authors themselves regard as tentative. Life-cycle estimates and Joshi's 1986 study of single as well as married women are discussed in the text.
2. Elasticities are evaluated at sample means unless otherwise stated.
3. 1974 GHS sample of 3877 married women. Participation and hours modelled as joint decision. Probability function estimated for participation. Labour supply function specified using predicted wage of wife. No account taken of tax system. Results reported are those in Table 2, p. 159.
4. 1971 GHS sample of 4453 married women. Note that participation and hours of work decisions are treated as independent, with specified participation and labour supply functions with allowance for non-linearities in budget constraints. OLS estimation. Results are those reported in Table 3, p. 307.
5. Greenhalgh reports the elasticity of couples net income if wife were not in work (both husbands income and unearned income are therefore included).
6. 1974 GHS sample of 3495 married women using a CES direct utility function with complete budget constraint. MLE.
7. As in note 6, with allowance for optimization errors.
8. The studies reported, other than Greenhalgh (1980), calculate elasticities of hours worked conditional on participation.

Additional evidence can be cited on the effects of age and children on female labour supply. Given that childrearing responsibilities tend to fall on women it is hardly surprising that the presence of dependants appears to reduce both participation and hours worked. Greenhalgh (1980) concluded that 'for the parents of young children, the extra financial burden is not sufficient to lead to increased working by the wife, since the time required for care of the children is of paramount importance, whereas in families with teenagers the financial pressures dominate' (p. 308). Layard *et al.* (1980) produce a similar finding, that after about age fourteen children cease to have much downward impact on participation. More recent work by Zabalza (1983) and Arrufat and Zabalza (1986) confirms that it is young children which dramatically reduce the probability of participation. Typical results are reproduced in Table 1.3. These estimates are based on 1974 General Household Survey (GHS) data.

There has been much work in the United States investigating the economics of fertility. It is argued that family structure cannot be considered totally exogenous in determining labour supply, since decisions on these matters are simultaneous. If this is the case, elasticity estimates are to be treated with extra caution for younger married women (Greenhalgh and Mayhew, 1981). Some recent work by Sprague (1988) has attempted to model the joint labour force participation/childbirth decision for the UK, using time series data.

Table 1.3   The effect of children on the probability of participation

Family composition	Age of Wife	
	25–34	*35–44*
Base case	0.728	0.707
1 child aged 0–2	0.242	0.222
1 child aged 3–5	0.582	0.556
1 child aged 14–15	0.815	0.798
2 children aged 0–2	0.021	0.018
2 children aged 0–2 and 3–5	0.133	0.120
2 children aged 0–2 and 14–15	0.334	0.320

Source: Arrufat and Zabalza (1986) Table IV, p. 60.

Note:
These probabilities are evaluated for a married women with gross hourly earnings of £0.58, whose husband's net earnings are £41.63 per week, with net unearned family income of £4.92 per week, who is white, and enjoys good health.

She shows that male earnings affect participation with a negative coefficient and fertility with a positive one. The converse is true of female earnings. For the youngest group (16–19) in her sample, wages make no contribution to labour force activity. Other important explanatory variables include male earnings, education, vacancies and numbers of children. It is clear that family commitments are closely bound up with the labour supply decisions of married women, and that consequently it is particularly difficult to model fully this group's behaviour.

Married Women with Unemployed Husbands

The studies above are for households in which the husband is employed. What if this is not the case? Layard *et al*. (1980) found that 'wives with unemployed husbands are 31 percentage points less likely to work than otherwise similar wives with husbands at work'. Dilnot and Kell (1989) in a similar vein conclude that the benefit system has a significant disincentive effect on women whose husbands are unemployed, and that this group does respond to marginal changes in incentives: in 1984, 60 per cent of wives participated in the labour market when the household head was employed, but only 25 per cent participated when the head was unemployed.

Single Women

Largely because of the restriction imposed by availability of data, virtually no work has been done specifically on single women. One attempt by Joshi (1986) using the 1980 'Women and Employment' study estimated a (compensated) own-wage elasticity of 0.35 for single women (0.45 for married) and an unearned income elasticity of −0.10 (−0.32). On this evidence unmarried women would appear to be slightly less responsive.

The Elderly and the Disabled

In addition to the above studies there is some evidence available as to the responsiveness of some special groups – the elderly and the disabled – which might be important for policy measures, particularly social security proposals.

In response to the declining labour force participation of older people a number of studies have been undertaken (mainly in the US) to analyze the supply decisions of this group. Generally this has focused on the retirement decision, rather than labour supply per se. The only major study conducted with UK data is that of Zabalza *et al.* (1980), applied to a large 1977 sample of 1483 men and 1207 women, aged 50–73. Using maximum likelihood estimation (MLE) of a CES utility function, they find wage elasticities to be small (−0.02 for men and 0.37 for women), and income elasticities of −0.023 for men and −0.38 for women. Those just under pensionable age tend to be more responsive, with poor health being a significant factor in the retirement decision. Thus, on this limited evidence, it would appear that elderly men at least are not very different from their younger colleagues in the labour force.

As with the elderly, the responsiveness of disabled workers has received little attention. The only evidence available is for the United States where Hausman (1985) and Halpern and Hausman (1986) have developed models of the decision to apply for disability insurance. The latter is a social security programme paying disabled workers an amount equal to what they would receive on retirement. Allowing for uncertainty as to whether or not someone is accepted into the programme, it is shown that 'individuals in the sample behave much as other prime age males have been estimated to behave' (Halpern and Hausman, 1986). Needless to say the applicability of these results to the United Kingdom is open to question.

Implications for Policy

We draw the following conclusions from the preceding survey of empirical labour supply literature: first, it seems clear that the responsiveness of prime age males to own-wage changes is relatively small; second, married women are probably more responsive to wage changes; third, there is some limited evidence to suggest that the elderly and disabled are not very much different from those not in these groups.

What does this summary of likely supply side responses imply for the successful application of policies designed to improve incentives for the low paid? There are two obvious difficulties. First, as we have shown, there is a wide range of estimates. Second, the simple fact that the specifications of labour supply used to obtain these are often very different makes it difficult to gauge the probable policy impact (Blundell *et al.*, 1988). Given this, it may be that one is ill-advised to derive policy implications that are too firm. What we have surveyed are estimates of an *individual's* labour supply decision focusing on the role of net labour income. It is not at all clear that the *aggregate* effect of policy changes on labour supply can be inferred. It is not a straightforward matter to translate, for example, wage and income elasticities into tax–benefit elasticities. There may be factors at work other than simply the monetary: for example, Blank (1985) has found that in the United States welfare income has a stronger negative effect on hours worked than does other non-labour income, implying that it is treated somewhat differently by individuals. People may also be inadequately informed about expected wage rates and their benefit entitlements. Many of the labour supply studies cited thus far have been conducted specifically in order to simulate the effects of tax and benefit changes. These are by construction the most relevant for policy analysis in terms of specification and estimation. Even then, however, they are generally designed to simulate marginal changes in policy. Since many of the policy prescriptions often suggested involve large changes in wage rates or income, it is possible that there might be a large supply response in aggregate.

2   LOW PAY AND PARTICIPATION: THE BRITISH PICTURE

In this section we provide some background on the incidence of low pay, and on participation rates for Britian. We should begin by noting that the definition of low pay is essentially arbitrary, because it allows a person's status to fall into only one of two categories rather than a whole range of conditions. Non-participants in the labour market are in danger of being ignored. However, if one takes average gross weekly earnings of £110 in 1988 as the cut-off level, one finds that about 11 per cent of full-time adults on adult rates fall in the 'low paid' category using the New Earnings Survey (NES) (this cut-off is about 60 per cent of median male earnings, which is a little lower than the level chosen by the Low Pay Unit, for instance; it is of the same order of magnitude as the level at which minimum wage legislation applies in the United States). This figure is only 5 per cent for men, but 23 per cent for women. The occupations with the highest proportion of low-paid men are catering (20 per cent), farming (14 per cent), miscellaneous (12 per cent), and selling (11.5 per cent). The corresponding list for women is catering (52 per cent), selling (50 per cent), making/repairing (45 per cent) and materials processing (41 per cent). Amongst industries, the highest proportions of both low-paid men and low-paid women are in distribution (18 per cent and 62 per cent respectively). Indeed, this industry accounts for about one-third of the low-paid. Of the broad occupational categories, clerical workers account for nearly 30 per cent of the low-paid (this occupation covers considerably more workers than catering). Further details are reported in tables 1.4 and 1.5. As far as individual characteristics are concerned, it is clear that women are more at risk of being low-paid than are men. This is also true of part-time workers (whose *hourly* rates of pay tend to be lower than those of full-timers), young people (because of lack of education, training, and experience), and ethnic minorities.

Changes in the structure of industry between 1983 and 1988 have tended to increase very slightly the proportion of the low-paid. The number of low-paid according to the definition used above was about 1.4 per cent higher in 1988 than it would have been had the employment pattern across industries not changed from 1983 (assuming no change in the proportion of low paid *within* each single digit industrial order). This effect was more pronounced for men, both manual and non-manual, than for women. There was a tendency for industries with higher proportions of the low-paid to have faster employment growth. The change in the structure of occupations can be analyzed in a similar way, and had hardly any effect on the number of low-paid workers (increasing it for men by 2.3 per cent but reducing it for women by 3.5 per cent).

Turning now to the potentially low-paid, data on participation or activity rates provide some indication of the scope for increased labour force participation in response to improved incentives. Table 1.6 shows that female activity rates in the UK increased between 1975 and 1986 by over six percentage points. This more than made up for the decline in male activity rates, brought about mainly by early retirement. The experiences of other countries is not dissimilar, but it demonstrates that greater participation in the labour force is possible for certain demographic groups in the UK. It is interesting to observe that the US and Sweden have much higher activity rates amongst the over-54s, particularly amongst women, despite their higher per capita income levels (suggesting that there must be some quite powerful substitution effect at work to counteract the obvious income effect on work/retirement decisions). Overall, British female activity rates appear to be around the average, but they have not increased as rapidly since 1975 as they have in France, Sweden, and the US. Youth activity rates are high in the UK; the development of

Table 1.4 Low pay and participation: analysis by industry, 1988

Industry	FT adults on adult rates 'Low-paid'			FT manual males on adult rates 'Low-paid'			FT manual females on adult rates 'Low-paid'		
	% of total	% of industry	% of total low-paid	% of total	% of industry	% of total low-paid	% of total	% of industry	% of total low-paid
0 Agriculture	0.8	13.2	1.0	2.4	13.2	4.9	NA	NA	NA
1 Energy	3.5	0.7	0.2	5.4	0.3	0.3	NA	NA	NA
2 Extraction Industry	4.9	5.8	2.6	7.6	2.8	3.3	5.4	30.2	3.7
3 Metal Goods	13.9	5.5	7.0	21.0	2.8	9.1	16.3	26.4	9.8
4 Other Manufacturing	11.3	14.5	15.0	15.5	5.9	14.2	31.9	44.2	32.1
5 Construction	5.2	5.0	2.4	9.9	3.8	5.8	NA	NA	NA
6 Distribution	13.7	25.5	32.0	12.5	17.7	34.2	16.2	61.7	22.8
7 Transport	7.9	3.8	2.7	12.9	1.9	3.8	3.7	15.1	1.3
8 Banking	12.6	9.0	10.4	2.8	9.8	4.2	NA	NA	NA
9 Other Services	26.2	11.2	26.7	10.0	13.0	20.2	26.6	49.8	30.3
6–9 All Services	60.4	13.1	71.5	44.1	10.6	62.4	46.3	50.6	53.7
2–4 All Manufacturing	30.1	9.0	24.3	38.2	3.9	26.4	51.6	37.4	44.2

Source: New Earnings Survey (1988), Department of Employment

Note
NA = not available.

Table 1.4 (cont.)

Industry	FT non-manual males on adult rates 'Low-paid'			FT non-manual females on adult rates 'Low-paid'		
	% of total	% of industry	% of total low-paid	% of total	% of industry	% of total low-paid
0 Agriculture	NA	NA	NA	NA	NA	NA
1 Energy	3.6	0.3	0.3	1.9	3.1	0.3
2 Extraction Industry	4.1	1.0	1.2	2.1	15.0	1.8
3 Metal Goods	13.0	0.9	3.6	5.1	16.8	4.9
4 Other Manufacturing	7.3	2.1	4.7	5.2	20.7	6.1
5 Construction	4.2	2.0	2.6	1.5	26.0	2.2
6 Distribution	13.8	10.1	42.6	14.7	41.2	34.7
7 Transport	6.3	1.6	3.1	4.4	12.2	3.1
8 Banking	19.2	3.9	22.8	20.8	14.7	17.6
9 Other Services	28.5	2.2	19.1	44.4	11.5	29.3
6–9 All Services	67.4	4.3	87.9	84.1	17.5	84.5
2–4 All Manufacturing	24.3	1.3	9.6	12.3	18.1	12.8

Table 1.5 Low pay and participation: analysis by occupation, 1988

Occupation	FT adults on adult rates: % of total occupation	FT adults 'Low-paid': % of occupation	FT adults 'Low-paid': % of total low-paid	FT males on adult rates: % of total occupation	FT males 'Low-paid': % of occupation	FT males 'Low-paid': % of total low-paid	FT females on adult rates: % of total occupation	FT females 'Low-paid': % of occupation	FT females 'Low-paid': % of total low-paid
II Prof Management	7.5	0.7	0.5	8.8	0.5	0.9	4.6	1.5	0.3
III Prof Educational	10.7	7.3	7.1	5.9	2.1	2.5	20.1	10.3	9.0
IV Art, Sport	0.9	4.2	0.4	1.0	2.0	0.4	0.8	9.6	0.3
V Prof Scientist	6.2	1.1	0.6	8.6	0.8	1.4	1.4	4.6	0.3
VI Management	6.1	3.3	1.8	7.5	1.7	2.6	3.2	11.0	1.5
VII Clerical	20.9	15.6	29.3	9.6	6.5	12.6	42.9	19.5	36.3
VIII Selling	5.1	26.3	12.1	4.8	11.5	11.1	5.8	50.3	12.6
IX Security	2.0	2.6	0.5	2.8	2.6	1.5	0.4	2.7	0.1
X Catering	5.6	36.7	18.6	4.1	20.3	16.9	8.5	52.3	19.2
XI Farming	1.3	14.3	1.7	2.0	14.3	5.8	NA	NA	NA
XII Materials Processing	2.7	12.4	3.0	3.3	6.5	4.4	1.3	41.0	2.4
XIII Making/Repairing	4.6	16.9	7.0	5.0	5.2	5.2	3.9	45.4	7.8
XIV Process Metals & Elec	11.2	3.2	3.2	16.3	2.2	7.2	1.3	27.7	1.5
XV Repetitive Assembly	4.5	17.1	7.0	4.2	6.2	5.3	5.1	34.6	7.7
XVI Construction	2.5	4.4	1.0	3.7	4.4	3.3	NA	NA	NA
XVII Transport, Salvage	7.0	7.9	5.0	10.2	6.9	14.2	NA	NA	NA
XVIII Miscellaneous	1.2	12.3	1.4	1.9	12.3	4.7	0.7	36.9	1.1
ALL NON-MANUAL	58.4	9.6	51.0	48.3	3.3	32.2	78.3	17.4	59.0
ALL MANUAL	41.6	13.0	49.0	51.7	6.5	67.8	21.7	43.7	41.0

Source: New Earnings Survey (1988), Department of Employment.

Note:
NA = not available.

education and training programmes for young people, together with demographic changes, will tend to reduce the potential contribution of young people to the labour market.

3 THE TAX AND SOCIAL SECURITY SYSTEMS

The debate on incentives has tended to focus on the role of the tax and social security systems and their interaction since these are the most visible and active policy instruments. We consider the UK record on these policies in this section. However, if we accept that the factor determining an individual's decision to participate in labour market activity is his or her potential net income (compared to his or her minimum acceptable wage) then this has two components: the gross wage determined in the labour market; and the amount paid in taxation and received from social security payments. We consider the former in section 4. Before we proceed, though, a number of qualifying points need to be made. First, it is not a straightforward matter to judge the impact of the social security and tax systems on incentives. There can be no simple (quantitative) measure of their effect. Policies have not been implemented in a vacuum. Second, even if it can be demonstrated that certain (dis)incentives have existed in the past, or are currently operational, there is no guarantee that individuals will respond to these; nor, indeed, does it necessarily follow that the aggregate effect of policy changes can be inferred with much certainty. Third, there are many government policies that affect, intentionally or otherwise, incentives for the low-paid. The provision of healthcare and education, training initiatives, equal opportunities legislation, as well as a whole gamut of macroeconomic policies, are just a few examples. Rarely are such issues considered in any detail in the context of incentives, even though they may be important. Fourth, there are many other influences on an individual's participation decision that are, at least to some extent, independent of government such as the nature of employment contracts offered by employers, the type of jobs available and their quality and so on. Of course it is not possible to review all potentially important policy considerations but our arguments in this and the following section are intended to provide a balanced assessment of recent policies.

From the 1960s, incentive effects have taken a more prominent place in discussion of taxation and social security, as a larger

Table 1.6 Low pay and participation: activity rates, 1975 and 1987

Year	United Kingdom*			West Germany*			Sweden			France			Japan			USA		
	Total	M	F	Total	M	F	Total	M	F	Total	M	F	Total	M	F	Total	M	F
1975																		
-15	0.0	0.0	0.0	0.5	0.5	0.5	0.1	0.2	0.1	0.8	1.0	0.5	0.5	0.7	0.3	0.6	0.8	0.4
15-19	56.1	57.6	54.6	63.2	63.2	63.3	35.4	35.7	35.1	37.2	40.3	34.1	35.0	35.4	34.6	40.1	45.2	34.9
20-24	75.2	89.0	60.9	77.5	85.6	69.0	65.6	71.7	59.3	74.3	84.3	63.9	77.9	82.6	73.1	71.2	84.0	58.1
25-44	75.1	97.9	51.7	74.6	97.1	49.8	74.4	93.3	54.5	72.5	96.5	46.8	76.9	98.3	55.7	72.3	95.2	49.8
45-54	79.3	97.6	61.4	69.8	94.8	48.5	75.2	93.1	57.4	70.4	92.9	48.0	81.1	97.5	66.1	75.1	92.6	58.8
55-64	64.0	90.8	39.9	48.1	77.8	27.6	58.4	80.9	36.4	54.5	72.1	38.9	67.5	88.6	50.4	60.9	80.3	43.9
65+	11.0	18.7	6.1	9.2	15.1	5.6	9.7	17.1	3.8	8.4	12.5	5.7	32.3	50.2	18.3	15.2	24.3	8.9
TOTAL	46.2	60.0	33.1	45.3	60.1	31.7	44.3	56.3	32.3	42.2	55.6	29.3	51.5	63.3	40.1	44.2	56.3	32.7
1987																		
-15																		
15-19	57.4	58.2	56.5	43.7	47.0	40.1	46.3	44.6	48.2	13.8	15.7	11.8	17.1	17.4	16.6	43.3	43.7	42.8
20-24	77.1	84.8	69.2	77.7	80.9	74.4	81.0	81.9	80.0	64.9	65.7	64.2	72.4	71.3	73.6	75.7	79.0	72.3
25-44	80.5	93.9	66.9	79.2	94.4	63.6	92.5	94.7	90.4	84.9	96.8	73.0	78.3	96.9	59.6	82.1	91.3	72.9
45-54	80.7	91.6	69.9	75.3	95.0	54.9	92.8	95.1	90.6	78.2	92.8	63.7	80.6	96.4	65.2	78.2	90.0	67.1
55-64	50.4	67.0	34.9	40.4	59.5	24.7	69.3	75.0	64.2	39.2	47.6	31.5	63.0	82.6	45.1	53.9	66.9	42.4
65+	4.6	7.5	2.7	3.2	5.1	2.1				3.0	4.7	1.9	23.6	35.5	15.4	10.5	15.7	6.9
TOTAL	48.2	57.5	39.5	47.9	60.6	36.3				44.3	51.8	37.3	49.8	60.9	39.1	50.0	57.2	43.1

Source: ILO Yearbooks (1978, 1988).

21

Notes:

* Latest year's data are for 1986.

USA Economically active population figures related to persons 16 years of age and over are annual averages.
Total population figures relate to persons 15 years old and over are based on mid year estimates.
Economically active population figures include 1,706,000 resident members of the armed forces (1,551,000 males and 155,000 females) for whom age distribution is not available.

Japan 1975 data based on labour force sample surveys, 1987 based on census data.

France 1975 data based on a 20 per cent sample tabulation of census returns.
1987 economically active population figures do not include persons on compulsory military service.
1987 data based on labour force sample survey.

West
Germany Data based on labour force sample survey.

Sweden 1985 economically active population figures do not include persons on compulsory military service and persons seeking work for the first time.
Figures relate to persons aged 16 to 64 years of age who have worked at least 1 hour per week.
1987 economically active population figures do not include persons on compulsory military service.
All data based on labour force sample survey.

UK 1975 data are 'de jure' data. Official mid-year estimates.
1986 data are 'de jure' data. Economically active population figures relate to persons 16 years of age and over.
Based on census data.

proportion of the population has been drawn into the tax and benefit systems. Since 1979, spurred on by the 'supply side revolution' among economists, the reduction of perceived adverse incentive effects has been one of the major forces driving economic policy. Below (and in the Appendix), we review some of the most important changes to the tax and social security systems over the past decades, and then look at the evidence of their impact. We focus our discussion on two groups: the working low-paid (particularly those with families) and the unemployed.

The Working Low-paid

The earliest welfare state measures, whilst providing limited benefits for the unemployed and those suffering due to absence from work because of injury, did not attach any priority to the working poor despite the evidence of Rowntree (1901) that low earnings were a major cause of poverty. This neglect continued until after the Second World War. Beveridge's social insurance principle meant flat rate contributions above a lower earnings level with benefits for poverty caused by unemployment, sickness, injury, maternity, and retirement. Means-tested National Assistance (renamed Supplementary Benefit in 1966) was to provide a safety net. There was little discussion of poverty among working households. Writing in the shadow of the Depression, Beveridge believed that very few men's wages were insufficient to cover at least two adults and one child (Beveridge, 1942, p. 155, quoted in Atkinson, 1983, Chapter 11). Family allowances were introduced in 1945 for families with two or more children but subsequently failed to keep pace with rising wages. At the same time, the proportion of the working population liable for direct taxation rose dramatically – from 20 per cent in 1939 to over 50 per cent by the end of the War (1945). In 1939 *average* wages were around £180 per annum, but there was no liability to tax for a married couple with earnings below £225 per annum (Kay and King, 1986, Chapter 2). Throughout the post-war period, as tax allowances declined relative to wages, large numbers of low-paid workers were brought into the tax system. (It was not until the Rooker–Lawson–Wise amendment to the Finance Bill in 1977 that allowances were linked by statute to prices.) Table 1.7 clearly illustrates the dramatic shift in tax incidence (including National Insurance contributions) from middle and high income groups to the lower-paid: between 1956 and 1978 the tax burden doubled for those

Table 1.7   Income Tax and National Insurance contributions as percentages of gross earnings

Multiples of average earnings	Single			Married		
	1956–7	*1978–9*	*1988–9*	*1956–7*	*1978–9*	*1988–9*
2/3	14.0	27.5	26.3	8.6	21.9	21.9
1	18.9	31.5	28.9	13.5	27.8	26.0
2	26.0	33.7	30.1	23.1	31.4	27.8
5	41.0	52.2	36.1	39.4	50.5	35.1
10	22.4	67.5	38.0	54.4	66.5	37.6

Source: *Hansard*, WA (29 April 1988) cols 318–19.

on two-thirds of average earnings whilst increasing by around a quarter or less for those at twice the average or above.

During the late 1960s and 1970s concern began to mount about the incidence of poverty among the low-paid. Various benefits were introduced in an attempt to ameliorate the situation, such as rent and rate rebates (began in the 1960s with modifications and extensions in 1972) and Family Income Supplement (1971). By 1986, there were well over thirty benefits with different rationales and structures. These confronted potential recipients with a wide variety of eligibility criteria and benefit tapers (the progressive reduction of a benefit as the relevant measure of income increases). Administrative costs were correspondingly higher and efficiency of benefit delivery was impaired. Government estimates of take-up suggest only 50 per cent of those entitled to Family Income Supplement and 70 per cent of those entitled to rent and rate rebates actually claimed their entitlement (Dilnot, Kay, and Morris, 1984, Table 2 p. 49). Many households found themselves facing high effective marginal rates of taxation because receipt also brought with it a 'passport' to other benefits such as free school meals, prescriptions, and dental treatment. Dependence on social security grew significantly throughout the post-war period: by the early 1980s an estimated 30 per cent of the population were receiving means- or income-tested benefits and a further 10 per cent were probably eligible (Parker 1989, p. 40).

The problems created by these new benefits were compounded by the replacement of flat rate National Insurance contributions in 1975. Instead employees had to pay a percentage of *all gross earnings* once they moved above the lower earnings limit (originally this was set at 5.5 per cent for employees but had reached 9 per cent – for those not contracted out of the State Earnings Related Pension Scheme – by 1985). This change led to a severe disincentive problem: just below the lower earnings limit no National Insurance contributions were payable, yet the payment of 1p over the lower earnings limit meant all gross earnings were liable, a massive jump in liability. Dilnot and Webb (1988), reviewing the distribution of earnings, show that the system resulted in a bunching of individuals just below the lower earnings limit, evidence of this disincentive effect being operational. The proliferation of means testing and the change in National Insurance liability meant that in extreme cases it was possible for household net income to fall with a rise in gross income (i.e. a marginal rate of taxation of more than 100 per cent). The 'poverty trap' – marginal rates of taxation approaching or exceeding 100 per cent – was potentially a severe disincentive to work extra hours or to switch to a marginally higher paid job. We examine the extent of the problem below.

The belief that these disincentive effects were important was part of the motivation for the overhaul of the social security system which took place in 1988, following the passage of legislation two years earlier. The Green Paper (DHSS, 1985) specified five main defects of the system that had developed as a result of the 'forty years of tinkering' since Beveridge: complexity, lack of targeting, the poverty and unemployment traps, inadequate freedom of choice, and concerns about the future burden of the system. After a short period of consultation, the 1986 Social Security Act was passed. In the event the changes in structure were far from fundamental, leaving the basic 'Beveridge plus tinkering' system relatively undisturbed. There was some simplification of the system, and a rationalization of the relationship between tax and National Insurance liability and benefit entitlement. Income Support replaced Supplementary Benefit, and Family Credit replaced Family Income Supplement, with the retention of a reduced form of Housing Benefit. The reforms were, at least in part, specifically designed to redirect resources towards poor families with children. Most significantly for incentives, the basis of assessment for each benefit was to be the same, with benefit entitlement calculated sequentially on *net* income. This reduced rates of benefit withdrawal below 100 per cent, eliminating the extreme version of the poverty trap, and removing kinks in the benefit withdrawal schedule, but at the cost of increasing effective marginal rates of taxation for many recipients.

In addition to the above reforms there have also been changes designed to reduce the disincentive caused by the sudden jump in National Insurance liability. In 1985 the jump was reduced (with 5 per cent of all gross earnings above the lower earnings limit being liable), but at the expense of introducing two further jumps. The greatest gainers from this change were families with gross incomes between £50 and £150 per week. In 1989, however, it was announced that the system would change again: employees were now to pay 2 per cent of the lower earnings limit (£43) once their earnings exceeded this level, and 9 per cent of the excess of earnings up to £320. This change should help reduce the disincentive effects of NICs on low-paid employees (Dilnot and Webb, 1989b), but there is still a deterrent to part-timers to work a number of hours that takes their earnings over the lower earnings limit. Additionally, the 1985 and 1989 reforms have not removed the incentive on the demand side for employers to hire part-timers.

It is not possible to estimate precisely the number of people whose labour supply is actually affected by adverse incentives. Recent changes have attempted to remove the worst anomalies. Official estimates of the number of families currently facing high marginal tax rates are shown in Table 1.8. It should be noted that no details of calculation procedures are given but presumably they take account of the 1985 National Insurance contribution reforms, and the 1986 Social Security reforms that came into effect in 1988, although not the reduction in the standard rate of income tax to 25 per cent that transpired. The official estimates clearly demonstrate two important points: first the numbers actually affected by high marginal rates of tax as a proportion of all working families is relatively small, and second, whilst the Fowler reforms reduced the number facing marginal rates of tax higher than 100 per cent, the number of families with children facing marginal rates between 50 and 100 per cent has risen. (It should be noted that the *latest* official estimates are reported by Atkinson in this volume. They show 415,000 affected by marginal rates of tax of more than 70 per cent, but this figure is for the number of working heads of tax units rather than for families.)

Some scepticism is warranted. Simulations by the Institute for Fiscal Studies using their tax–benefit model (which is based on Family Expenditure Survey data) show that around 500,000 tax units faced a marginal rate of tax above 60 per cent in 1985 (about 2 per cent of total tax units), but that the 1986 reforms of social security would lead to a significant *increase* in the number of tax units facing high marginal rates of tax: from 310,000 to 1,400,000 facing 60–80 per cent

Table 1.8　Poverty trap: number of working families affected, pre- and post-Fowler

Marginal tax rate-% per £1 of extra gross earnings	Nov. 1985 (000)	Apr. 1988[1] (000)
(a)　Families with children		
Above 100	70	0
90 but less than 100	60	60
80 but less than 90	110	370
70 but less than 80	0	75
60 but less than 70	100	*
50 but less than 60	140	NA
	480	505
(b)　Families without children		
Above 100	0	0
90 but less than 100	0	10
80 but less than 90	50	10
70 but less than 80	0	20
60 but less than 70	60	0
50 but less than 60	90	0
	200	40
Totals with and without children	680	545

Source: Parker (1989) quoting *Hansard*, WA (21 October 1987) col. 809, and *Hansard*, WA (19 November 1987) cols 647–8.

Notes:
*　　Less than 5000.
　　NA: not available.
1.　The April 1988 figures assume income tax at 27 per cent and income tax allowances uprated in line with RPI.

rates, and from 150,000 to 700,000 for 80–100 per cent rates, although none would face the extreme poverty trap (Dilnot and Stark, 1986, Tables 2 and 5). The wide variation in the various estimates of the numbers in the poverty trap suggests a need for cautious interpretation. Certainly, given all the attention this aspect of the incentive debate has attracted, the figures put the problem in some perspective: the overall numbers affected are small. Nonetheless the interaction of the tax and benefit systems does adversely affect an important minority. Table 1.8 shows that families with children tend to be affected to a greater extent than those without children. Similarly a breakdown of the Institute for Fiscal Studies figures by demographic

Table 1.9   High marginal tax rates (1985) by group

	Marginal rate of tax		
	60–80 (%)	80–100 (%)	100+ (%)
Single-parent families	35 (3.7)	35 (3.7)	40 (4.2)
Couples with 1 or 2 children	105 (1.9)	35 (0.6)	40 (0.7)
Couples with 3+ children	35 (2.8)	35 (2.8)	35 (2.8)
Pensioners	25 (0.4)	10 (0.2)	0
Childless units	110 (0.9)	35 (0.3)	0
	310	150	115

Source: Dilnot and Stark (1986) Table. 2.

Note:
Figures (for tax units) are in 1000, with the per cent of relevant population in parentheses. The figures assume full take-up.

group (Table 1.9) shows how some groups are more affected than others. For example, single parents tend to be badly affected by high marginal rates of tax because of the way Supplementary Benefit/ Income Support is calculated, and because this group mainly consists of women concentrated in lower paid occupations. Calculations by Parker (1989) show that a typical lone mother could only slightly improve her net income by going out to work, provided she did not have childcare costs.

A potentially important disincentive not revealed in Table 1.9 concerns part-time work, and is due largely to the National Insurance system. The jump in liability at the lower earnings limit is likely to encourage employees to ensure their hours are such that this level of earnings is not exceeded (and by doing so may lose some of their employment rights, see below). Hart and Trinder (1986) also highlight the impact on employers, arguing that the change to earnings related employers' National Insurance contributions has made the hiring of full-time workers more expensive relative to part-timers. Indeed there are large cost savings in employing two part-timers instead of one full-timer when both the former are kept below the lower earnings limit, because total National Insurance liabilities are reduced. However there may be additional fixed costs incurred by using more part-time workers. There is some limited survey evidence to suggest that some employers do reduce the hours worked by their employees below the National Insurance contributions threshold as a means of reducing labour costs; the number of part-timers below the National Insurance lower earnings limit has increased over the last decade or so. Schoer (1987) (using the Labour Force and New Earnings Surveys) estimates that about 28 per cent of the male and 29 per cent of the female total of part-time employees falls below the National Insurance contribution threshold and are not liable. Their hourly rates of pay tend to be lower as well.

The Unemployed

The group for which concern over incentives has been strongest in recent years has been the unemployed. Throughout the last sixty years benefits for the unemployed in the UK have developed along two separate tracks: a contributory benefit and a means-tested benefit. The former was first introduced in 1911 (Unemployment Insurance Act) for workers in certain industries, entitlement being dependent on contributions. The enactment of the Beveridge Report basically continued this system, with benefits in theory financed by National Insurance contributions. In 1966 an Earnings Related Supplement to unemployment benefit was introduced, whereby benefit became partly dependent on earnings as well as contributions. (The Earnings Related Supplement was calculated as one-third of weekly earnings in the previous tax year between the National Insurance lower and upper earnings limits; for details see Egginton, 1987.) After Beveridge some of the unemployed (those who were ineligible for Unemployed Benefit due to insufficient contributions) qualified for National Assistance (Supplementary Benefit from 1966). However, the unemployed were initially the smallest group in receipt of Supplementary Benefit. With the dramatic rise in the 1970s and early 1980s in the numbers of unemployed, particularly the long-term unemployed who had exhausted their unemployment benefit entitlements, this situation changed. By 1982 around two-thirds of the unemployed were on Supplementary Benefit and they represented the largest single group of claimants for that benefit (Bradshaw and Huby, 1989).

The traditional measure of the incentive to seek work has been the replacement ratio (or replacement rate), which compares net income in and out of work. When levels of benefit are high relative to potential earnings in work, the financial incentive to work is low. However there are major problems both with the construction of replacement ratios and with their interpretation. On the measurement side, replacement ratios are normally defined for a hypothetical household (typically a married man with non-participating or unemployed wife and two children), and with a range of assumptions about past and potential earnings, housing costs, benefit take-up (nearly always assumed to be 100 per cent for the sake of simplicity), position in the tax year and refund claims, as well as about the interpretation of social security laws (such as changes in the likelihood of being disqualified from Unemployment Benefit). The latter may be particularly important in recent years given the large number of administrative changes, mostly restrictive, placed on the receipt of benefit (Atkinson and Micklewright, 1989). Thus there are a large number of possible methods of calculating replacement ratios (see Atkinson and Micklewright, 1985, Table 5.1, p. 113 for some alternatives). For measuring the incentive to return to work it is necessary to make assumptions about the prospective earnings a person is likely to receive, and the probability of obtaining a job. We reproduce one estimate of replacement ratios for the unemployed in Table 1.10 (Dilnot and Morris, 1983). Since it is based on Family

Table 1.10   The replacement ratio[1] over time, with constant population[2], 1980

	13-week average			53rd week marginal[3]		
	Average	% >0.9	%<0.5	*Average*	%>0.9	%<0.5
1968	0.870	35.2	0.5	0.537	2.8	30.7
1975	0.751	17.2	5.9	0.498	2.5	50.5
1978	0.790	21.0	2.3	0.519	2.2	44.0
1980	0.727	12.0	8.0	0.503	1.9	47.8
1982	0.597	3.2	28.0	0.510	2.2	52.3
1983	0.600	2.9	21.0	0.504	1.9	53.2

Source: Dilnot and Morris (1983) Table 6 p. 332.

Notes:
1. Figures refer to ratio of net incomes in and out of work for family head. Full benefit entitlement is assumed to be taken up; individual expects all benefits and tax allowances to be uprated year-on-year with Retail Price Index. Earnings of spouse are taken into account but only on the assumption that he or she does not alter earnings during a period of unemployment of the family head. For full details see Dilnot and Morris, 1983.
2. Tax and benefit systems in each year are applied to the 1980 population at 1980 prices.
3. Marginal replacement ratios imply the monetary loss from an additional week's unemployment.

Expenditure Survey data covering individuals with a variety of different characteristics, it probably provides a fairly accurate indication of the development of replacement ratios. The figures are calculated on the basis of a 'constant' population in order to isolate the effects of changes in the tax benefit regime from changes in the demographic structure of the population.

The replacement ratio has fallen since 1978, largely due to the government measures discussed below. It is important to draw the distinction between the short- and long-term replacement ratios (when entitlement to Unemployment Benefit is exhausted). The figures in Table 1.10 show that there has never really been a tax–benefit incentive problem in the UK for the latter (although other factors certainly suggest that this group is engaged in less active job search than the short-term unemployed). These results are not dissimilar to those obtained (also using Family Expenditure Survey data) by Atkinson and Micklewright (1985).

Interpretation of replacement ratios requires considerable caution. The calculation of a high replacement ratio for a supposedly typical case may provide little guide to actual income levels. Replacement ratio calculations need to take full account of the interrelationships between benefits: in some cases entitlement to one benefit may reduce that from another (see Egginton, 1987, p. 96). Simply because the replacement ratio may be close to 100 per cent it does not necessarily mean a particular individual will not take a job offered to him (Atkinson and Fleming, 1978). The latter decision will almost certainly depend on many factors other than the short-term monetary prospects. The possession of a job is often highly valued and there are important factors such as human capital considerations, family status, and the work ethic, which will affect an individual's decision to seek work. In any case a high level of benefits may actually facilitate more active job search, counteracting to some extent the likely increase in reservation wages. It is interesting to note that Wadsworth (1989) concludes that, after controlling for personal characteristics, those receiving benefits tend to use more methods of job search than do non-receivers. It may be, too, that the incentive depends on the absolute level of benefit rather than its relative value. Recently, Jenkins and Millar (1989) have argued that an unemployed individual making the transition to work faces not just a change in his/her potential income but also in income *risk*. Income whilst on benefits is relatively certain, but at the time of the participation decision potential income may be uncertain. Thus, even if replacement ratios are low, risk averse individuals may not participate because of the income risk. More empirical work is needed to test this idea; the important point is that an average replacement ratio by itself does not give an adequate measure of the incentives faced by the unemployed.

Other evidence on the impact of the social security and tax systems on unemployment can be found in the literature that has attempted to assess the extent to which unemployment during the 1970s and 1980s was 'voluntary'. These studies typically produced estimates of the responsiveness of the unemployed to changes in the replacement ratio, i.e. they measured the incentive to return to work (rather than to quit an existing job). As one might anticipate there are numerous methodological difficulties in empirical work, to say nothing of the conceptual problems associated with 'voluntary' unemployment. Atkinson *et al.* (1984) surveyed the evidence available at that time and concluded that it was far from robust. Another sceptical survey can be found in Micklewright (1986). Elasticity estimates vary greatly, especially in time series studies, ranging from Minford's total elasticity of unemployment with respect to real benefits of between 2 and 3 (Minford, 1983, 1985) to Nickell and Andrews's (1983) finding of an insignificant response. The labour demand equations of the former have been subject to widespread criticism: for example on the grounds that no productivity related variables are included. Layard and Nickell (1986) estimate a total elasticity of unemployment to the replacement ratio of about 0.7 at the same mean (p. S165). Cross-sectional data produce little more consistency. Atkinson and Micklewright (1985) using Family Expenditure Survey data for 1972–7 show that it is possible to generate a variety of results, suggesting a lack of robustness and that 'there is no firm evidence of a quantitatively large disincentive effect' (p. 240).

Replacement ratios for most groups have fallen over the last ten years. Atkinson and Micklewright (1989) show that whilst unemployment benefit rose more or less in line with the Retail Price Index it shows a marked decline relative to average earnings. The Earnings Related Supplement to Unemployment Benefit was abolished in 1982, and Unemployment Benefit was made taxable. The 1986 reforms have also acted to improve incentives due to the new alignment of Family Credit and Income Support assessed on net income, together with larger earnings disregards (Dilnot and Webb, 1989a). The standard rate of tax has fallen and National Insurance contributions have been reformed. As noted earlier, there have also been numerous changes in the administration of benefits (such as changes to the 'willingness to work' test) that are extremely difficult to model; whatever their precise quantitative effect, it seems reasonable to believe that these have further reduced any disincentives either to quit work and claim benefit or to undertake prolonged job search when unemployed.

The evidence reviewed above suggests that the scope for improving incentives for the unemployed is rather limited. However, any aggregate picture can obscure special cases that might be important. For example, there is evidence to suggest that the tax and benefit systems work in a particularly disadvantageous way for married women with unemployed husbands. Dilnot and Kell (1989) show that in some cases (when the unemployed man is on Supplementary Benefit, and there are children) there is very little incentive for the wife to participate in labour force activity.

4 THE LABOUR MARKET

The incentive to work more hours depends on the gross wage as well as the tax and social security systems. In the simplest theoretical framework this is set by the demand for and the supply of labour. The reality, however, is more complex, with the presence of monopolistic employers and unions, government intervention, and various institutional rigidities. The underlying philosophy in government policy since 1979 has been to make the labour market more competitive. Hence, we review some of the measures introduced to this end and attempt to gauge the impact of policy on incentives for the low-paid.

'Good' jobs and 'bad' jobs

Attention was drawn earlier to the fact that some industries have higher proportions of low-paid workers than others. The pattern of interindustry wage differentials shows a remarkably similarity across time and across countries (see, for instance, Krueger and Summers, 1988; Slichter, 1950, noted this a long time ago). Katz and Summers (1989) consider relative wages amongst various manufacturing industries in nine countries in 1983. They limit their analysis to the single occupational group of operatives in order to control for differences in occupational structure (skill mix) across countries. The correlations of relative hourly wages are high, typically between

0.6 and 0.9. The UK's structure is particularly close to those of Japan (correlation of 0.95), West Germany (0.93) and the US (0.86). This gives rise to the suspicion that characteristics of industry product markets are reflected in the rates of pay offered to workers. Of course, low rates of pay may reflect a lower quality of worker (despite the attempts to standardize for occupational mix) or higher non-pay benefits of the job. US economists have been able to investigate this further using very detailed data on individual workers drawn from the US Current Population Survey (see, *inter alia*, Dickens and Katz, 1987). They tend to find persistent industry wage differentials even after controlling for numerous characteristics which are likely to be correlated with ability, skills, and non-wage benefits. The pattern of differentials is very similar whether or not the controls are applied, so the raw industry differentials point to the good jobs and bad jobs. It appears to be better to be a secretary or a fork-lift truck driver in the petroleum industry than in the clothing industry, for instance. People who change jobs (but not occupation) tend to experience changes in pay reflecting the differential between the industry they leave and the industry they join (see Katz and Summers, 1989, Thaler, 1989). This is contrary to the simple competitive model of the labour market.

There is still considerable doubt about the cause of these inter-industry wage differentials. Most theories invoke revenue sharing arrangements between employers with some monopoly power and their existing workforce ('insiders'), in response to efficiency wage considerations or implicit threats of disruption. The situation in the UK is clouded by the absence of the type of individual data which would allow one to test the various hypotheses in the way in which they have been in the States. However, if it *is* true that workers in some industries are receiving what amount to rents from their employment relationships, the possibility exists that employment is too low in high-wage industries because of this non-competitive setting of wages. If this is the case, it is appropriate to encourage the expansion of the high-wage industries. Thus some of the low-paid could be more productive (and better paid) if they were offered the incentive of job openings in the 'good' industries. This does not happen automatically via the functioning of a market in jobs because employers tend to treat members of their existing workforce differently (better) than outsiders (whose abilities are more uncertain and who do not possess firm-specific skills or the leverage of potential collective action). Whether this line of reasoning, which points towards an activist industrial policy, is valid or not, considering it

reminds us of the pitfalls of assuming that the labour market
functions like a simple auction market.

Direct Administrative Intervention in Wage Setting

Since 1979, there has been no official incomes policy, although some
guidelines have been implicit in the budgeting decisions regarding
public sector pay awards, and restraint in wage bargaining has been
urged by Ministers.

Apart from incomes policy, the major direct influence on wage
setting in the UK has been via wages councils. Before we examine
their operation, however, we should mention two other measures of
direct importance to the low paid: Schedule 11 of the 1975 Employment Protection Act and the Fair Wages Resolution. The Fair Wages
Resolution (dating from 1891 and established in its modern form in
1948) was abolished by the government in 1983. This was aimed at
preventing firms contracted by the government from paying wages
below those recognised in the sector or locality concerned. Its
abolition was an integral part of the government's determination to
see the privatization of local government services succeed. The
Employment Protection Act enabled trade unions and employers'
associations to make a claim to ACAS (the Advisory, Conciliation
and Arbitration Service) on behalf of employees whose pay was
considered to be low, as compared with similar employees in the
same occupation or similar circumstances. 90 per cent of awards were
to employees whose pay was less than the median (Bazen, 1985). This
was repealed in August 1980 as part of the government's drive to
remove restrictions on the operation of the labour market.

Wages Councils provide the closest approximation in the UK to a
statutory national minimum wage. The origin of the bodies was the
1909 Trade Boards Act, which set up four boards in manufacturing
('sweated' trades) to establish minimum rates of remuneration. They
were composed of equal numbers of employer and worker representatives, with an uneven number of independents. The system was
extended and amended and at its peak in 1953 there were 66 councils
covering some 3.5 million workers in Great Britain (a separate
system developed in Northern Ireland). In addition there were
another 750,000 workers protected by the Agricultural Wages
Boards. Over the last three decades the number of councils has been
cut via abolition and amalgamation (see Annex 3, Department of
Employment, 1988, for details). In 1988 there were 26 councils
(although two of these were in abeyance) covering 2.5 million

workers or 11 per cent of the total workforce, in 376,000 establishments. Three sectors predominate: retailing, clothing and catering
account for 94 per cent of the coverage. Two-thirds of the workers
are part-time, about three-quarters are women, and the young
predominate.

Ever since their introduction, Wages Councils have attracted
criticism from some employers (who resented the interference in
wage setting), some trade unionists (who considered them a block on
the development of collective bargaining), and some campaigners
against poverty (who saw them as institutionalizing low pay), as well
as from government. The Conservative government has been un-
sympathetic to the concept of the determination of wages by official
committees and it came as some surprise that Wages Councils were
not abolished altogether in 1985. Until that time the UK was bound
by the ILO (International Labour Office) Convention 26 (8), article
(1) of which requires the maintenance of 'machinery whereby
minimum rates of wages can be fixed for workers employed in certain
of the trades or parts of the trades in which no arrangements exists for
effective regulation of wages by collective agreement or otherwise, or
wages are exceptionally low'. The government believed that regulation was inimical to flexibility in the labour market, and that Wages
Councils impeded the creation of jobs by keeping wages too high.
('Wages Councils decisions [continue to] prevent employers from
developing pay systems wholly in accordance with the best interests
of their business. In that way the councils reduce jobs and increase
unemployment', Department of Employment, 1988.) As a result of
the Wages Act 1986 the Councils have been restricted to setting a
minimum hourly rate (at the time of writing between about £2 and
£2.50 per hour), one overtime rate, and a limit on the amount an
employer can charge for accommodation. Also, Wages Councils were
required to consider the employment effects of their decisions. In
fact, a 1988 consultation document makes clear (Department of
Employment, 1988) the majority of Councils 'generally seem to have
operated without regard to their clarified remit'. IRS (1988) found in
a survey of the Act's effects that there had been some convergence of
the statutory minima laid down in different orders for different
sectors. Perhaps the centrepiece of the Act was the deregulation of
the youth labour market: all young people under 21 (then about
500,000) were removed from scope of Wages Councils' decisions.

The view that the Wages Councils destroy jobs is not a new one,
but the evidence for this assertion is inconclusive. It is, of course,
extremely difficult to predict what would have transpired in the

absence of Councils. Craig *et al.* (1982), examining the effects of the *abolition* of Wages Councils in six industries (Paper Box, Jute, Baking, Stamped or Pressed Metal, Cutlery, and Industrial Canteens) by surveying some 220 firms between 1977 and 1979, found that there were no major increases in relative wage rates, nor did collective bargaining develop to provide protection for employees. Some 18 per cent of firms were found to be paying below the old Council rates, and there was considerable prima facie evidence of a deterioration in pay and conditions for a minority of workers in a minority of firms after abolition. It has been estimated that the average minimum rate laid down by the top seven Councils represents around 40 per cent of the male median wage and 60 per cent of the female median wage (Bazen, 1985, Table 4.3, p. 43; Bazen, 1988). However, when comparisons are made with the median wage in each sector the figures are somewhat higher, at around 60 per cent for full-time men and 75 per cent or more for full-time women. Hence abolition may help to maintain low-paid employment. The Department of Employment (1988, paragraph 15, p. 4) believes that 'probably as many as one third [of covered workers] continue to be paid at the minimum rate', and that 'such clustering of pay levels around a particular figure is evidence that council minima continue to be above the levels required to fill jobs'. The initial government estimate of the consequences of the 1986 Act was that between 50,000 and 100,000 jobs would be created or saved (Brosnan and Wilkinson, 1987, p. 14).

Collective Bargaining

The policy of the government since 1979 has been to reduce regulation in the setting of wages. In promoting free collective bargaining, however, there have been a series of measures which might have shifted significantly the balance of power away from the unions in the bargaining process and in doing so may well have affected the attitudes of both unions and management. The major measures introduced – the 1980, 1982, and 1988 Employment Acts and the 1984 Trade Union Act – have limited the extent of 'closed shop' agreements, constrained secondary industrial action, and required ballots before industrial action. The new legislation has been only modestly used by employers although its *threatened* use may have had a more significant impact. To the extent that changes have taken place in the structure and processes of collective bargaining, these can largely be put down to economic rather than legislative change: the large rise in unemployment in the early 1980s and subsequent restructuring of industry meant a shift in employment away from the traditional areas of strength of British unions. Since 1979 manufacturing employment has fallen by nearly 30 per cent (some 2 million jobs) whilst the number in the service sector has risen substantially (1½ million more jobs). Much of the growth concentrated in private services has been in small firms, and there have been increases in the use of part-time, temporary and casual workers, as well as in self-employment. All these growth areas lack an established union presence, and are more difficult for unions to organise.

Employment Protection

In the 1960s and 1970s a number of measures were introduced in order to give employees some protection in their jobs. The most important pieces of legislation were: the 1965 Redundancy Payments Act which introduced a statutory payment when a worker was made redundant; the 1970 Equal Pay Act which outlawed sexual discrimination in pay; the 1971 Industrial Relations Act which established protection against unfair dismissal for all employees; the 1974 Trade Union and Labour Relations Act and the 1974 Health and Safety at Work Act; the 1975 Employment Protection Act which extended the periods of notice required for redundancy; the 1975 Sex Discrimination Act and the 1976 Race Relations Act which extended rights against discrimination in recruitment, promotion, dismissal, redundancy, fringe benefits etc.; the 1978 Employment Protection (Consolidation) Act. The latter was the basis of many of the rights which are set out in Table 1.11 below. It has been argued that the protection which these Acts afforded workers had a number of potentially important incentive effects. On the demand side the legislation made it harder for firms to reduce the size of their workforces by introducing redundancy provisions and protection against unfair dismissal, but made them more cautious about taking hiring decisions. On the supply side it is possible that, if changes enhance employment protection, participation in the labour force is encouraged, and turnover of those in jobs might be reduced. The legislation might also have an important qualitative effect on the *type* of labour (part-time versus full-time, for example) that firms wish to hire, and labour force participants wish to provide. A wrong 'match' between a worker and a job is more costly. Attempting to quantify these effects is extremely difficult.

Over the last decade, there have been a number of changes designed to improve demand side incentives by removing restrictions on employers imposed by legislation. In 1978 a six-month qualifying period was introduced for employees before unfair dismissal rights were applicable, and the Conservative government extended this to a year in 1979, and to two years for employees in firms employing less than twenty people in 1980 and for all in 1985. The 1980 Employment Act also weakened unfair dismissal provisions by placing the onus on the worker to show that an employer was acting unreasonably, and made it possible for a woman to be fairly dismissed if it is not practicable to allow her to return to her former job (and she turns down suitable alternative employment). As Table 1.11 shows, most

Table 1.11   Rights at work linked to service[1]

	Working hours per week		
	Under 8	*8 but less than 16*	*16 or more*
Written statement of pay and conditions	X	**	(13 weeks)
Guaranteed paid leave	X	**	(1 month)
Medical suspension pay	X	**	(1 month)
Time off for antenatal appointment	+	+	+
Maternity pay	X	**	*
Right to return to work after maternity leave	X	**	*
Itemised pay statement	X	**	+
Redundancy payment	X	**	*
Unfair dismissal[2]	X	**	*
Dismissal/action short of dismissal for:			
TU membership/activities	+	+	+
sex/race discrimination	+	+	+
Written statement with reasons for dismissal	X	**	(6 months)

Source: LRD (1986) from Table 4, p. 21.

Notes:
1. As of January 1990.
2. See text for provisos.
X   No right.
*   Qualifying period of two years.
** Qualifying period of five years.
+   No qualifying period.

rights are linked to length of service, with different stipulations depending on the number of hours worked per week.

As Table 1.11 illustrates, there are several rights for workers in Britain which require a qualifying period to be completed. This means that part-timers and temporary workers do not benefit from the same conditions of service as full-timers (see LRD, 1986 and 1987, for full details). After one month's employment, any employee has the right to guaranteed pay, medical suspension pay and statutory notice, but the former two rights are not available to employees under a contract of three months or less. Beyond this, rights are conditional on two or five years of more or less continuous employment. The former applies to those working sixteen hours a week or more, and the latter to those working between eight and sixteen. Those working less than eight have no additional rights.

These requirements affect a large number of low-paid workers, particularly women. Because the responsibilities of parenthood tend to fall on the mother, many women seek temporary and part-time work. It can be very difficult to build up enough service to meet the qualifying period for employment rights. Casey (1988) shows that three-fifths of temporary workers are excluded from legislation coverage because they do not work sufficient hours per week or have not established a sufficient length of service. Below we reproduce some further evidence confirming this from the Women in Employment Survey conducted in 1980 among over 3000 women. Table 1.12 shows that although the average number of hours worked was over the employment protection threshold of sixteen, some 37 per cent of part-time women worked less than this. Table 1.13 shows how this

Table 1.12 Full- and part-time working women (excluding those working very irregular hours) – percentages working the stated number of hours

Usual number of hours per week	Full-time	Part-time	All working women
Under 8 hours	–	10	4
8 but less than 16 hours	0	27	12
16 but less than 31 hours	8	57	29
31 hours or more	92	6	55
Average number of hours per week	37.4	18.5	29.2

Source: Martin and Roberts (1984) Table 4.1, p. 34.

Table 1.13   Proportions of full- and part-time employees covered by main employment protection legislation (excluding those working very irregular hours)

Hours of work per week; and length of service with present employer	Full-time	Part-time	All employees
16 or more hours; two or more years' service	67	52	61
8 but less than 16 hours; 5 years' service	–	8	3
Covered by legislation	67	60	64
16 or more hours; less than two years' service	33	11	24
8 but less than 16 hours; less than 5 years' service	–	19	8
Less than 8 hours	–	10	4
Not covered by legislation	33	40	36

Source: Martin and Roberts (1984) Table 4.3, p. 35.

distribution of hours translates into the application of employment rights: two-fifths are unprotected by legislation.

According to the 1988 New Earnings Survey, about 12 per cent of manual and 8 per cent of non-manual females work less than 8 hours; 29 per cent and 24 per cent work 8–16 hours, and 59 per cent and 69 per cent work 16–30 hours, figures broadly in line with those above. This aggregate picture, though, masks considerable variation between industries and occupations.

Tables 1.12 and 1.13 clearly show the potential for widespread incentive effects on both the demand and the supply side in relation to the type of labour hired (see for example Hart and Trinder, 1986). Employers can avoid numerous legal provisions by hiring on temporary contracts, or by recruiting part-timers rather than full-timers (there are also other cost advantages such as a reduction in employer National Insurance liability, as noted earlier). The government proposed (Department of Employment, 1986) reducing the hours thresholds to 12 and 20 hours, but as of January 1990, no action had been taken.

What is the evidence on the effects of employment protection legislation? We have two main sources: econometric analyses of unemployment and survey evidence from employers. In examining the unemployment-vacancy (u–v) ratio, Layard and Nickell (1986) argue that employment protection is a factor in determining search intensity. In their regression analyses of annual data they find that only about 3 per cent of the increased unemployment since the late 1950s (up to 1983) can be attributed to the *combined* impact of more liberal social security payments and improved employment protection (measured by outward shifts in the u–v curve).

The operational effects of Unfair Dismissal legislation on employment practices have been examined in three major surveys: Daniel and Stilgoe (1978), Clifton and Tatton-Brown (1979), and more recently Evans *et al*. (1985). The debate between employers and unions on the effects of protection has been going on since the mid-1970s. On the one hand, it has been claimed that Unfair Dismissal provisions impose unwarranted costs on firms, raising product prices and reducing the demand for labour. On the other hand, supporters of legislation have argued that Unfair Dismissal rights are beneficial: 'employees who feel less vulnerable to arbitrary action, more secure in their employment, identify more closely with the business and its management, and generally behave more co-operatively and productively' (Evans *et al*., 1985, p. 3).

In fact neither of these positions can claim much concrete backing on the basis of the survey evidence. All three produced broadly similar results. None found much indication of a significant employment effect: 2.3 per cent of firms claimed the legislation was a deterrent to hiring in Daniel and Stilgoe, and the figure was 8 per cent in both the other surveys. Employers were not favourable towards the legislation, and over three-fifths of managers in small firms thought that it had made workers harder to dismiss (Clifton and Tatton-Brown), but most claimed they did not let any personal hostility carry over to employment decisions. They regarded the risks of use of the Unfair Dismissal provisions as highly marginal. Of six firms – 8 per cent of the sample – which expressed reluctance to hire additional labour, three had previously lost Unfair Dismissal cases (Evans *et al*.). The conclusion was that 'there was very little sign that employment protection legislation was inhibiting industrial recovery or contributing to the high level of unemployment by discouraging employers from taking on new people' (Daniel and Stilgoe, p. 77). Interestingly, there was some suggestion of a qualitative effect, with employers becoming more careful with regard to the type of labour hired. 'There was equally little evidence of companies switching to forms of employment other than full time "permanent" employees for reasons of avoiding or lessening the obligations imposed by

Unfair Dismissal legislation' (Evans *et al.*, p. 66). None of the firms
employing more female part-timers said their decision was influenced
by the legislation (Clifton and Tatton-Brown), although this could
partly be explained by the widespread ignorance of detailed provisions of the legislation that all three surveys found. This lack of
information was matched amongst employees, with 78 per cent of
employees having no knowledge of changes made since 1978 (Evans
et al.).

One further piece of suggestive evidence comes from a CBI study
(CBI, 1984, cited by Layard, 1986, Table 18, p. 169) of 800 firms
which asked about *possible* legal changes that might affect the
numbers they employed. The results indicated that only 3 per cent
thought the abolition or reduction in Unfair Dismissal provisions
would definitely lead to an increase in employment, 7 per cent said an
increase was possible, but 77 per cent did not know. On other
changes, 75 per cent thought a change in redundancy entitlements
would have no affect on employment and more than two-thirds
believed a reduction in the collective rights of unions would have no
effect. Generally the picture would seem to be that economic factors
are more important than legal considerations in employment decisions. It would appear, therefore, that the behavioural effects of
legislation – at least on the demand side – have been relatively weak.

Measures Affecting the Participation of Women

In section 2 we noted that while female activity rates in the UK have
increased, they remain lower than in Sweden, France and the United
States. Although the reasons for this difference are complex (cultural
and historical as well as economic), it seems reasonable to suppose
that public policy has had some impact on participation. Of particular
relevance are the tax and social security benefits for mothers and
children, provisions for maternity leave, and the quantity (and
quality) of childcare available. The importance of these issues has
been demonstrated in a number of studies – the 'Women and
Employment' survey showed, for example, that a large proportion of
non-working women were constrained by commitments to their
families. 52 per cent of non-working women (18 per cent of all
women) gave 'looking after children' as the major reason for not
having a paid job (Martin and Roberts, 1984, Table 7.1 p. 81).

Despite the evidence no government since the war has given
priority to addressing this issue. Until 1977 a system of child tax

allowances and Family Allowance were the main system of support. Child Benefit – a tax-free benefit payable to mothers of children under 16 – replaced these. Since then Child Benefit has failed to keep pace with inflation and since 1985 has been frozen at £7.25 per child. In early 1990 no childcare expenses could be deducted from taxable income (in contrast to the US, for example, where there are Federal and sometimes State childcare tax credits, or France, where there are tax allowances for childcare expenses). Additionally there are two maternity benefits. Statutory Maternity Pay, a National Insurance benefit paid by employers, is available for 18 weeks, with a higher rate (dependent on length of service) of 90 per cent of gross weekly earnings for the first six of these 18 weeks. Part-timers and temporaries are thus at an obvious disadvantage, needing two years' employment with an employer and at least 16 hours work per week or five years if eight to 16 hours are worked. Statutory Maternity Allowance is available to those excluded from Statutory Maternity Pay but only if full rate National Insurance contributions have been paid for at least 26 weeks (for details see the Appendix). Expectant mothers may also qualify for payments from the Social Fund if they are receiving Income Support or Family Credit.

A woman expecting a baby, however, has no statutory right to leave. There are three basic rights: time off with pay for ante-natal appointments; a right not to be dismissed on the grounds of pregnancy; and a right to reinstatement. The right to return to work (whether the women had been dismissed or not) depends on fulfilling continuous service requirements (two or five years depending on hours as previously set out). Further limitations have also been introduced in recent years: the 1980 Employment Act meant that a women could be fairly dismissed if it was not reasonably practicable for her to return to her former job (and she has turned down alternative employment); employers with fewer than five employees were made exempt; and from 1985 all employees must have a minimum of two years' service to qualify for Unfair Dismissal protection. This situation is in contrast to developments elsewhere. In Sweden, for example, since 1974 a mother or father has the right to 'parenthood leave of absence' with some pay for twelve months, parents of children under eight can reduce their working day to six hours (with no financial compensation), and all employment rights apply equally to both full and part-timers. The European Commission has discussed a draft directive on parental leave which would provide time off work for parents looking after children up to age two, and the House of Lords Select

Committee on European Community Affairs recommended legislation. No action has yet been taken by the government, although there are some signs of employer initiative (Mottershead, 1988).

Evidently the incentives for women to work full- or part-time require the existence of childcare facilities. To a large extent family is the main provider of care: the 'Woman and Employment' survey revealed that 65 per cent of full-timers who made arrangements for pre-school children did so with their husbands, older brother or sister, grandmother or other relative, 23 per cent used a childminder, only 3 per cent an employer crèche or day nursery, and 7 per cent a Local Education Authority or Local Authority nursery; for part-timers the figures were 87 per cent, 11 per cent, 1 per cent, and 5 per cent respectively (Martin and Roberts, 1984, Table 4.10, p. 39). The main emphasis of policy has been on voluntary provision (except during the Second World War when expansion of nursery places became a national priority). There is considerable evidence, however, that there is inadequate supply of such facilities. Daniel (1980) found that although 22 per cent of women did not return to work because they preferred to look after their baby, 22 per cent did not return because there was no-one else to look after it, 13 per cent cited a lack of childminding facilities or the cost, 26 per cent said there was no job with convenient hours, and a further 5 per cent said they could not fit in with their husbands' hours. Simpson (1986) has estimated that there is a demand for up to 1.9 million places for under-5's, whilst Dex (1987) estimated a shortfall of nearly 570,000 day places for children under 3 and nearly 390,000 for 3–4 year olds in 1983. Recent government initiatives such as the 'Play Policy', established in 1985, have concentrated on providing information to parents about available facilities. Mottershead (1988) conducted a series of case studies and concluded that 'evidence suggests strongly that there is still a large unmet demand for appropriate childcare'. With spending restrictions on local authorities there is likely to be little improvement in this area. Additionally from March 1984 until the time of writing the Inland Revenue has treated a subsidised workplace nursery place as a taxable benefit, perhaps discouraging their use, and special capital allowances for workplace nurseries were abolished in 1980.

CONCLUSIONS

The evidence suggests that the labour supply decisions of many individuals are influenced by the net income they can obtain in work compared to what they can receive when not in employment. The effects of employment income and other sources of income differ. The structure of pay (influenced by labour demand), the tax system, and the social security system therefore all have an impact on how people allocate their time between work and leisure and across different occupations and industries. Such decisions are important determinants of output and productivity levels as well as of personal income and welfare. Consequently the policies of government, employers, and trade unions which influence these decisions have implications for the efficiency of the economy. The people most evidently in danger of being affected by this nexus of forces are those at the margins of economic activity – those in low-paying jobs, the unemployed and groups such as married women and the old, who are making decisions about whether to be involved in the labour market at all. Choices about whether to participate, about how many hours to work and about what sort of job to take are all at issue. Though we have argued that much more than the tax–benefit system is involved, it is groups such as these which may face high effective marginal tax rates and for whom, therefore, quite substantial disincentive effects may be present despite the often modest labour supply elasticities indicated by the research reported in this Chapter.

The elasticity of labour supply with respect to the net wage varies across demographic groups, so the quantitative impact of any given financial incentive will vary. The studies we have surveyed tend to show that married women are more responsive than men to a given financial stimulus – i.e. they generally exhibit higher labour supply elasticities. They also show a greater range of labour market response (non-participation, part-time work, full-time work). Family composition, particularly the number and age of children, also influences the effectiveness of a given incentive. The female labour force is disproportionately low-paid, whilst international comparisons indicate there is scope for increased female participation. Thus any discussion of incentives to the low-paid should pay particular attention to the way in which the tax–benefit system (e.g. child benefits, independent taxation of husband and wife) alters choices about labour supply within the family and also to the choice of jobs available to women. Likewise the issue of childcare provision is evidently relevant and merits research into its possible effects on labour supply in the UK.

Similarly, academic research and comparisons with other countries point towards the scope for stimulating the labour force participation of older people. Low pay is likely to have a particularly large disincentive effect within this group. Pension arrangements can do so as well. Further study of how the tax–benefit system affects the retirement decision in Britain would be useful.

Young people comprise a third important group at the margin of labour market activity. Here the issue is complicated by the existence of an alternative to work or leisure, education and training, which is particularly relevant to the age group. We have not considered the incentives to train, as these are considered by Keep and Ryan (Chapters 5 and 6 in this volume). There will be a reduced supply of labour from young people over the next few years. Thus incentives to acquire more human capital should be considered for groups for whom this has been a less obvious choice in the past.

Mention of training draws attention to the fact that expected pay relativities and the costs of acquiring skills are important determinants of the incentives facing the low-paid. One of the themes of this Chapter has been that a discussion of incentives should concern itself with the determinants of labour demand as well as labour supply. It cannot be assumed that employers' behaviour approaches the economist's archetypal state of perfect competition sufficiently closely for the demand side to be ignored. We have indicated that pay varies across firms and industries for very similar jobs. It is possible that the economy could be more productive if employment were greater in the high-wage sectors and less in the low-wage ones. Incentives to encourage and enable the low-paid to move in the right direction would be desirable if this is the case and would at the same time improve their welfare. Further investigation of this hypothesis is desirable. Public policy has also affected incentives through the demand side of the labour market; notably by differentiating between part-time and full-time workers and (particularly in the past) intervening in the wage setting process, for instance via incomes policy. The nature and effectiveness of incentives for the low-paid depend on how the labour market as a whole works, and thus the constraints on individuals imposed by the structure of labour demand should not be forgotten. Indeed it is perhaps in this area that the most serious increase in research effort is needed.

Appendix: The Social Security and Direct Tax Systems[2] – Late 1989

1 SYSTEM OF DIRECT TAX AND NATIONAL INSURANCE CONTRIBUTIONS

1. *Direct taxation*
   The *standard rate* of income tax 25 per cent, increasing to 40 per cent at a taxable income of £20,700. The single person and wife's earned income allowance **£2,785**, and the married man's allowance **£4,375**.

   The single *age allowance* **£3,400** (for ages 65–74) and the married age allowance **£5,385** (65–74); both of these higher for those aged 75 and over. The age allowance income limit **£11,400**.
2. *National Insurance contributions*
   Employees (from 5 October 1989) with earnings below £43 per week pay nothing. Those with earnings at or above £43 per week: 2 per cent on the first £43 and 9 per cent on the rest up to the *upper earnings limit* of **£323** per week.

   The employees', contracted out rebate: 2 per cent.

2 SOCIAL SECURITY BENEFITS

National Insurance/Non-means-tested Benefits

1. *Unemployment Benefit (UB)*
   Receipt dependent on previous *two* tax years' NICs. Payable for *one* year. After six months there is a 'Restart' interview; those refusing to attend may be disallowed benefit. Can be disqualified if left job 'voluntarily', or 'dismissed for misconduct', or if a suitable job/training place has been refused. Must be available for work. Weekly rates from April 1989: Insured person **£34.70**; Adult dependent **£21.40**.
2. *Statutory Sick Pay (SSP), Sickness Benefit, Disablement Benefit, Invalidity Pension, etc.*
   SSP is payable if ill for four days in a row and employed. Dependent on gross earnings: if £84.00 pw or more, benefit is **£52.10**: if earnings are between £43.00 and £84.00 pw, benefit is **£36.25**.
   If disbarred from SSP due to unemployment or because over pension age or because on a short-term contract get *sickness benefit*. Based on *two* years NICs. Insured person gets **£33.20** pw; adult dependent **£20.55**.

Disablement benefit is payable if still unable to work after 15 weeks due to an industrial accident/disease. Amount is dependent on extent of disablement, up to £71.20 pw.

If after 28 weeks of SSP or sickness benefit receipt still incapable of work then may be able to get: *Invalidity pension* – £43.60 pw for insured pension plus £26.50 for adult dependent plus £8.95 for each child; an *additional pension* (AP) dependent on NICs since April 1978; an *Invalidity* Allowance (IA) according to age – if under 40 £9.20, if 40–49 £5.80, if 50–59 (man) or 50–54 (woman) then £2.90.

3. *Child Benefit (CB)*
    Tax-free cash benefit for all children under 16 or up to 18 if still in full-time education. £7.25 per child per week paid to mother. One parent families get an additional £5.20 for first child.

4. *Statutory Maternity Pay (SMP) and Statutory Maternity Allowance (SMA)*
    SMP is payable at the rate of £36.25 pw for 18 weeks. There is a *higher rate* of 90 per cent of gross weekly earnings for the first 6 of 18 weeks *if* worked two years and at least 16 hours per week, or five years and 8–16 hours per week, (and must have paid NICs, i.e. earned more than the Lower Earnings Limit of £43.00 pw). Must have been employed for at least 26 weeks. SMP is paid by employer.
    Those who do not qualify for SMP should be eligible for *SMA* of £33.20 pw for 18 weeks. Again must have paid full rate NICs for at least 26 weeks. Maybe an additional '*maternity payment*' from the Social Fund if in receipt of Income Support or Family Credit.

5. *Widows*
    Widows are eligible for a number of payments – a lump sum *widow's payment*, a *widowed mother's allowance*, a *widow's pension* and an additional pension.

6. *Disabled*
    The Disabled may be eligible for a *mobility allowance* (£24.20), a *severe disablement allowance* (£26.20) as well as *invalidity pension* (above). If attendance of a carer is required than an *attendance allowance* (£34.90 for day and night attendance; £23.30 for day or night) may be payable. An *invalid care allowance* of £26.20 pw is paid to the carer of someone in receipt of attendance allowance.

7. *Retirement Pension and State Earnings Related Pension Scheme (SERPS)*
    The *basic single person's pension* of £43.60 pw is payable to those who have paid sufficient NICs over their working life. For those retiring after April 1979 with sufficient earnings and contributions since April 1978 there is a *State Earnings Related Pension*.

Means-tested Benefits

1. *Income Support (IS)*
    Payable to those with insufficient resources including those over 60, those unfit for work or unemployed. Entirely dependent on resources – assessed at various 'applicable' amounts. Cannot get if spouse works 24 hours or more pw.

2. *Family Credit (FC)*

A weekly payment added to present family income as long as there is at least one child and one of adults is working 24 hours or more pw. FC should be payable if the *net* family income is below £54.80 pw. Adult credit is **£33.60** with additions for children, (varying by age). Receipt means *loss* of entitlement to free school meals.

3. *Housing Benefit (HB)*

Consists of payments to council tenants (rent rebates), to private tenants (rent allowances) and to both tenants and owner occupiers (rate rebates).

4. *Social Fund*

A system of loans and grants for specific purposes. For example a maternity payment of **£85.00** (lump sum) is payable to those receiving IS or FC, payments for funeral expenses, budget and crisis loans, and cold weather payments.

Notes

1. This chapter expresses the opinions and judgements of its authors. It does not represent any official view of the National Economic Development Office.
2. Sources: various Government departments and Labour Research Department, *State Benefits, 1989*. Figures as of December 1989. The information above is *not* exhaustive. As the details given make clear the system of benefits is extremely complex with numerous qualifying provisions, etc.

References

Arrufat, J. and Zabalza, A. (1986) 'Female labour supply with taxation, random preferences, and optimization errors', *Econometrica*, 54: 47–64.

Ashworth, J. S. and Ulph, D. T. (1981a) 'Endogeneity I – Estimating labour supply with piecewise linear budget constraints', in Brown, C. V. (ed.), *Taxation and Labour Supply* (London: Allen & Unwin).

Ashworth, J. S. and Ulph, D. T. (1981b) 'Household models' in Brown, C. V. (ed.), *Taxation and Labour Supply* (London: Allen & Unwin).

Atkinson, A. B. (1983) *The Economics of Inequality* (Oxford: Clarendon Press) 2nd edn.

Atkinson, A. B. and Fleming, J. S. (1978) 'Unemployment, social security and incentives', *Midland Bank Review* (Autumn 1978): 6–16.

Atkinson, A. B., Gomulka, J., Micklewright, J. and Rau, N. (1984) 'Unemployment benefit, duration and incentives in Britain: how robust is the evidence?', *Journal of Public Economics*, 23 (1/2): 3–26.

Atkinson, A. B. and Micklewright, J. (1985) *Unemployment Benefits and Unemployment Duration* ST/ICERD occasional paper, 6.

Atkinson, A. B. and Micklewright, J. (1989) 'Turning the screw: benefits for the unemployed 1979–88', in Dilnot, A. and Walker, I. (eds), *The Economics of Social Security* (Oxford: Oxford University Press).

Atkinson, A. B. and Stern, N. H. (1980) 'On the switch from direct to indirect taxation', *Journal of Public Economics*, 14(2): 195–224.

Atkinson, A. B. and Sutherland, H. (1988) 'Introduction', in Atkinson, A. B. and Sutherland, H. (eds), *Tax–Benefit Models*, ST/ICERD occasional paper, 10.

Atkinson, A. B. and Sutherland, H. (1989) *Taxation, the Poverty Trap and the 1989 Budget*, Taxation Review Background Paper, 4 (April 1989) (London: Fabian Society).

Bazen, S. (1985) *Low Wages, Family Circumstances, and Minimum Wage Legislation*, Family Income Support, part 10, no. 643 (May) (London: Policy Studies Institute).

Bazen, S. (1988) *Minimum Wage Legislation: the Likely Impact on Earnings, Poverty, and Employment in the UK*, Phd. thesis, London School of Economics and Political Science (May 1988).

Becker, G. S. (1965) 'A theory of the allocation of time', *Economic Journal*, 75: 493–517.

Beenstock, M. *et al.* (1987) *Work, Welfare and Taxation* (London: Allen & Unwin).

Beveridge, Lord (1942) *Social Insurance and Allied Services* (London: HMSO).

Blank, R. (1985) 'The impact of state earnings differentials on household welfare and labour force behaviour', *Journal of Public Economics*, 28: 25–58.

Blundell, R., Meghir, C., Symons, E. and Walker, I. (1984) 'On the reform of taxation of husband and wife: are incentives important?', *Fiscal Studies*, 5 (4): 1–22.

Blundell, R., Meghir, C., Symons, E. and Walker, I. (1986) 'A labour supply model for the simulation of tax and benefit reforms', in Blundell, R. and Walker, I. (eds), *Unemployment, Search and Labour Supply* (Cambridge: Cambridge University Press).

Blundell, R., Meghir, C., Symons, E. and Walker, I. (1988) 'Labour supply specification and the evaluation of tax reforms', *Journal of Public Economics*, 36: 23–52.

Blundell, R. and Walker, I. (1982) 'Modelling the joint determination of household labour supplies and commodity demands', *Economic Journal*, 92: 351–64.

Blundell, R. and Walker, I. (1983) *Limited dependent variables in demand analysis: an application to modelling family labour supply and commodity demand behaviour*, Discussion Paper, ES126 (Department of Econometrics and Social Statistics, University of Manchester).

Blundell, R. and Walker, I. (1986) 'A lifecycle consistent model of family labour supply using cross-section data', *Review of Economic Studies*, 53: 539–58.

Blundell, R. and Walker, I. (1988) 'Taxing family income', *Economic Policy*, (April).

Bradshaw, J. and Huby, M. (1989) 'Trends in dependence on supplementary benefits', in Dilnot, A. and Walker, I. (eds), *The Economics of Social Security* (Oxford: Oxford University Press) Chapter 3.

Brosnan, P. and Wilkinson, F. (1987) Cheap Labour: Britain's False Economy (London: Low Pay Unit) (September).

Brown, C. V., Levin, E. and Ulph, D. T. (1976) 'Estimates of labour hours supplied by married male workers in Britain', *Scottish Journal of Political Economy* 23 (3): 261–77.

Brown, C. V. *et al.* (192–3) *Direct Taxation and Short run Labour Supply*, H M Treasury Project, Working Papers nos 1–12 (Department of Economics, University of Stirling.

Brown, C. V. *et al.* (1986) 'Payment systems, demand constraints and their implications for research into labour supply', in Blundell, R. and Walker, I. (eds), *Unemployment, Search and Labour Supply* (Cambridge: Cambridge University Press).

Brown, C. V. *et al.* (1987) *Taxation and Family Labour Supply*, Final Report of H M Treasury project (Department of Economics, University of Stirling).

Browning, M., Deaton, A., and Irish, M. (1985) 'A profitable approach to labour supply and commodity demands over the life cycle', *Econometrica*, 53 (3): 503–44.

Casey, B. (1988) *Temporary Employment: Practice and Policy in Britain* (London: Policy Studies Institute).

Clifton, R. and Tatton-Brown, C. (1979) *The Impact of Employment Protection Laws on Small Firms*, Department of Employment Research Paper, 6 (London: HMSO).

Confederation of British Industry (CBI) (1984) *Attitudes towards Unemployment* (London: CBI Social Affairs Directorate) (November).

Craig, C., Rubery, J., Tarling, R. and Wilkinson, F. (1982) *Labour Market Structures, Industrial Organisation and Low Pay* (Cambridge: Cambridge University Press).

Daniel, W. W. (1980) *Maternity Rights. The Experience of Women* (London: Policy Studies Institute).

Daniel, W. and Stilgoe, E. (1978) *The Impact of the Employment Protection Laws, XLIV* 577 (London: Policy Studies Institute).

Department of Employment (1986) *Building Business – Not Barriers*, Cmnd. 9794 (London: HMSO).

Department of Employment (1988) *Wages Councils*, Consultation Document. (London: HMSO).

Department of Health and Social Security (DHSS) (1985) *Reform of Social Security* (Green Paper) 1 Cmnd 9517 (London: HMSO).

Dex, S. (1987) *Women's Labour Supply and the Demand for Childcare Provisions in the WES*, Report to Equal Opportunities Commission (London).

Dex, S. (1988) *Women's Attitudes Towards Work* (London: Macmillan).

Dickens, W. T. and Katz, L. F. (1987) 'Inter-industry wage differences and industry characteristics', in Lang, K. and Leonard, J. S. (eds), *Unemployment and the Structure of Labour Markets* (New York: Basil Blackwell).

Dilnot, A., Kay, J., and Morris, C. (1984) *The Reform of Social Security* (Oxford: Oxford University Press).

Dilnot, A. and Kell, M. (1989) 'Male unemployment and women's work', Chapter 8 in Dilnot, A. and Walker, I. (eds), *The Economics of Social Security* (Oxford: Oxford University Press).

Dilnot, A. and Morris, C. (1983) 'Private costs and benefits: measuring replacement rates', in Greenhalgh, C., Layard, R. and Oswald, A. (eds), *The Causes of Unemployment* (Oxford: Clarendon Press).

Dilnot, A. and Stark, G. (1986) 'The poverty trap, tax cuts and fowler', *Fiscal Studies*, 7 (1): 1–10.

Dilnot, A., Stark, G. and Webb, S. (1988) 'The IFS tax and benefit model', in Atkinson, A. B. and Sutherland, H. (eds), *Tax–Benefit Models*, ST/ICERD occasional paper, 10.

Dilnot, A. and Webb, S. (1988) 'Reforming NICs', *Fiscal Studies*, 9 (4): 1–24.

Dilnot, A. and Webb, S. (1989a) 'The 1988 Social Security Reforms', in Dilnot, A. and Walker, I. (eds), *The Economics of Social Security* (Oxford: Oxford University Press).

Dilnot, A. and Webb, S. (1989b) 'Reforming National Insurance Contributions: a progress report', *Fiscal Studies*, 10 (2): 38–47.

Doeringer, P. B. and Piore, M. J. (1971) *Internal Labor Markets and Manpower Analysis* (Lexington: D. C. Heath).

Egginton, D. (1987) A historical analysis of labour supply incentives', in Beenstock, M. *et al.*, *Work, Welfare and Taxation* (London: Allen & Unwin).

Evans, S., Goodman, J. and Hargreaves, L. (1985) *Unfair Dismissal Law and Employment Practice in the 1980s*, Department of Employment research paper, 53 (London: HMSO) (July).

Greenhalgh, C. (1980) Participation and hours of work for married women in Great Britain', *Oxford Economic Papers*, 32: 296–318.

Greenhalgh, C., and Mayhew, K. (1981) 'Labour supply in Great Britain: theory and evidence', in Hornstein, Z., Grice, J. and Webb, A. (eds), *The Economics of the Labour Market* (London: HMSO).

Halpern, J. and Hausman, J. A. (1986) 'Choice under uncertainty: labour supply and the decision to apply for disability insurance', in Blundell, R. and Walker, I. (eds), *Unemployment, Search and Labour Supply* (Cambridge: Cambridge University Press): 294–302.

Hart, P. E. and Trinder, C. (1986) 'Employment protection, national insurance, income tax and youth unemployment', in Hart. P. E. (ed.), *Unemployment and Labour Market Policies* (Aldershot: Gower): 29–51.

Hausman, J. A. (1980) 'The effect of wages, taxes, and fixed costs on women's labor force participation', *Journal of Public Economics* 14: 161–94.

Hausman, J. A. (1985) 'The econometrics of nonlinear budget sets', *Econometrica*, 53(6): 1255–82.

Heckman, J., Killingsworth, M., and MaCurdy, T. (1981) 'Empirical evidence on static supply models: a survey of recent developments', in Hornstein, Z., Grice, J. and Webb, A. (eds), *The Economics of the Labour Market* (London: HMSO).

Industrial Relations Service (IRS) (1988) 'Wages Councils after the Wages Act', *European Industrial Relations Review*, 171 (April): 21–2.

Jenkins, S. and Millar, J. (1989) 'Income risk and income maintenance: implications for incentives to work', in Dilnot, A. and Walker, I. (eds), *The Economics of Social Security* (Oxford: Oxford University Press).

Joshi, H. (1986) 'Participation in paid work: evidence from the Women and Employment Survey', in Blundell, R. and Walker, I. (eds), *Unemployment, Search and Labour Supply* (Cambridge: Cambridge University Press).

Katz, L. F. and Summers, L. H. (1989) 'Industry rents: evidence and implications', *Brookings Papers on Economic Activity*.

Kay, J. and King, M. (1986) *The British Tax System* (Oxford: Oxford University Press) 4th edn.

Killingsworth, M. R. and Heckman, J. J. (1986) 'Female labor supply: a survey', in Ashenfelter, O. and Layard, R. (eds), *Handbook of Labour Economics* (Amsterdam: North-Holland).

Krueger, A. B. and Summers, L. H. (1988) 'Efficiency wages and the interindustry wage structure', *Econometrica*, 56 (March): 259–93.

Labour Research Department (LRD) (1986) *Part-time Workers* (London: LRD).

Labour Research Department (LRD) (1987) *Temporary Workers* (London: LRD).

Layard R. (1978) *Hours Supplied by British Married Men with Endogeneous Overtime*, discussion paper, 30 (Centre for Labour Economics, London School of Economics).

Layard, P. R. (1986) *How to beat Unemployment* (Oxford: Oxford University Press).

Layard, P. R., Barton, M. and Zabalza, A. (1980) 'Married women's participation and hours', *Economica*, 47: 51–72.

Layard, P. R. and Nickell, S. (1986) 'Unemployment in Britain', *Economica*, 53: S121–70.

Martin, J. and Roberts, C. (1984) *Women and Employment: A Lifetime Perspective* (London: Department of Employment and Office of Population Censuses and Surveys).

Micklewright, J. (1986) 'Unemployment and incentives to work: policy and evidence in the 1980s', in Hart, P. E. (ed)., *Unemployment and Labour Market Policies* (Aldershot: Gower).

Minford, P. (1983) 'Labour market equilibrium in an open economy', in Greenhalgh, C., Layard, R. and Oswald, A. (eds), *The Causes of Unemployment*, (Oxford: Clarendon Press).

Minford, P. (1985) *Unemployment: Cause and Cure* (Oxford: Basil Blackwell) 2nd edn.

Minford, P. and Ashton, P. (1989) 'The Poverty Trap and the Laffer Curve – What can the GHS tell us?', CEPR discussion paper (London).

Mottershed, P. (1989) *Recent Developments in Childcare: A Review*, Equal Opportunities Commission (London: HMSO).

National Economic Development Office (NEDO) (1988) *Young People and the Labour Market – A Challenge for the 1990s* (London: NEDO).

Nickell, S. and Andrews, M. (1983) 'Trade unions, real wages and employment in Britain 1951–79', in Greenhalgh, C., Layard, R. and Oswald, A. (eds), *The Causes of Unemployment* (Oxford: Clarendon Press).

Parker, H. (1989) *Instead of the Dole: An Enquiry into Integration of the Tax and Benefit Systems After 1990* (London: Routledge).

Pencavel, J. (1986) 'Labor supply of men: A survey', in Ashenfelter, O. and Layard, R. (eds), *Handbook of Labour Economics* (Amsterdam: North-Holland).

Rowntree, B. (1901) *Poverty – a Study of Town Life* (London: Macmillan).

Ruffell, R. J. (1981) 'Endogeneity II: direct estimation of labour supply functions with piece-wise linear budget constraints', in Brown, C. V. (ed.) *Taxation and Labour Supply* (London: Allen & Unwin).

Schoer, K. (1987) 'Part- time employment: Britain and West Germany', *Cambridge Journal of Economics*, 11: 83–94.

Simpson, R. (1986) 'The cost of childcare services', in Cohen, B. and Clarke, K. (eds), *Childcare and Equal Opportunities: Some Policy Perspectives* (London: Equal Opportunities Commission).

Slichter, S. H. (1950) 'Notes on the structure of wages', *Review of Economics and Statistics*, 32 (February).

Sprague, A. (1988) 'Post War fertility and female labour force participation rates', *Economic Journal*, 98: 682–700.

Thaler, R. H. (1989) 'Interindustry wage differentials', *Journal of Economic Perspectives*, 3 (2) (Spring).

Thurow, L. C. (1975) *Generating Inequality* (New York: Basic Books).

Wadsworth, J. (1989) *Unemployment Benefits and Search Effort in the UK Labour Market*, discussion paper, 333 (January) (Centre for Labour Economics, London School of Economics).

Zabalza, A. (1983) 'The CES utility function, nonlinear budget constraints and labour supply: results on female participation and hours', *Economic Journal*, 93: 312–330.

Zabalza, A., Pissarides, C. and Barton, M. (1980) 'Social security and the choice between full-time work, part-time work, and retirement decisions', *Journal of Public Economics*, 14: 245–76.

2 Scaling the 'Poverty Mountain': Methods to Extend Incentives to all Workers

Tony Atkinson and Holly Sutherland

1 INTRODUCTION: HIGH MARGINAL TAX RATES FOR LOW-INCOME FAMILIES

A person on £35,000 a year who earns another £50 a year pays 40 per cent of the extra in income tax. There may be a further deduction for contributions to an occupational pension scheme, and possibly an increase in the parental contribution assessed for student grants, but leaving these aside such families keep 60 per cent of their marginal earnings. In contrast, a person earning only a quarter of this amount may face a much higher marginal tax rate. Someone with two children aged 12 and 14, with savings below £3000, is eligible for Family Credit on an income of up to some £9000 a year. This generates a marginal tax rate of at least 70 per cent. (All figures relate to the situation in January 1990.)

To see how this comes about, consider a person with earnings of £8000 a year. On an extra £50, the additional income tax is less than for the higher rate taxpayer, 25 per cent, but there are National Insurance contributions of a further 7 per cent (contracted out of the State Earnings Related Pension Scheme or SERPS) or 9 per cent (not contracted out). Taking the latter, as we do in these calculations, brings the marginal tax rate to 34 per cent. So the gain in net income from an extra £50 a year is

$$£50 - £12.50 - £4.50 = £33$$
income tax NIC

When, however, Family Credit come, to be re-assessed, it will be reduced by 70 per cent of the gain in net income, or

70 per cent of £33 = £23.10

So that the gain in net income falls to £9.90, which implies that the marginal tax rate is

$$(£50 - £9.90) / £50 = 80.2 \text{ per cent}$$

This family keeps less than 20 per cent of marginal earnings.

Nor is this the only way in which high marginal tax rates may arise. The family may be receiving Housing Benefit. If the husband of the family described above had been earning £6000 a year, if he were not contracted out of the State Earnings Related Pension Scheme, and there was no other income apart from child benefit and Family Credit, and they paid rent of £25 a week and rates of £10 a week, then a £50 a year rise in earnings would lead to a £8.42 reduction in Housing Benefit, calculated as

> 65 per cent of (£50 − £12.50 − £4.50 − £23.10) reduction in rent rebate

and

> 20 per cent of (£50 − £12.50 − £4.50 − £23.10) reduction in rate rebate

The final marginal tax rate is 97 per cent.

The effective marginal tax rate on small increases in earnings may indeed exceed 100 per cent – even after the April 1988 changes in benefits. This may happen where the entitlement to Family Credit or to Housing Benefit falls below the minimum payment or where entitlement is lost to passport benefits. The receipt of Family Credit, for example, is a 'passport' to receipt of benefits such as legal aid, maternity or funeral expenses from the social fund, free prescriptions, glasses, and dental treatment. The value of these benefits depends on the family's circumstances, but once the entitlement to Family Credit falls to zero, they are lost, causing a discrete fall in net income. Similarly, in the case of Housing Benefit, the amount assumed to be contributed by non-dependent members of the household (for example, a grown-up son or daughter living at home) depends on his or her gross income. If this income rises from below £52.10 to above it, then the amount deducted increases from £3.85 to £9.15. In terms of the total position of the household, this may generate a sizeable disincentive at this point. Or a low-paid worker may be caught by the remaining notch in the National Insurance contribution schedule. If a person moves from below £43 a week to above it, then they pay not only 9 per cent (not contracted out) on the earnings above £43 but also 2 per cent on the entire £43.

The high marginal rates of tax for low-income families – commonly referred to as the 'poverty trap' – are illustrated in Figure 2.1 for the case of the two-child family described above. This diagram is the reverse of the usual one (for example Chart 5.17 in *Social Trends 1988*) in that we show on the horizontal axis different levels of net income and on the vertical axis the amount of gross income necessary to generate the net income after allowing for taxes and benefits. The slope of the curve indicates how much gross income has to be raised in order to increase net income by £1. A higher rate taxpayer has to earn £1.67 in order to increase his net income by £1 (since the Chancellor takes 40 per cent of £1.67 = 67p). Before the 1988 Budget, this figure was £2.50, so that the gradient has been made significantly easier. But for the low-income taxpayer on Family Credit the additional gross earnings needed are £5.05, or more than three times that for the higher rate taxpayer. If the family is also receiving Housing Benefit, then the increase in gross income could be as high as £33.67.

This means that the slope of the curve is much steeper for the low-paid family. This family has a real mountain to climb, so for this reason we have christened this curve 'the poverty mountain'. There are indeed 'overhangs' where the person has to go backwards – i.e. where the marginal tax rate is greater than 100 per cent.

The picture shown in Figure 2.1 is a hypothetical one, in the sense that it describes the position *if* families had certain earnings, numbers of children, housing costs, etc. The quantitative importance depends on how many families are in fact in the situation where there is a high marginal tax rate. This is the subject of section 3. Before this, we examine in section 2 the different work decisions that may be affected by high marginal rates. What are the different routes by which a family may seek to climb the mountain?

2 DIFFERENT DIMENSIONS OF WORK DECISIONS

Our concern here is with decisions by individual workers already in employment, or self-employment, which lead to a permanent increase in their real earnings level. In other words, we are not concerned with the incentive to seek employment in the first place, so

Figure 2.1   The poverty mountain

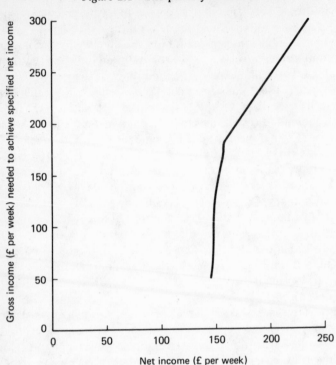

that we do not consider the 'unemployment trap'; nor are we concerned with the effect of annual wage increases.

A worker may increase real earnings in a wide variety of ways. He (or she) may work more intensively at a given job, putting in more effort, as is possible for employees under a piece-rate system, or for the self-employed. Employees may decide to increase hours of work: for example, choosing more overtime. They may decide to take on a second job or to work freelance in the evenings/at weekends. Married women may decide to work full-time rather than part-time. A worker may seek promotion to a better-paid job in the same organisation or transfer to another job. Such changes in job may involve the acquisition of new skills or training. There are a number of dimensions to work decisions.

One of the key factors affecting such decisions will be the net financial gain from increasing gross earnings; and it is for this reason that the calculations of marginal tax rates are relevant. At the same time, the marginal increase in earnings that we should be considering is probably not the £1 a week (£50 a year) taken earlier. The switch to full-time rather than part-time work, or seeking promotion to a better job, or taking on a second job, are all likely to involve a discrete gain in earnings. For this reason, it may be more relevant to calculate the marginal tax rate on a discrete increase: for example £20 a week. In terms of the poverty mountain, this means that the gradient is measured by taking two points some distance apart. In this case, it is the general nature of the terrain that is relevant, rather than the detail of the notches.

Three further considerations need to be borne in mind. The first is that the income-tested benefits are assessed on the basis of the family unit, and take account of contributions by non-dependant members of the household. For Family Credit, it is the joint income of husband and wife that determines the amount payable. This means that we cannot draw any conclusions from the level of earnings of one partner. There may be low-paid men who are not subject to high marginal rates because their wives earn enough to take them above the Family Credit level. At the same time, it does not follow that they both face the same marginal tax rate. The wife's separate income tax allowance for example means that the wife may not be subject to income tax at the margin; she may also have retained the right to pay the reduced National Insurance contribution rate for married women. Where the husband is receiving National Insurance unemployment benefit or a retirement pension, there is a cut-off for the wife's earnings, and if her earnings rise above this level the entitlement to a dependant's addition is lost. These factors mean that we should consider the marginal tax rates separately for husbands and wives.

The second consideration is that work decisions may be taken collectively rather than individually. This may be informal, as for example where there is a group consensus in the workplace about the level of effort or about such matters as accepting new working practices. It may be formally part of collective bargaining, with for example productivity agreements being negotiated by the union on behalf of its members. In these cases the impact of income-tested benefits depends on the proportion of the work-force affected. There may be a critical mass such that if sufficient are subject to high rates of withdrawal, then it becomes a factor in the negotiations. In this respect the extension of family means-tested support since April 1988 may be significant.

The third consideration is that take-up of income-tested benefits is incomplete. According to the official figures for 1985/6 (Department of Social Security, 1989a), only 54 per cent was in fact spent of the money which would have been paid out in Family Income Supplement (now replaced by Family Credit) had everyone claimed. In terms of case-load, which is what is relevant to determining the numbers with high marginal rates, 48 per cent of those entitled to FIS actually claimed it. The official estimate of the take-up rate for the new Family Credit is 50 per cent on a case-load basis (House of Commons Social Services Committee, 1989, p. xi). In the case of housing benefit, the take-up in 1985 in terms of case-load was 78 per cent, although the take-up for standard housing benefit by non-pensioners – the figure most relevant here – was 53 per cent (Department of Social Security, 1989b, Tables 2 and 6). About half of those in principle subject to high marginal tax rates may therefore not have been affected because they do not claim their entitlement.

3   QUANTITATIVE IMPORTANCE OF THE PROBLEM

The quantitative importance of high marginal tax rates for low-income families could be assessed by considering administrative data on the number of people with the conjunction of circumstances that generates high marginal tax rates: for example, receipt of Family Credit. This would mean that the non-take-up of benefit is allowed for, since non-claimants would be excluded. In April 1989, 286,000 families were receiving Family Credit and they constituted 4.2 per cent of all families with children (*Hansard*, WA, 15 November 1989). When allowance is made for those receiving the maximum amount (who are not subject to a 70 per cent withdrawal rate on small increases in income), the proportion of families affected appears still quite small – although it is larger than with the previous Family Income Supplement: in 1987/8 the average number in receipt of Family Income Supplement was 220,000 (HM Treasury, 1989, Table 15.6).

There are however four problems in interpreting these figures:

(a)   the administrative data tend to provide information about only one element of the system: for example Family Credit records do not indicate whether Housing Benefit is received,

(b)   from knowledge of the receipt of benefit it may be possible to deduce the marginal tax rate on a £1 increase in earnings, but the effect of discrete changes, such as a £20 increase, cannot be calculated,

(c) receipt of benefit may be based on income in a previous period (Family Credit is paid for 26 weeks on the basis of earnings in a 5-week or 2-month period), and circumstances may have changed,

(d) the data do not typically allow one to distinguish the marginal tax rate of wives from that of husbands.

For these reasons, most studies make use of sample survey data from the Family Expenditure Survey (FES). In the past, the government has published estimates of the number of working families with children which face 'theoretically high marginal tax rates'. The qualification 'theoretical' is used to draw attention to the fact that Family Income Supplement (and now Family Credit) was not immediately adjusted to increases in earnings; the rates apply therefore to the permanent earnings increase that we are considering. A selection of the official estimates for the late 1970s and early 1980s is given in Table 2.1.

In considering these figures it needs to be borne in mind that they are based on very small numbers in the original survey (the figure of 10,000 for example corresponds to some 3 or 4 families actually interviewed) and that they are surrounded by sizeable sampling error. It may therefore be better to concentrate on the total figure for

Table 2.1 Official estimates of the number of working families with children facing theoretically high marginal tax rates, 1977–81

Marginal tax rates (%)	No. in December		
	1977	1979	1981
50–74	150,000	130,000	200,000
75–99	60,000	60,000	50,000
100–	50,000	30,000	10,000
Total	260,000	220,000	260,000

Sources: HM Treasury, Evidence to House of Commons Treasury and Civil Service Committee Sub-Committee 12 May 1982 para A6 for 1977, Supplementary Evidence submitted by the DHSS for 1979, and *Social Trends 1985*, p. 85.

marginal rates in excess of 50 per cent. On this basis, there appeared at this time to be around a quarter of a million, or less than 5 per cent of families with children headed by a person in full-time work.

Rather higher figures have been given by the Institute for Fiscal Studies. According to Dilnot and Stark (1986), 395,000 families with children faced marginal tax rates for the family head in excess of 60 per cent, and 115,000 faced rates in excess of 100 per cent. (The date to which these calculations relate is not given.) Their figures are in part higher because they assume 100 per cent take-up of means-tested benefits. Other factors which may lead the estimate to be different are the definition of population covered, the difference between current entitlement and current receipt, the range of benefits taken into account, and the definition of the 'margin' (see below). Without further information about the method of calculation, it is not possible to explain the difference.

The Institute for Fiscal Studies also give figures covering those without children as well as those with children, which shows an overall total of 540,000 facing marginal tax rates of 60 per cent or more (leaving out pensioners). The corresponding figures given by the government at the same time, allowing for incomplete take-up, is 450,000 (*Hansard*, WA, 15 January, 1986, col. 594). These figures suggest that families with children accounted for around two-thirds of the total problem.

The Institute for Fiscal Studies in their calculation of the marginal tax rate consider a range of possible increases in earnings, and base their results on a weighted average (Davis and Dilnot, 1985), in contrast to the government figure just quoted, which is based on £1 increase in gross earnings. Atkinson, King and Stern (1982) in their calculations for 1980 compare the marginal tax rate on an earnings increase of 15 per cent with that on the conventional £1 increase. With a discrete change in earnings, the number of families facing marginal rates of 50 per cent or higher is lower by a quarter. The same study calculates marginal tax rates for wives and finds that relatively few faced high marginal rates at that date.

The evidence described above may be summarized as suggesting that 'the numbers in the poverty trap form a small proportion of all workers' (*Social Trends 1985*, p. 85) and that the quantitative significance of the problem should not be exaggerated. On this basis, there may appear to be more urgent disincentive issues – such as the substantial disincentive for the wives of unemployed men in receipt of Income Support to enter employment.

Two qualifications need however to be entered. The first is that the number of people in different income ranges may itself be affected by the tax and benefit system. As it is put by Dilnot and Webb, 'the fact that there are relatively few people in the poverty trap may in fact imply that high marginal tax rates *are* important and that individuals have adjusted their labour supply accordingly' (1988, p. 40). We have however to consider what form the behavioural response is likely to take. In the case of Family Credit, such an adjustment cannot involve the primary earner leaving the labour force, since entitlement is then lost (these benefits *improve* the unemployment trap). The result seems likely to be a clustering of earnings at the lowest levels as primary workers do not seek to improve their earnings and spouses do not enter the labour force.

Secondly, the problem of high marginal tax rates for low income families has been affected by the April 1988 changes, which reduced the numbers with marginal rates in excess of 100 per cent, but at the cost of increasing the number with rates of 70 per cent or higher. The official prediction of the impact was as follows:

Marginal rate (%)	Change	After-reform numbers
50–69	Fall of 300,000	90,000
70–99	Rise of 350,000	570,000
100–	Fall of 70,000	nil

(*Hansard*, WA, 15 January 1986, col. 594).

The 1989/90 position is shown in Table 2.2, which also reflects the changes which have been made to income tax and National Insurance contribution rates. There are 415,000 heads of tax units facing marginal rates of 70 per cent or higher, of whom the great majority (88 per cent) have dependent children. Moreover, the primary means-tested benefit for those in full-time work has become Family Credit, not least because of the reductions made in housing benefit (the structural change involved a reduction in housing benefit for an estimated 390,000 families with children (*Hansard*, WA, 18 December 1987, col. 918).

Overall, the size of the problem of rates in excess of 50 per cent appears to have remained much the same; the most important change is that now – even more than in the past – it is a problem affecting families with children.

Table 2.2   Official estimates of the number of working heads of tax units facing high marginal tax rates, 1989–90

Marginal tax rates (%)	Families with children	Others	Total
70–9	170,000	35,000	205,000
80–9	155,000	10,000	165,000
90–9	40,000	5000	45,000
100–	nil	nil	nil
Total	365,000	50,000	415,000

Source: House of Commons Social Services Committee (1989) p. xii.

4   POLICY OPTIONS TO IMPROVE INCENTIVES FOR LOW-INCOME FAMILIES

We turn now to considering the possibility of reducing the marginal tax rates faced by low-income families by reforms of the tax–benefit system. We begin with one option which has been much advocated but which can make little contribution – the raising of the income tax threshold. The fact that many families are both receiving Family Credit and paying income tax – an estimated 11 per cent in March 1989 (*Hansard*, WA, 18 July 1989, col. 146w) – has led to the proposal that the slope of the poverty mountain could be eased by raising income tax personal allowances. However, the contribution which this can make is very limited and indeed has become more limited·in the past decade.

The role played by income tax may be seen if we consider the position of a person paying basic rate tax at rate t and receiving Family Income Supplement/Family Credit with a withdrawal rate w. (National Insurance contributions and other deductions are left out here for simplicity of exposition.) Under Family Income Supplement, the withdrawal rate of 50 per cent was applied to gross income, so that the total marginal tax rate was $(t + w)$, which with income tax at the rate of 33 per cent (in 1978–9) came to 83 per cent overall. In this situation, raising the tax threshold so that the family were no longer liable for income tax would have led to a major reduction in the marginal tax rate – from 83 per cent to 50 per cent. In contrast, under Family Credit the withdrawal rate is applied to *net* income, so that the overall marginal rate is $[t + (1-t)w]$. This is equal to $[t(1-w)+w]$, so that a reduction in t has much less impact (it is multiplied by $1-w$)). The overall marginal rate with a basic rate of 25 per cent and a withdrawal rate of 70 per cent is 77.5 per cent. Taking the family out of tax reduces this only to 70 per cent.

What about National Insurance contributions? A reduction in the rate of NIC would have little impact for the reason just given. The main scope for reform in this area is to eliminate the one remaining 'notch' at the lower earnings limit. To make the lower limit into an exemption would avoid people immediately becoming liable for a tranche of contributions on passing the limit.

It is however clear that the problem of high marginal tax rates for low-income families is largely due to the existence of income-tested benefits for families with children, and it is here that a solution must be sought. There seems to be two main possibilities. The first is to reform Family Credit by reducing the rate of withdrawal below 70 per cent. In other words, a means-tested structure would be retained but the taper made significantly less severe. The second is seek to reduce the number dependent on Family Credit by raising child benefit. It is not possible here to consider both of these in depth, but in the following two sections of the chapter we examine some of their implications.

In both cases, we present calculations for a scheme costed in October 1989 terms. These calculations are based on the TAXMOD model developed at LSE, which incorporates the results of several years work on the underlying Family Expenditure Survey data. We have for example made corrections for the omission of certain information and for the under-reporting of certain types of income. We have applied grossing-up factors that take account of differential non-response, and we have uprated the data to an October 1989 basis. (For further information, see Atkinson and Sutherland, 1988.) The calculations take as their base the tax and social security system in force in January 1990 with two exceptions to take account of policy changes: (a) the tax treatment of married couples is that introduced in April 1990, and (b) local taxation takes the form of a poll tax at a rate of £275 per person per year.

5 REFORMING FAMILY CREDIT

The marginal tax rate faced by families in receipt of Family Credit could be reduced if the rate of withdrawal were decreased. Suppose for example that the taper were halved. This would reduce the marginal tax rate faced by a person paying the basic rate of tax (and NIC at 9 percent) to

$$34 \text{ per cent} + (66 \text{ per cent} \times 35 \text{ per cent}) = 57.1 \text{ per cent}$$

compared with 80.2 per cent today. This would represent a major improvement.

On the assumption that the government would not want to reduce the maximum Family Credit payable to those with incomes below the income threshold, such a reduction in the taper would extend Family Credit further up the income scale. With a taper of 35 per cent, a family with two children aged 12 and 14 would be eligible for Family Credit with an income of up to around £15,000 per year. The poverty mountain would become less steep for those currently in receipt but the reform would steepen the slope for those who became eligible.

The estimates made using the TAXMOD model suggest that reducing the taper to 35 per cent would increase the number of recipients (assuming the same take-up rate) by a factor of nearly 4. The expenditure would rise by less but would increase by a factor of more than 3, which would be a very sizeable increase in the cost of the scheme. (It should be stressed that these estimates are surrounded by a considerable margin of error.) The estimated number of family heads facing marginal tax rates of 70 per cent or higher would fall from around 400,000 to around 190,000, but there would be a substantial increase in the number facing marginal rates between 50 and 60 per cent. The estimated number facing marginal rates of 50 per cent or higher would in fact rise from 400,000 to about 1 million. (The marginal tax rates quoted here and below refer to a £1 week increase in gross earnings.)

The central feature of this approach is that by reducing the Family Credit taper one is extending the benefit to many more families. High marginal rates would become less severe but they would affect many more people.

6   RAISING CHILD BENEFIT TO REDUCE DEPENDENCE ON FAMILY CREDIT

The second approach is to raise child benefit while reducing Family Credit by a corresponding amount so as to reduce the number dependent on this means-tested benefits. This approach has also the merit of reaching some of the poorest families – those who are eligible for, but do not claim, means-tested benefit (whereas there does not appear to be a take-up problem with child benefit).

The increases in child benefit that we consider are a £7.30 increase for all children coupled with a new payment of £10 per week for all families with children. The first of these amounts is equal to the Family Credit for children aged under 11 and thus replaces Family Credit in these cases; the second allows the adult credit to be reduced to £23.60 from £33.60. These changes are not sufficient to float all families off Family Credit, since those with net incomes below £88.50, or higher amounts with older children, are still entitled to Family Credit. But the number of recipients should be substantially reduced. According to the estimates made using TAXMOD, the number of families receiving Family Credit would fall to around one-third of its 1989 level.

As a result, the number of family heads facing marginal tax rates of 70 per cent or higher would fall to around 225,000, or quite close to that achieved by reducing the Family Credit taper to 35 per cent. But in this case there would be no offsetting rise in the 50 to 60 per cent range. The same would be true for wives, where there would be a – not very large – decrease in the proportion facing marginal tax rates of 50 per cent or higher.

The problem with this approach lies in its cost. The cost of these changes is estimated using the TAXMOD model to be £7.2 billion. The gross cost of the child benefit and new family benefit is £8.4 billion, but there is a saving of £1.2 billion on income-tested benefits. (This is very largely a saving on Income Support and rent/poll tax rebates.) The cost arises because the higher benefits are paid to all families with children. There are several ways in which it could be reduced by targeting the spending more effectively: for example, by making the child benefit taxable as the income of the mother (in a two-parent family), or by grading child benefit according to the age of the child or the number of children in the family. These illustrate the point that targeting is not synomymous with means-testing and should clearly be investigated further.

7 MORE RADICAL APPROACHES

The changes to the social security system just described are modest in comparison to some of the radical alternatives that have been proposed, particularly those that aim to integrate income taxation and social security. Such integration has evident attractions. At present there is duplication of functions between the tax and benefit systems. The income tax through tax allowances and reliefs provides the equivalent of benefits. The income tests operated in Family Credit, Income Support and housing rebates are equally a parallel system of taxation.

Integration has been put forward in two rather different forms. The first, negative income taxation, proposed by Lees (1967), Institute of Economic Affairs (1970) and Minford (1984), among others, is based on an assessment of income for each family. The resulting tax calculation is either positive (in which case tax is paid as at present) or negative (in which case the taxpayer receives a payment). The negative tax payments replace all social security benefits and income tax allowances. The second version is the basic income or social dividend scheme, proposed by Rhys Williams (1943) and Meade (1972), among others. This too abolishes all existing benefits and tax allowances, but replaces them with a system of basic incomes paid to everyone, differentiated according to personal characteristics. There would then be a separation of function, with income tax being collected on all income, possibly at a progressive rate.

Neither of these pure forms of integration seems to offer the prospect of resolving the problem of high marginal tax rates. The negative income tax would have to have a high rate of withdrawal if the negative tax supplements are to be sufficient to replace the existing benefits. In the proposal of Minford (1984) for example the tax rate is 70 per cent. The basic income would similarly have to be at a high level to allow existing schemes to be abolished and the tax rate necessary to finance a full basic income is likely to be at least 70 per cent (Parker, 1989, p. 137). In view of this, we consider a compromise form of basic income which does not abolish all existing benefits and which retains a basic tax rate of 25 per cent.

This *partial basic income* scheme in effect 'cashes out' the personal income tax allowances, abolishing the single allowance, the married couple's allowance (so that there would be fully independent taxation of married couples), the additional allowance for single parents, and the age allowance. The resulting increase in tax revenue would be used to introduce basic incomes. If, for example, the level of the basic income were taken to be £13.40 per adult, this would correspond to the value of the January 1990 single person's allowance to a basic rate taxpayer. Since twice this amount is more than the value of the present allowances to a one-earner couple (£21.03), one-earner couples would gain overall. It would not, on the other hand, be enough to compensate two-earner couples, who would receive less than at present since they would lose the married couple's allowance. Other losers would be higher rate taxpayers, who would lose since the present allowances are more valuable to them (the single allowance is worth £21.40 a week). The partial basic income is intended to replace in part existing social security benefits, so that these benefits would at the same time be reduced by £13.40 per person.

Such a partial basic income may be seen either as a compromise solution or at the first stage along the route to a full basic income. (It should be noted that this version of the partial basic income is a simplification of the more fully-developed proposals of Parker (1989); for analysis in more detail, see Atkinson and Sutherland, 1989). Our concern here is with its effectiveness in floating families off Family Credit and other income-tested benefits. As far as children are concerned, the basic income is the same as child benefit, and in the same way it could be used to reduce dependence on Family Credit. With a basic income per child of £14.55 a week (the same amount as the increased child benefit in the previous section) we would achieve much the same reduction in the number of Family Credit recipients and in the number of family heads facing a marginal tax rate of 70 per cent or more. Again this would represent a substantial transfer towards families with children, but this may be more easily achieved within a more general redistribution, as would be entailed by the partial basic income scheme.

8   CONCLUDING COMMENTS

The principal conclusions of this chapter may be summarised briefly:

- the problem of high marginal tax rates for low-income families in work is now very largely one of families with children faced with high rates as a result of the 70 per cent taper in Family Credit,
- very little can be done to solve the problem by raising the income tax threshold,
- to reduce the rate of taper of Family Credit to 35 per cent would reduce the numbers facing marginal tax rates of 70 per cent or more, but at the expense of increasing much more the number facing marginal rates in the range from 50 to 60 per cent,

- the problem can effectively be solved only by reducing the role of means-tested benefits,
- in such a strategy an increase in child benefit is likely to play an important role, but at a sizeable budgetary cost,
- the substantial transfer towards families with children which this would involve may be more easily achieved as part of a more radical redistribution of the kind implied by a partial basic income scheme.

References

Atkinson, A. B. King, M. A. and Stern, N. H. (1982) 'Memorandum', House of Commons Treasury and Civil Service Committee Sub-Committee, *The Structure of Personal Income Taxation and Income Support*, Appendices (London: HMSO).

Atkinson, A. B. and Sutherland H. (1988) 'TAXMOD', in Atkinson, A. B. and Sutherland, H. (eds.), *Tax-Benefit Models*, STICERD occasional paper, 10.

Atkinson, A. B. and Sutherland, H. (1989) 'Analysis of a Partial Basic Income', in Atkinson, A. B., *Poverty and Social Security* (Hemel Hempstead: Harvester).

Davis, E. and Dilnot, A. (1985) 'The Restructuring of National Insurance contributions in the 1985 Budget', *Fiscal Studies*, 6: 51–60.

Department of Social Security (1989a) *Family Income Supplement Take-Up 1985–86*.

Department of Social Security (1989b), *Housing Benefit Take-Up 1985*.

Dilnot, A. and Stark, G. (1986) 'The Poverty Trap, tax cuts and the reform of Social Security', *Fiscal Studies*, 7: 1–10.

Dilnot, A. and Webb, S. (1988) 'The 1988 Social Security Reforms', *Fiscal Studies*, 9: 26–53.

HM Treasury (1989) *The Government's Expenditure Plans 1989–90 to 1991–92* Cm 615 (London: HMSO).

House of Commons Social Services Committee (1989) *Social Security: Changes Implemented in April 1988*, Ninth Report, 1988–89 (London: HMSO).

House of Commons Treasury and Civil Service Committee Sub-Committee (1983) *The Structure of Personal Income Taxation and Income Support*, Third Special Report (London: HMSO).

Institute of Economic Affairs (1970) *Policy for Poverty* (London).

Lees, D. (1967) 'Poor families and fiscal reform', *Lloyds Bank Review*, 86 1–15.

Meade, J. E. (1972) 'Poverty in the Welfare State', *Oxford Economic Papers*, 24: 289–326.

Minford, P. (1984) 'State expenditure: A study in waste', *economic Affairs*, 4, i–xix.

Parker, H. (1989), *Instead of the Dole* (London: Routledge).

Rhys Williams, J. (1943) *Something to Look Forward to* (London: Macdonald).

Social Trends 1985 (1986) (London: HMSO).

Social Trends 1988 (1989) (London: HMSO).

3 The Tax and Benefit Systems, and Their Effects on People With Low Earnings Potential

Hermione Parker

1 DEFINITIONS

For the purposes of this chapter the term *unemployment trap* refers to the situation whereby paid work is not worthwhile by comparison with life on the dole, with the latter defined to encompass all out-of-work benefits, including invalidity benefit and income support for lone parents as well as unemployment benefits. The term *poverty trap* refers to the situation whereby extra earnings are barely worthwhile, due to loss of means-tested benefits, extra tax liability and (sometimes) extra work expenses. *Low earnings* means low in relation to benefit entitlement when not in paid work, after deduction of income tax, National Insurance contribution (NIC), local authority rates/community charge, and work expenses.

2 THE NEED TO TAKE A WIDE VIEW OF THE PROBLEM

Most current discussion of the 'traps' concentrates on readily available, easily quantifiable information of the sort that lends itself to state-of-the-art, computer modelling techniques. The results are confusing because they over-simplify. Some components of the unemployment and poverty traps can be evaluated using computer models, others have to be left out, either because they are non-quantifiable, or because there is insufficient information about them. These omissions are important. They include liability to maintain laws and family breakdown (non-quantifiable), travel-to-work, child-care costs and behavioural change (quantifiable but insufficient information available).

Before we can begin to understand how those at the margins of

73

economic activity could be brought into more effective competition in the labour market, it is necessary to include descriptive as well as computer analysis. Descriptive analysis fills the gaps that computer models cannot reach, especially in regard to reform proposals. A proposal that looks cost-effective in year one, using computer analysis, may look quite different by year 10, after its behavioural effects have worked their way through. Using descriptive analysis the scale of those effects remains unknown, but not the direction.

Taking a wide view of tax and benefit reform is not easy. Both systems are heavily departmentalized, and the information is often hard to come by. On the tax side, it is no use looking just at income tax. NICs and local authority rates/Community Charge are at least as important, since they remove a proportionately larger chunk from the earnings of people at the bottom of the income distribution than they do from the better off. On the benefit side it is misleading to look just at Department of Social Security (DSS) benefits. Department of Employment, Department of Education (DES) and local authority benefits, grants and allowances also play a part.

Those affected by disincentive are not just the unemployed. Anyone with low earnings potential is at risk. By disaggregating the problem it can be shown that low earnings (defined in relation to out-of-work benefit entitlement) correlates with family responsibilities, disability and lack of skills. Most at risk are the following:

- anyone who is unskilled or only semi-skilled,
- people with disabilities, and those who care for them,
- families with young children, especially lone-parent families and single-earner, two-parent families,
- young people,
- older people, especially those with chronic disability, and those with skills that are no longer in demand.

In Britain today an unskilled family man in poor health has almost no chance of becoming financially independent. The more children he has and the higher his rent, the fewer his chances. In 1985 some 40 per cent of those with families of four or more children were out of work (sick or unemployed), and those in work were heavily concentrated towards the upper end of the earnings distribution (*Hansard*, WA, 21 January 1988, Cols. 836–40). Family credit (FC) is supposed to encourage such families into the labour market, but it does not give them economic independence, it merely replaces the unemployment trap by the poverty trap. Family Credit has little or no effect on the labour market participation of lone mothers with childcare costs to pay. They cannot afford to work unless either their earnings potential is well above the average for female workers, or they know someone who will look after their children for free. Over 60 per cent of lone parents are on Income Support (*Hansard*, WA, 24 July 1989, Col. 564).

The disability trap is at least as potent as the unemployment and lone-parent traps, even for claimants without children. Invalidity Benefit is higher than National Insurance unemployment benefit, and tax free. Between 1983–4 and 1989–90, while the number of people receiving Unemployment Benefit went down (from 1 million in 1983–84 to an estimated ½ million in 1989–90), the number of Invalidity Benefit pensioners went up – from ½ million in 1983–4 to 1¼ million in 1989–90 (PEWP, CM 615, Table 15, Treasury, January 1989).

Looking at the figures, it is tempting to politicise them. Did disability really increase by so much in so short a time? Are all those people really unable to work? Are they 'scroungers'? Or is it the system that traps them into inactivity? Did the earlier unemployment figures include 1 million people with disabilities who have now given up all hope of paid work?

One effect of 'scrounger bashing', whether through tighter controls or verbally, is to send unemployed claimants with low earnings potential to safer havens. Another effect is to conceal the issues. Every society has its layabouts – some rich and some poor. In societies where the state guarantees a minimum income, the key issue is not whether a tiny minority manage to cheat the system, but the price at which the great majority are motivated to sell their labour. What is needed is a system that will keep the unit costs of unskilled labour in line with its marginal product, without poverty- or unemployment-trap effects, without jeopardizing the living standards of those most in need, and with the least possible invasion of privacy and autonomy.

If people with low earnings potential are to be reintegrated into mainstream society, one of the first priorities is to consult those most affected. The existing tax and benefit systems are out of touch with the way people at the bottom actually live. Most reform proposals are devised by middle-class intellectuals (academics, politicians and/or civil servants) with no experience of what it is like to be really poor. Administrative convenience takes priority, and claimants are packaged into boxes which bear no relation to contemporary lifestyles.

Those worst affected are those most in need. Often inarticulate and scared of officialdom, yet usually rather practical about their needs and abilities – ask them what they want and they will say work. Work and a secure income. Both together, not as alternatives. Because paid work (for men) and paid work or having children (for women) are badges of citizenship without which they feel second class. It may sound old fashioned but that is the way they see it. The flaw in Beveridge-style social security is that it presupposes full employment and a life that is well ordered, yet the very poor have never had either. So they are excluded. When jobs are very plentiful some do clamber in, but when jobs are scarce they are soon pushed outside.

3   RIGIDITIES IN THE EXISTING SYSTEM

Some components of the 'traps' can be traced to design faults in the Beveridge Plan, some to the way it was implemented, and others to changes, particularly tax changes, since 1948. In this section I shall not attempt a complete list. Nor shall I examine benefits other than Department of Social Security benefits. In reality the 'traps' are functions of countless overlaps between a host of DSS and non-DSS benefits, the three main taxes mentioned above, housing shortage, lack of pre-school and out-of-school care, transport policy and even health policy. Every time a universal benefit is replaced by means-tested provision (dental care, eye care, school milk, school meals, or the short-lived minimum grant for students), every time rent, rates, interest rates or fares to work increase faster than net earnings, the problem gets a new twist. But it is necessary to simplify.

When asked in Parliament how many families are subject to high marginal tax rates, the standard reply gives numbers receiving Family Credit and/or housing benefit – i.e. those caught in the poverty trap. The most recent estimate is 415,000 with marginal tax rates above 70 per cent (Hansard, WA, 2 May 1989, Cols. 94-5). But this is misleading because it excludes families receiving non-Department of Social Security grants/allowances, it excludes families not taking up their benefit entitlements, and it excludes out-of-work families. Far more families are caught in the unemployment, invalidity and lone-parent traps than in the poverty trap. Many face implied marginal tax rates of over 100 per cent. But the number cannot be safely estimated because nobody knows what wages they might be offered or what their prospective work expenses might be.

As explained above, some components of the traps are quantifiable, and others non-quantifiable. Here I shall concentrate on the following:

Quantifiable

(a) Earnings rules.
(b) Tax beyond ability to pay.
(c) Fragmented family income support.

Non-quantifiable

(d) Availability for work rule.
(e) Family breakdown.
(f) Childcare (and other work expenses).
(g) Complexity.

Earnings Rules

These are intrinsic to Bismarck- and Beveridge-style social security systems, all the main benefits being paid as replacement for loss or interruption of earnings. To be eligible the claimant must be unable to work on account of sickness or old age, or be out of work but available for work. Only widows can build on their benefits by doing paid work.

To allow people to claim out-of-work benefits when they are in work would clearly be nonsensical, yet the system has undesirable consequences. For each claimant it creates a wages floor below which paid work is not worthwhile. Beveridge-style, flat-rate benefits with their dependency and housing additions have more perverse effects than Bismarckian earnings-related benefits, but both systems are flawed. For each claimant the wages floor has to be grossed up for tax and work expenses. For employers it has to be grossed up again for payroll taxes and other statutory levies, resulting in unit labour costs for unskilled labour that are uncompetitive in world markets, or with machinery.

For twenty years successive British governments have tried to overcome the unemployment trap by introducing means-tested benefits for the lower paid. The main result has been the poverty trap. For families with children the Family Credit ceilings operate as markers below which paid work is a form of drudgery, offering little or no reward. Table 3.1 gives examples. Disposable income is defined as gross earnings *plus* benefits, less Income Tax, NIC, rent and rates. Net spending power is defined as disposable income *less* fares to work and childcare costs. In each case the model families are assumed to pay average local authority rents and rates. The amounts for fares to work are hypothetical (no official figures being available). The amount for childcare costs is based on minimum charges for 1989 recommended by the National Childminding Association.

For owner occupiers, whose mortgage interest is paid in full when they are out of work but who get at most rate rebates when in work, the unemployment trap is much deeper than the figures suggest. Likewise for people with higher benefit entitlements than those assumed (e.g. Invalidity Benefit pensioners), or those with higher work expenses. In Table 3.1, if a job offer involved fares to work of £15, the father would need to earn £165 a week in order to be £10 a week better off than on the dole – *without* taking into account union dues, superannuation, etc. For people with low earnings potential the message is simple: find a job near home, otherwise keep your head down.

From time to time proposals are made to soften the unemployment trap by liberalizing the earnings rules, but this would make matters worse by adding to the number of 'unemployed' people. The only lasting solution is to change the basis of entitlement from out-of-work status to assessed basic need.

Tax Beyond Ability to Pay

When Beveridge wrote his Report he could not foresee the huge changes in tax incidence that would take place. These changes, at the expense of the lower paid and families with children generally, are the second most important reason for the unemployment and poverty traps and perhaps the single most important reason for the increase in welfare dependency (see Figures 3.1 and 3.2).

In 1949, a two-child, single-earner family could earn 123 per cent of average male, manual earnings before their Income Tax liability exceeded their family allowance. Forty years later the break-even point (excluding NIC and local authority rates, both of which have increased faster than Income Tax) is £142 a week, or about 62.4 per cent average male manual earnings (*Hansard*, WA, 15 May 1989, Col. 18).

Most families receiving Family Credit are also paying tax. If they

Table 3.1 The unemployment and poverty traps, 1989–90

(1) Single-wage married couple plus two children aged 4 and 6

	Not working	Working part-time		Working full-time						
	(£)	(£)	(£)	(£)	(£)	(£)	(£)	(£)	(£)	(£)
Gross earnings	0.00	20.00	40.00	80.00	100.00	120.00	140.00	160.00	180.00	200.00
Income support	+70.30	55.30	35.30	0.00	0.00	0.00	0.00	0.00	0.00	0.00
Child benefit	+14.50	14.50	14.50	14.50	14.50	14.50	14.50	14.50	14.50	14.50
Income tax	− 0.00	0.00	0.00	0.00	3.97	8.97	13.97	18.97	23.97	28.97
NI contribution	− 0.00	0.00	0.00	4.19	5.99	7.79	9.59	11.39	13.19	14.99
Rent	−21.50	21.50	21.50	21.50	21.50	21.50	21.50	21.50	21.50	21.50
Rent rebate	+21.50	21.50	21.50	2.65	0.00	0.00	0.00	0.00	0.00	0.00
Rates	− 9.00	9.00	9.00	9.00	9.00	9.00	9.00	9.00	9.00	9.00
Rate rebate	+ 7.20	7.20	7.20	1.40	0.55	0.00	0.00	0.00	0.00	0.00
Family credit	+ 0.00	0.00	0.00	33.49	23.53	14.29	5.05	0.00	0.00	0.00
Free school meals	+ 2.70	2.70	2.70	0.00	0.00	0.00	0.00	0.00	0.00	0.00
Free welfare milk	+ 1.83	1.83	1.83	0.00	0.00	0.00	0.00	0.00	0.00	0.00
Disposable Income	=87.53	92.53	92.53	97.35	98.12	101.56	105.49	113.64	126.84	140.04
Work expenses	− 0.00	0.00	0.00	5.00	5.00	5.00	5.00	10.00	10.00	10.00
Net spending power	=87.53	92.53	92.53	92.35	93.12	96.56	100.49	103.64	116.84	130.04

Table 3.1 *(cont.)*
(2) Lone mother with two children aged 4 and 6

	Not working	Working part-time		Working full-time						
	(£)	(£)	(£)	(£)	(£)	(£)	(£)	(£)	(£)	(£)
Gross earnings	0.00	20.00	40.00	80.00	100.00	120.00	140.00	160.00	180.00	200.00
Income support	+49.10	44.10	24.10	0.00	0.00	0.00	0.00	0.00	0.00	0.00
Child benefit	+14.50	14.50	14.50	14.50	14.50	14.50	14.50	14.50	14.50	14.50
One-parent benefit	+ 5.20	5.20	5.20	5.20	5.20	5.20	5.20	5.20	5.20	5.20
Income tax	− 0.00	0.00	0.00	0.00	3.97	8.97	13.97	18.97	23.97	28.97
NI contribution	− 0.00	0.00	0.00	4.19	5.99	7.79	9.59	11.39	13.19	14.99
Rent	−21.50	21.50	21.50	21.50	21.50	21.50	21.50	21.50	21.50	21.50
Rent rebate	+21.50	21.50	21.50	0.00	0.00	0.00	0.00	0.00	0.00	0.00
Rates	− 9.00	9.00	9.00	9.00	9.00	9.00	9.00	9.00	9.00	9.00
Rate rebate	+ 7.20	7.20	7.20	0.00	0.00	0.00	0.00	0.00	0.00	0.00
Family credit	+ 0.00	0.00	0.00	33.49	23.53	14.29	5.05	0.00	0.00	0.00
Free school meals	+ 2.70	2.70	2.70	0.00	0.00	0.00	0.00	0.00	0.00	0.00
Free welfare milk	+ 1.83	1.83	1.83	0.00	0.00	0.00	0.00	0.00	0.00	0.00
Disposable income	=71.53	86.53	86.53	98.50	102.77	106.73	110.69	118.84	132.04	145.24
Fares to work	− 0.00	0.00	0.00	5.00	5.00	5.00	5.00	10.00	10.00	10.00
Childcare	− 0.00	0.00	0.00	60.00	60.00	60.00	60.00	60.00	60.00	60.00
Net spending power	=71.53	86.53	86.53	33.50	37.77	41.73	45.69	48.84	62.04	75.24

Source: Disposable incomes: *Hansard*, WA (26 July 1989) cols 763–5.
Net spending power: own calculations

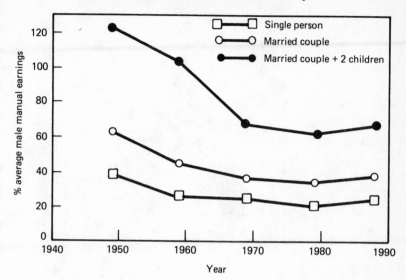

Figure 3.1   Tax thresholds and break-even points

were not, the need for Family Credit would greatly diminish. Gradually the principle of tax *according* to ability to pay has been replaced by the illusion that tax *regardless* of ability to pay is harmless, provided the 'really' poor (unquantified and undefined) can claim means-tested rebates. Community Charge exemplifies this trend. Community Charge benefit will exacerbate both 'traps'.

Figure 3.2 illustrates the changes in tax incidence since 1956. The figures refer to single people. They show tax liability (Income Tax + NIC) at two-thirds, twice, five times and ten times average earnings as percentages of tax liability at average earnings. The black columns represent the average, single earner. The last set of columns may be disregarded (until later).

Notice how by 1988–9 (existing system) all the columns are telescoped together.

Tax regardless of ability to pay results in *tax-induced poverty* and the social security authorities acquire a new function. Originally their job was to remove poverty due to lack of earnings, but today's Department of Social Security also has to deal with poverty due to tax. Figure 3.3 illustrates the problem. The horizontal axis represents gross income and the vertical axis net income. The 45° line tracks net incomes assuming there are no benefits and no income taxes. It is not

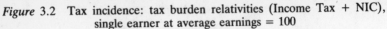

Figure 3.2   Tax incidence: tax burden relativities (Income Tax + NIC), single earner at average earnings = 100

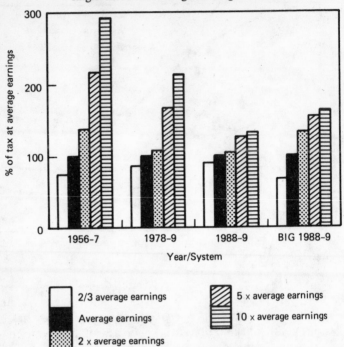

Sources: Rhys Williams (1989); Hansard, WA, 29 April 1988, col. 318.

Notes:
Average earnings in 1988–9 estimated to be £244.70 a week.
BIG 1988–9: PBI is £26 a week, BI contribution is at a flat-rate 35 per cent, earned-income tax discount is £8.75.

necessary to put figures to the poverty line. It can be at subsistence level (however defined) or can be extended to include social necessities.

The original aim of social security was to fill the gap between the 45° line and the poverty line, the *PAO* triangle in Figure 3.3a. In Figure 3.3b the line *PA* is the line of disposable income, after adding in benefit and assuming a benefit withdrawal rate of 70 per cent. Tax does not come into it, because poor people are assumed not to pay tax. Figure 3.3c illustrates the situation once poll tax is introduced. The line *BC* shows how net incomes are dragged below the 45° line, as a result of which the poverty gap, and the poverty trap, are greatly

Figure 3.3   Tax-induced poverty

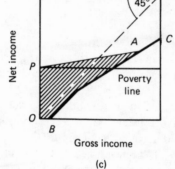

(a)

(b)

(c)

Source: Parker (1989)

Notes: a   No tax or benefit
b   Poverty gap filled by benefit
c   Enlarged benefit area due to tax slippage.

enlarged. The number of people entitled to welfare benefits grows disproportionately, partly because the assumed 70 per cent taper causes benefit leakage to people with incomes above the poverty line, and partly because point *A* (where benefit ceases to be payable) is pushed into more thickly populated areas of income distribution.

Fragmented Family Income Support

For the purposes of this chapter, Family Income Support is defined as the extra Income Tax allowances available for spouses and children *plus* the grossed up values of Family Allowance/Child Benefit.

Additions payable with means-tested benefits are not included because they have more to do with poverty relief.

Britain has never had an explicit policy, or set of policies, for families with children. Family Income Support is fragmented between in-/out-of-work families, single-/two-earner families, and one-/two-parent families. Two-earner couples do relatively well, single-earner couples drag behind. Lone parents do well by comparison with parents who stay together, but their earnings potential is so low, and so few receive maintenance, that most are caught in the 'traps'. The solution is an explicit family policy with the following characteristics: a symmetrical Income Tax system; Child Benefits at least as high as the Income Support allowances for children; good quality childcare at affordable prices; and much tougher liability to maintain laws.

Families with children are among those worst affected by the 'traps'. For three reasons:

- Failure of the coalition government in 1945 to introduce Family Allowances at rates sufficient to avoid the need for child dependency additions when National Insurance and National Assistance benefits were introduced in 1948.
- Gradual redistribution of tax and cash expenditures away from single-earner, two-parent families, due to erosion of Family Allowance/Child Benefit, changes in the relative values of the personal Income Tax allowances, and introduction of lone-parent benefit and the additional personal allowances for lone parents.
- Accelerating trend towards owner occupation and the fact that mortgage interest is payable with Income Support but not for people in work.

Inclusion of mortgage interest within the Family Credit 'net income' formula (or in housing benefit) seems the minimum change necessary to make lower paid work worthwhile. In 1989–90 *a working family* got £7.25 Child Benefit for each child and could claim mortgage interest tax relief on a loan up to £30,000. If they were *out of work*, the guaranteed minima were £54.80 for the parents, £11.75 per child under age 11, £17.35 per child aged 11–15, and £20.80 per child aged 16–17; plus a family premium of £6.50, passport benefits (free school meals/free welfare milk, etc.), 80 per cent of their rates bill and mortgage interest with no upper limit.

Table 3.2 summarizes the changes in family income support for working families since 1939. Single person's tax allowance is the

Table 3.2   Family Income Support, 1939, 1959, 1979 and 1989, taxpaying families

April	SPA (%)	MMA (%)	WEIA (%)	CTA (%)	Tax-free CB grossed up for tax (%)
				Relative value of main personal tax allowances and child benefit/equivalent, SPA = 100	
1939	100	180	45	60	–
1959	100	171	100	107 (age 16+)	–
				89 (age 11–16)	*
				71 (age 0–11)	
1979	100	156	100	–	60
1989	100	157	100	–	54

Notes:
* Value of Family Allowance not calculable on comparable basis.
SPA = Single Person's Allowance.
MMA = Married Man's Allowance.
WEIA = Wife's Earned-Income Allowance.
CTA = Child Tax Allowance.
CB   = Child Benefit.

reference point and no account is taken of means-tested benefits. For *two-earner* families with children family income support is higher now than in 1939. Before the Second World War an earning wife could not put more than 80 per cent of her earnings against tax, with maximum relief equal to 45 per cent of the Single Person's Allowance. This maximum was raised to equal Single Person's Allowance in 1942. In 1973 all earned-income fractions were removed and Wife's Earned-Income Allowance (WEIA) became the same as Single Person's Allowance. By contrast, for most *single-earner* (two-parent) families, non-means-tested family income support is less today than before the Second World War. Gainers are those on low earnings, who would not be able to use up their tax allowances if Child Benefit were replaced by Child Tax Allowances.

The Wife's Earned Income Allowance helps all two-wage (legally married) couples, whether or not they have children. Jointly they get *257 per cent* of the Single Person's Allowance. For those with children the Wife's Earned-Income Allowance helps offset the costs of childcare. But those who have done best during the post-war period are two-earner couples *without* children, who do not have childcare costs.

After April 1990 all two-*income* married couples get 257 per cent of the allowance for a single person, whether the second income is earned or unearned. But single-income married couples continue to get only 157 per cent, including those with young children, because the spouse without income will forfeit his or her personal allowance.

Table 3.3 shows the effects of tax and benefit changes since 1979. The relative net incomes of *lone* parents (boosted since 1976 by one-parent benefit) have drawn ahead of the net incomes of single-wage, *two-parent* families at the same earnings levels. The net incomes of two-earner couples *without* children have overtaken the net incomes of single-wage couples *with* children, even at the lowest earnings levels.

Almost all the families with children caught in the 'traps' are single-earner families, either one- or two-parent. Another Parliamentary Answer (Table 3.4) confirms the model family analysis in Table 3.3. Figures based on the average net incomes (including means-tested

Table 3.3   Relative net incomes, 1979, 1988, 1989

	Net income of single-wage married couple + 2 children, as % of the net incomes of:		
	Single person	Two-wage married couple	Single person + 2 children
At two-thirds average earnings			
1979–80	121.9	101.9	97.0
1988–89	117.4	99.8	96.7
1989–90	116.2	98.8	96.8
At average earnings			
1979–80	115.3	100.7	97.8
1988–89	112.0	100.1	97.6
1989–90	111.3	99.1	97.7
At twice average earnings			
1979–80	108.0	103.4	98.8
1988–89	107.4	102.6	98.7
1989–90	107.0	101.6	96.7
At three times average earnings			
1979–90	106.7	99.3	99.1
1988–90	105.4	99.7	99.0
1989–90	101.6	99.0	99.0

Source: Hansard, WA (13 April 1989) cols. 625–6 and own calculations.
Earnings Assumptions (average earnings of full-time men):
£109.30 in 1979; £254.10 in 1988; £273.10 in 1989.

Table 3.4   Net income relativities, 1979 and 1986

Year	swMC	swMC1	swMC2
1979	100	112	119
1986	100	99	112

Year	swMC1	2wMC1
1979	100	120
1986	100	142

Year	swMC2	2wMC2
1979	100	121
1986	100	129

Source: *Hansard*, WA (11 April 1989) cols 505–6

Notes:
SW = Single wage.
2w = Two wages.
MC = Married couple.
MC1 = Married couple with one child, etc.

benefits) of families interviewed for the 1979 and 1986 Family Expenditure Surveys (FES) show big changes in net income relativities, always at the expense of single-wage families. To stop the rot Britain needs an explicit family policy and a symmetrical tax/benefit system.

A symmetrical tax/benefit system (Figure 3.4) would take the individual (married or single) as the assessment unit. Unfortunately there are major difficulties so long as the existing tax allowance system is retained. *Non-transferable Income Tax allowances* would be symmetrical, but would push even more single-wage couples into the 'traps', as non-earners forfeited the value of their allowance. Increases in child benefit could offset this effect for families with children but not for those without. *Transferable Income Tax allowances* avoid the problem for married couples, but they are assymmetrical between married and unmarried couples. And they would be hard to administer. Mr Lawson's *married couples' allowance* (*MCA*) is the least symmetrical of all. Unless changed, the April 1990 tax changes will redistribute money where it is least needed. Married couples will get 25 per cent more Income Tax relief than unmarried couples (whether or not they have children), and two-income married couples will get 157 per cent more than single people.

The only solution I know of that is symmetrical, easy to administer and incentive neutral is a *partial Basic Income* combined with an

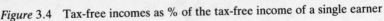

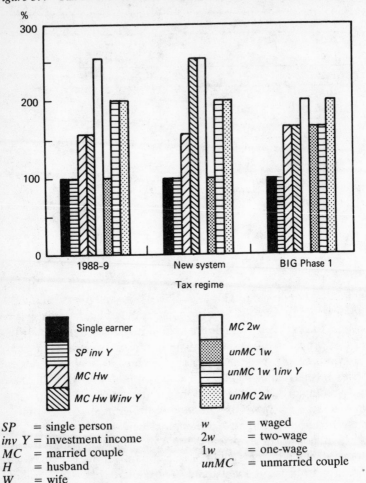

Figure 3.4   Tax-free incomes as % of the tax-free income of a single earner

SP	= single person
inv Y	= investment income
MC	= married couple
H	= husband
W	= wife

w	= waged
2w	= two-wage
1w	= one-wage
unMC	= unmarried couple

Source: Parker (1989) Figure 20.2

earned-income tax credit. This is illustrated in the third set of columns in Figure 3.4.

Availability for Work Rule

Like the earnings rule the availability for work rule is an integral part of Beveridge-style social security and a major, though largely unquantifiable, component of the unemployment and poverty traps. To be eligible for Unemployment Benefit or Income Support an able-bodied claimant, in addition to being out of work, must also be registered for work, available for work and actively seeking work. These rules follow logically from a benefit system based on replacement benefits, but their impact on skill levels is disastrous. As explained, both 'traps' correlate with low educational attainment and/or lack of skills, yet here is a benefit system that *discourages* 16 year olds from staying on at school, leaves students and trainees without any sort of guaranteed income, and deters the long-term unemployed from getting into the regular labour market through voluntary work (*Hansard*, Social Security Bill, Clause 7, 25 April 1989, Cols. 973–98).

For Department of Social Security purposes sixth-formers are treated as children, their mothers continue to draw child benefit, but the school student gets nothing; school leavers who take trainee jobs also get nothing, nor do their mothers; but sixteen year olds who join Youth Training Scheme get a weekly allowance of £29.50. Until recently school leavers could draw the dole, so the Youth Training Scheme is a big improvement, but why treat YTS trainees more favourably than school students or non-scheme trainees?

Income maintenance for students and trainees is fragmented, just like family income support. The *Department of Social Security* availability for work rule excludes students and (non-Department of Employment) trainees of all ages from benefit, no matter how low their educational attainments, or how small their incomes. The *Department of Employment* pays allowances to its own trainees, but the number involved is a drop in the ocean compared with industry's needs. The *Department of Education and Science* has its own (ever-changing) regulations for mandatory grant/loans, but only for first-degree and post-graduate students. The *local authorities* are empowered to pay grants to students not covered by the Department of Education and Science, but the grants are non-mandatory.

This mish-mash provision leaves huge areas of no-mans-land for which no government minister is responsible. *Employers* are expected to pay trainee wages that can compete with the dole grossed up for tax. *Parents'* expenditures are not even tax deductible. *Claimants* are deterred from improving their earnings potential.

Family Breakdown

For better or for worse the traditional family (two-parent, once-married, and supported by the single wage of the father) is being replaced by arrangements that are much more fluid. This is a world-wide trend, but in Britain it is reinforced by the tax and benefit systems. A second wage reduces the chances of being caught in the 'traps', but family breakdown has the reverse affect. In 1985 out of 1½ million out-of-work families, nearly half were lone parent families (*Hansard*, WA, 21 January 1988, Col. 836).

Less publicized but not to be lightly dismissed are the effects of two-earner parenting by an assortment of natural/step/common law parents on the upbringing and future earnings potential of their children. About 12 per cent of British children are being reared in lone-parent families. A further, *unknown* number are being reared in 'two-parent' families where one is not the natural parent. When both 'parents' are in full-time jobs they usually manage to keep out of the poverty trap, but they have little time for parenting. The children skip school, skip home work, leave school at the earliest opportunity, and end up in the 'traps'.

The links between family breakdown, benefit dependency and the tax and benefit systems are unquantifiable, with two main elements:

- Inadequate support for single-earner families.
- Tax benefit laws that subsidize marriage break up and unmarried parenthood.

In Downing Street there is a firm belief that mothers should not go out to work, an equally firm belief that families with children should not be subsidized by other taxpayers (unless the families are 'really' poor), and an overriding commitment to the merits of owner occupation. Whether or not one agrees with these policy objectives, they are incompatible. The withering away of non-means-tested family income support and the escalating costs of owner occupation push mothers into paid work, whether they like it or not. Analysis of the 1985 Family Expenditure Survey shows a clear correlation between single-earner status and low income. Out of 390,000 working families with earnings below £120 per week (about two-thirds average earnings in April 1985) only 90,000 were two-earner families; 40,000 were lone-parent families and 260,000 were single-earner, two-parent families (*Hansard*, WA, 21 January 1988, Cols. 836-40).

Table 3.5   Penalties for marriage: Income Support

| | Income Support (IS), 1989 rates; per week | | |
Marital status	˙IS allowances and premiums	Total (£)	Child/separation bonus (£)
1. Single person aged 18–24	27.40	27.40	
2. Single person +1 child	57.05	57.05	+29.65
3. Married couple +1 child	73.05	73.05	
4. Dad moves out:			
Mother +1 child	57.05⎫		
Dad	34.90⎭	91.95	+18.90
5. Married couple +2 children	84.80	84.80	
6. Dad moves out:			
Mother +2 children	68.80⎫		
Dad	34.90⎭	103.70	+18.90
7. Dad takes 1 child:			
Mother +1 child	57.05⎫		
Dad +1 child	57.05⎭	114.10	+29.30

Assumptions:
Mother aged 18 or over , Dad aged 25+, child under 11. No allowance for housing.

Family breakdown is disproportionately experienced by people at the bottom of the income distribution – i.e. those already most at risk of the 'traps'. Just as the tax and benefit systems push mothers into paid work, so the benefit system encourages women with low earnings potential to have babies, and families with low earnings potential to split up. With Income Support there are huge 'separation bonuses' (Table 3.5). Nobody knows the extent to which families respond to these financial stimuli, but the figures are not reassuring. Between 1979 and 1986 the number of lone-parent families increased from 840,000 to just over 1 million, and the proportion dependent on Supplementary Benefit increased from 40 to 60 per cent (*Hansard*, WA, 11 July 1989, Col. 440). Between 1980–1 and 1988–9 benefit expenditure for lone parents (excluding Child Benefit) rose from £1200 million to almost £3000 million at constant 1988–9 prices (*Hansard*, WA, 2 March 1989, Col. 324).

One way to strengthen the traditional family would be to treat it more generously. A further (but not alternative) way would be to review the laws of liability to maintain. Only a fraction of benefit expenditure on lone parents is recouped from the absent parents. No maintenance at all is received by 77 per cent of lone parents on

Income Support (*Hansard*, WA, 11 July 1989, Col. 440). Elsewhere in Europe the laws of liability to maintain are usually much stricter. Social assistance benefits are recouped from the nearest liable relative.

Childcare (and Other Work Expenses)

None of the tax/benefit model tables produced by the Department of Social Security has ever shown the effects of work-related childcare costs on the disposable incomes of families with children. Until 1987 a notional figure was included for 'fares to work', but this is now omitted on the grounds that it was too arbitrary.

Work expenses are a major, though largely unquantifiable, component of both 'traps'. If it were not for the high cost of childcare, many more lone parents would be in paid work and many more single-earner families would enjoy a second wage. The fact that neither is tax deductible, nor taken into account for Family Credit, compounds the problem.

Detailed information about travel-to-work and childcare costs is not separately recorded in the Family Expenditure Survey. Rather little is known about either. In their Cohort Study of unemployed men the DHSS reported very low travel-to-work costs in previous jobs (DHSS, 1982, p. 42). But those results beg the question. What we need to know is not just the fares the unemployed men had paid, but also whether they would have taken their previous jobs if the fares had been higher. Even if information about fares to work and work-related childcare costs were recorded separately in the Family Expenditure Survey (which in my view they should be), the data would need to be used very carefully.

In her report for the European Commission's Childcare Network, Bronwen Cohen showed that less than 40 per cent of the 0–4 age group is catered for, and much of this provision (e.g. playschools) is for short periods once or twice a week. Most UK mothers rely on husbands, grandmothers and childminders to look after their children. (European Commission, 1988). Elsewhere in the EC there are wide divergencies. In the 0–2 age group, generally speaking at most 4 per cent are catered for, but in France and Belgium the figure is 20–25 per cent, and in Denmark 44 per cent. In the 3–4 age group, France and Belgium provide for 95 per cent of children. In the UK about 44 per cent of 3–4 year olds are provided for, about half for 2½ hours a day and the rest for 6–6½ hours a day. Only Portugal has less provision than the UK. Italy and Spain appear to be streets ahead. Compulsory schooling starts at age 5 in the UK, Netherlands and Luxembourg, at 5½ in Greece, but at 6 in all other Member States except Denmark, where it is 7. In many countries school hours are very short. Out-of-school care is difficult to arrange and very costly.

From an incentive point of view, the case for a major initiative on childcare is unanswerable (Figure 3.5). Allowing lone parents to deduct childcare costs for Family Credit would help, but would not solve the problem, and would be unfair to second earners in two-parent families. A mixture of public sector, voluntary sector and private initiatives would be encouraged if parents and employers were allowed to set their costs (up to fixed ceilings) against tax, and if

Figure 3.5   Lone parent trap, 1988–9, with and without work expenses

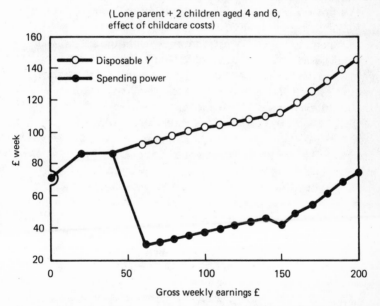

Sources: Disposable income: Hansard, WA, 26 July 1989, cols. 763–4.
Net spending power: As above *less* (a) £5 pw fares to work when working full-time earning £60–£140, then £10 pw; (b) £60 pw childcare costs (£40 for younger child, £20 for school child) when in full-time work.

Assumptions:
Earnings of £20 and £40 pw are for part-time work. Rent £21.50. Rates £90. Means-tested benefits taken up in full. No allowance for passport benefits other than free school meals and welfare milk.

employers were allowed to include *tax-free childcare vouchers* as part of the wage package. The now removed tax on workplace nurseries was a major impediment. Last year it was estimated to bring the Exchequer an average of £500 extra revenue per child per year (*Hansard*, WA, 17 May 1988, Col. 435), compared with £377 per child per year in child benefit.

Complexity

Complexity in the context of the 'traps' refers not just to the tax and benefit regulations and the constant changes to them, but also to the complexity of claimants' lives, with which the regulations are often in conflict. Although non-quantifiable and of its nature hard to fathom, complexity is a main component of both 'traps'.

The present system is a nightmare because it goes against the grain of human nature instead of with it. Most people want to work, but the system penalizes them. Most want to save but the system makes fools of small savers. Most want a stable family life, but the system dangles carrots in the opposite direction. Administration of the tax and benefit systems (including duplication) will cost the taxpayer about £4000 million gross in 1990 – enough to increase child benefit by £7 per week, although the net cost (due to low take-up) will be considerably less. What nobody knows is the amount of taxpayer's money going to claimants who fit the Department of Social Security regulations, but whose 'poverty' is behavioural or 'pre-arranged'.

For those who have not worked in local Department of Social Security offices, or stood in line to make their claims, or worked with poor families, it is hard to understand the countless, small, narking ways by which claimants are reduced to long-term dependency. Their helplessness (and hopelessness) is seldom reduced by tightening up benefit regulations, or increasing the vigilance of Department of Social Security fraud investigators. The 'clever Dicks' find ways round most regulations, the rest are terrorized.

Many people think the answer to complexity is automation, but that is wishful thinking. Real simplification requires low compliance costs, low marginal tax rates and the minimum of restrictive legislation – i.e. a system that can be automated without fear of abuse. Computerization works well for benefits that are age-related, like child benefit and old age pension. It can reduce the workload for officials operating conditional and withdrawable benefits, but it can never replace the traditional case office because it can never discover *why* people are poor.

4 EFFECTS OF 1988 SOCIAL SECURITY REFORMS

Mr Norman Fowler's Social Security Review had three main objectives: improved 'targeting', improved incentives and simplification. Unfortunately these objectives are incompatible. In the event the Social Security Review did almost nothing for incentives.

Poverty Trap

On paper the poverty trap was improved, the peaks and troughs induced by Family Income Supplement being replaced by a (very) gently rising curve. Family Credit operates like a negative income tax (NIT) with a 24-hour work condition. The continuing imposition of Income Tax, NIC and local authority rates/poll tax on income levels *below* the Family Credit ceilings adds to the number of families who need it, and produces marginal tax rates that destroy incentive (except in the underground economy). Top marginal tax rates are around 97 per cent (compared with 40 per cent for the highest earners in the land). These apply to families getting Housing Benefit as well as Family Credit. Where housing costs are low, Housing Benefit is extinguished before Family Credit, after which the marginal tax rates fall to 80–81 per cent until Family Credit is extinguished. Where housing costs are high, Housing Benefit continues above the Family Credit ceilings, in which case marginal tax rates can stay above 80 per cent on earnings above £200. Families without children get only Housing Benefit. They face marginal tax rates of 85–90 per cent so long as they are receiving rent and rate rebates, but the taper is so steep that not many are (at present) affected.

Figure 3.6 (taken from Table 3.1) illustrates the position of a family with two children in 1989–90, after the April 1989 NIC changes. The net spending power figures assume £5 a week for work expenses on earnings below £150, then £10 a week (hence the kink). The Income Support guaranteed amount (after housing costs) is £87.53. Both sets of figures assume the family pays £21.50 a week rent and £9 a week rates.

In its *Tax/Benefit Model Tables* the Department of Social Security has always assumed average local authority rents and rates, an assumption that is becoming increasingly unrealistic as local authority accommodation becomes harder to find, and more families become owner occupiers. The worst poverty trap effects occur when rents and rates are high. With high rent both lines in Figure 3.6 remain flat on

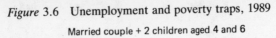

Figure 3.6   Unemployment and poverty traps, 1989

Married couple + 2 children aged 4 and 6

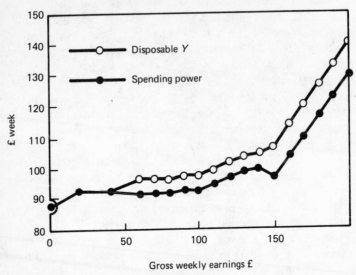

Gross weekly earnings £

earnings up to £150 (the Family Credit ceiling). Following abolition of rent controls and introduction of poll tax, large families, families with teenage children, and families living in inner cities may find themselves with marginal tax rates of more than 80 per cent on earnings above £200.

For those caught in the poverty trap, it makes scant difference how much they earn. The couple in Figure 3.6 have a disposable income of £107 a week from earnings of £150, compared with £97 from earnings of £60. If the job paying £150 a week involved higher fares to work, the apparent gain could turn into a net loss.

According to a recent estimate, only 3 per cent of families working more than 24 hours a week are affected by the poverty trap (*Hansard*, WA, 8 May 1989, Col. 309). But this figure assumes low take-up, excludes families affected by non-Department of Social Security benefit withdrawals, and excludes the much larger numbers of out-of-work men and women (unemployed, lone parents and people with disabilities), who would be affected by the poverty trap if they were not caught in the unemployment trap. Moreover the assumption that attitudes to work improve if lower paid workers make tuppence a week rather than nothing out of each extra £ earned is questionable.

Table 3.6   Poverty trap: numbers of working families affected

Marginal tax rate % per £ of extra gross earnings	November 1985 (000)	April 1989 (000)
Families with children		
Above 100	70	0
90 but less than 100	60	40
80 but less than 90	110	155
70 but less than 80	0	170
60 but less than 70	100	*
50 but less than 60	140	*
40 but less than 50	na	10
	480	405
Families without children		
Above 100	0	0
90 but less than 100	0	5
80 but less than 90	50	10
70 but less than 80	0	35
60 but less than 70	60	5
50 but less than 60	90	5
40 but less than 50	na	25
	200	85
Total with and without children	680	490

Sources: November 1985: *Hansard*, WA (21 October 1987) col. 809; April 1989: *Hansard*, WA (8 May 1989) col. 309.

Note:
* Fewer than 5000.
na   not available

The post-April 1988 poverty trap looks better on paper, but not to claimants (see Table 3.6).

Unemployment Trap

The effects of the 1988 benefit changes on the unemployment trap are even more disquieting. This is by far the more important of the 'traps'. Table 3.7 summarizes replacement ratios in 1988–9. In April 1988 average male manual earnings were £196 a week and average female manual earnings £119. The figures are taken from the Department of Social Security *Tax/Benefit Model Tables 1988*. Replacement ratios of 70 per cent or over are printed in bold type (a danger signal). In the case of the lone mother, even 70 per cent is too high unless she knows someone who will look after her children free of charge. Once again the Department of Social Security presents the

Table 3.7   Replacement ratios 1988 (Net income after housing costs when unemployed and in receipt of IS, as a % of net income when in work at various levels of gross earnings. Average local authority rents and rates; no work expenses)

Gross earnings in full-time work at weekly earnings of:	60	75	90	105	120	135	150	165
Single householder (aged 25+)	81	80	64	55	47	41	36	33
Single person + 1 child aged 3	70	67	64	63	61	57	52	47
Single person + 2 children aged 4 and 6	76	73	70	69	67	65	61	56
Married couple	90	82	79	76	66	59	53	48
Married couple + 1 child aged 3	86	85	85	84	81	76	69	63
Married couple + 2 children aged 4 and 6	90	90	89	88	85	82	78	71
Married couple + 3 children aged 3, 8, 11	94	93	92	90	87	85	83	81
Married couple + 4 children aged 3, 8, 11, 16	96	96	93	91	89	88	86	84

Source: DSS Tax/Benefit Model Tables (December 1988) Table B, p. 68.

best possible case, all the families being assumed to be tenants in average-cost local authority housing, without work expenses. And once again the figures oversimplify. Many out-of-work people have much higher replacement ratios than those in the table. It all depends on their marital status, housing costs and tenure, work expenses and earnings potential. For mortgagors replacement ratios are regularly above 100 per cent.

Why the Failure?

There are four reasons why the Social Security Review did so little to improve the 'traps':

– Incompatible objectives.
– Terms of reference too narrow.
– Too doctrinaire.
– Disregard for behavioural factors.

Incompatible Objectives

The Social Security Review's *explicit* aims were improved 'targeting', improved incentives and simplification. The *implicit* aim was tax cuts, 'targeting' being a euphemism for increased reliance on means-tested benefits – an approach which produces major difficulties. First, the known 'trap' effects of means-tested benefits. Second, the 'underclass' syndrome. And third, the incompatibility of means-tested benefits with simplification.

Terms of Reference

The Social Security Review was a departmental review, it should have been inter-departmental. It did not look at students grants or training allowances or childcare provision. It did not look at tax reform, despite the impact of tax on the Department of Social Security case load. It could have questioned the fundamentals of Beveridge-style social security, but it did not. Instead it took all except child benefit for granted. It avoided the key questions (e.g. earnings rules, availability for work rules, liability to maintain, women's emancipation, break up of traditional labour markets), and it avoided any examination of alternative systems.

Too Doctrinaire

The review process was marred throughout by the presumption in favour of 'targeted' benefits, and the automatic equation of 'targeting' with means testing – as though other forms of targeting did not exist. No attempt was made to measure the longer-term effects of means-tested benefits on incentives to work and save. At their disposal the Department of Social Security have two main types of simulation model, whose functions are dissimilar but complementary: *actual family analysis*, which gives aggregate effects on families (or groups of families) participating in the Family Expenditure Survey; and *model family analysis*, which shows in very great detail how the net and disposable incomes of selected hypothetical families would be affected by any given set of tax or benefit changes. *Model family analysis* has well known and important limitations. It is nevertheless an invaluable indicator of the likely long-term effects of change. Yet for some reason unknown to me, the DHSS seems to have relied entirely on *actual family analysis*. Always the published figures showed expenditure savings, aggregates of gainers and losers in year one and aggregates of numbers affected by high marginal tax rates. At no stage were any tables published showing the effects on model families. And when the late Sir Brandon Rhys Williams MP tabled a Parliamentary Question to get the information it took weeks to arrive.

Behavioural Poverty

The danger with all conditional benefits is that they create their own demand. We pay people for not working, for being poor, for setting up their own households and for being lone parents, and are surprised when 'poverty' goes up, when there is housing shortage and when more children are born out of wedlock. Poverty programmes, if they are not to destroy self-reliance, need much, much more than money. They need the active involvement of case officers. And they need changes to Britain's liability to maintain laws, which are among the oddest in Europe.

This is how married and unmarried couples were defined in the 1986 Security Bill:

> 'married couple' means a man and woman who are married to each other *and are members of the same household*; ... 'unmarried couple' means a man and woman who are not married to each other but are living together as husband and wife otherwise than in prescribed circumstances (Social Security Bill 1986, Part II, Schedule 12, my emphasis).

Both definitions downgrade marriage and family life. Absent parents and 'parents' who turn their teenage children onto the streets are not held responsible for them. Only 23 per cent of lone parents on Income Support receive maintenance payments (*Hansard*, WA, 11 July 1989, Col. 440). When they do, they lose Income Support £ for £, so why bother? On the other hand, men and women sharing accommodation are counted by the Department of Social Security as married (with a mutual liability to maintain) although they have not made the marriage commitment. If one takes a job they both lose Income Support, no matter how low the pay. If one applies for Family Credit the income of the other is added in, whether or not he or she is a natural parent of the child.

5   INTEGRATED SYSTEMS

Within the existing dual systems of tax and social security, poverty prevention is perpetually stymied by the need to preserve a gap between incomes in and out of work. There are only three ways open, each of which raises major problems:

- increase net incomes from lower-paid work,
- reduce net incomes on the dole,
- compulsory workfare.

An alternative approach is to integrate the tax and benefit systems. Integrated systems improve incentives for people with low earnings potential by changing the basis of entitlement from out-of-work status and contribution record to legal residence and assessed basic need. All earnings rules go and benefit becomes a platform on which to build, instead of a trap. The labour market implications are immense.

In order to understand the debate about integration it is important to know the terminology, and the differences between:

- Full, spurious and partial integration.
- Negative Income Tax (NIT) and Basic Income (BI).
- Full Basic Income (FBI), Partial Basic Income (PBI) and Transitional Basic Income (TBI).
- Basic Income (BI) and Basic Income Guarantee (BIG).

Figures 3.7–3.10 illustrate the main differences. All the graphs are to scale, all refer to a single person in 1985–6, and all assume a poverty line of £60 a week (including housing). The maximum gross income on the horizontal axis is £200 a week, and the tax break-even point (A) is marked with double arrows. Figure 3.7 shows the existing system. (A) is below the poverty line and the tax allowance (G) is of no value to those without the income to set against it.

Full Integration

A fully integrated tax/benefit system has two main criteria

- *First criterion*: replacement of all existing cash benefits and Income Tax reliefs by a unified structure of Guaranteed Minimum Incomes and personal income taxation, the payment and financing of which becomes the responsibility of a single government agency.
- *Second criterion*: harmonization of all administrative regulations, below and above the break-even levels (A) at which people pay more in tax than they receive in Guaranteed Minimum Income.

Figure 3.7   Existing tax-benefit system

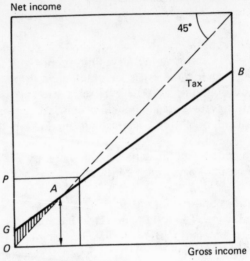

Source: Parker (1989) Figure 8.2.

The first criterion changes the tax-free amount (G) in Figure 3.7 from a tax allowance to a convertible tax credit. Everyone gets the same amount, either as a tax offset (if they have income of their own) or as a cash benefit (if they have no income, or only a small income). The first criterion also breaks the traditional link between benefit and out-of-work status, because (G) is credited unconditionally. The second criterion is the *sine qua non* of integration. It marks the frontier between integration and 'coordination' dressed up as integration. Most schemes that are said by their authors to be integrated are nothing of the sort. NIC may be combined with Income Tax, existing benefits may be consolidated into a single benefit, but taxpayers and beneficiaries are still subject to different regulations ('sheep and goat' effect).

The only system that meets both criteria is *Full Basic Income (FBI)* (Figure 3.8). With FBI every legal resident gets an unconditional, tax-free Basic Income (*BI*) sufficient to meet basic living costs. The amounts payable are age-related, with supplements for disability, but with no differences on account of work status or marital status. All existing benefits and Income Tax reliefs go. In most proposals the Basic Incomes are financed by an

Figure 3.8   Full integration

Full basic income

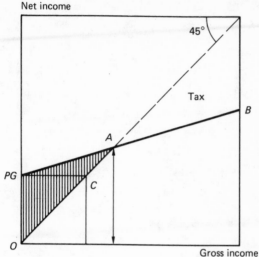

Source: Parker (1989) Figure 8.4

hypothecated Income Tax on all other income. All administrative regulations are harmonized, e.g. the assessment unit is the individual, the accounting period the year, the definition of income the same whether or not the individual is a *net* taxpayer or a *net* beneficiary, etc.

In theory a Full Basic Income removes both 'traps'. Benefit becomes a platform, benefit categories become exogenous, and paid work is always worthwhile. *In practice* a Full Basic Income would make the 'traps' worse than ever, because it is too expensive. Benefit leakage above the poverty line (triangle *GCA*), pushes the tax rate above 70 per cent for everyone – itself an intolerable disincentive.

Spurious Integration

During the 1960s, 1970s and early 1980s (starting with Milton Friedman's *Capitalism and Freedom* in 1962), various proposals were put forward for 'integration' of the tax and benefit systems through a *Negative Income Tax (NIT)*. By using family or household assessment

Figure 3.9   Spurious integration: negative income tax

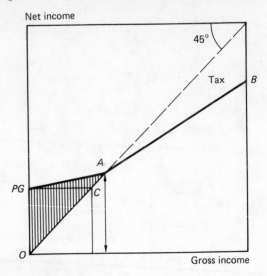

Source: Parker (1989) Figure 8.5.

units, and benefit withdrawal rates below the income break-even
level that are higher than the rates of positive tax above it, a Negative
Income Tax is supposed to be less expensive than Basic Income
(Figure 3.9). But only in year 1. Evidence from the North American
Negative Income Tax experiments of the 1970s suggests that the
combined effects of unconditional Guaranteed Minimum Incomes
plus high marginal tax rates and family-based assessment units would
be an ever-increasing case load.

A Negative Income Tax is most unlikely to improve incentives, and
would be extremely hard to administer. In fact it is not integrated at
all. It fails the second integration criterion, being much more like an
extension of the existing system (similar problems, but on a grander
scale). Incomes are topped up according to mathematical formulae,
and people who are poor are subjected to very high marginal tax rates
without any attempt to tackle the causes of their poverty. But a
Negative Income Tax does have some advantages. It does get rid of
the earnings rule, and it does rationalize family income support.

In 1983 Patrick Minford proposed a conditional Negative Income

Tax (Minford, 1983). It is not feasible. If part-time workers are allowed to get it, there is a disproportionate gain from part-time work. If they are not allowed to get it, part-time work is not worthwhile.

Partial Integration

Partial integration does not mean mixing together the characteristics of dual and integrated systems in a haphazard way. A system that is partially integrated is one with two or more components, *of which one is fully integrated*.

Partial integration (Figure 3.10) is a much more practical proposition than full integration. In the integrated part of the system (GAB) the Basic Incomes can be below subsistence level, because extra help is available through the non-integrated part of the system (not shown). These much smaller BIs are called *Partial Basic Incomes (PBIs)*. With partial integration the marginal tax rate for most people need not be more than 35 per cent (compared with Income Tax at 25 per cent and NIC at 9 per cent at present). In practice the PBI amounts and the tax rate would depend on how many of the non-personal

Figure 3.10   Partial integration

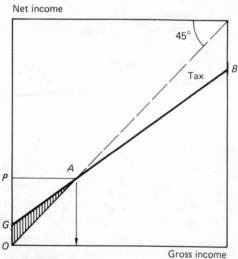

Source: Parker (1989) Figure 14.1.

Income Tax reliefs (e.g. mortgage interest and private pensions) were phased out.

With partial integration the question becomes how best to fill the GAP triangle. Most Partial Basic Income schemes use more than one instrument. Older people and people with disabilities may get Partial Basic Income supplements, which together with the Partial Basic Incomes can sum to a Full Basic Income, and which are withdrawn through the new Income Tax along with the PBIs. Low-income, able-bodied adults of working age get extra help through the non-integrated part of the system. That help depends on proof of need and may be conditional. It is withdrawn (along with the new Income Tax) at marginal tax rates which are much higher than in the integrated parts of the system. In some ways it sounds like the existing system, but the number of people affected by the high marginal tax rates *should* be much much smaller. This does not happen automatically. It depends on the detail of each scheme.

Not even a Partial Basic Income scheme could be introduced at a stroke. It would have to be done gradually, on the basis of consensus. During the early stages of transition the PBIs would be very small. These are called *Transitional Basic Incomes (TBIs)*.

Basic Income Guarantee (BIG)

This is the brand name of a series of Partial Basic Income schemes developed by the late Sir Brandon Rhys Williams MP and myself, and first officially referred to by Sir Brandon in evidence to the House of Commons Treasury and Civil Service Select Committee Sub Committee enquiry into *The Structure of Personal Income Taxation and Income Support (Proposals for a Basic Income Guarantee*, 21 July 1982).

All BIG schemes have two main administrative components, the *Transfer Income Account (TIA)* operated by central government, and the *Cash & Care departments (C&C)* operated by local authorities (Figure 3.11). The Basic Incomes are credited automatically each month to every legal resident by the Transfer Income Account, through the banking system. The Cash & Care benefits have to be applied for. This two-tier provision, with its strong distinction between the fully integrated, fully automated and fully individualized Basic Incomes, and the locally operated Cash & Care benefits, is a characteristic of all BIG schemes. The Cash & Care benefits are quite different to the Basic Incomes. They are withdrawable, the assessment

Figure 3.11   Basic Income Guarantee: administrative structure

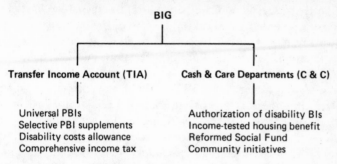

unit is the family, and they could be subject to a work test. The BIG recommendation that old-style case work be retained for all income-tested benefits is completely at variance with current Department of Social Security policy.

With all BIG schemes the adult Partial Basic Income equals half the Supplementary Benefit and Income Support allowance for a working-age married couple (e.g. £27.40 in 1989–90). The GAP triangle (Figure 3.12) is filled partly by selective Partial Basic Income

Figure 3.12   Partial Basic Income, break-even point at poverty line

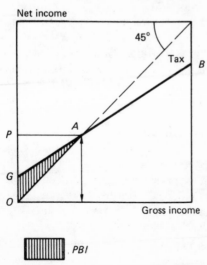

Source: Parker (1989) Figure 14.1.

supplements (for older people, people with disabilities and carers), and partly by Cash and Care benefits. The value of the Partial Basic Income supplements depend on the rate of the new Income Tax, on how many non-personal Income Tax reliefs are abolished, and on what happens to State Earnings Related Pension Scheme and personal pensions.

At £27.40 for every adult BIG Partial Basic Incomes are marriage neutral. But there is a problem, because £27.40 is £7.50 *less* than Income Support in 1989–90 for single people aged 25+. To prevent single, out-of-work householders from losing out, BIG housing benefit therefore includes a *householder element.* At nil own income the claimant gets rent and rates in full plus £7.50. Single, out-of-work *non*-householders aged 25+ lose £7.50 a week, everyone else either gains or breaks even.

Assuming income tax at 35 per cent and Housing Benefit withdrawn at 50 per cent of increases in net income, the disposable income marginal tax rate never goes above 67.5 per cent. The question is whether a gain of £32.50 from earnings of £100 is enough to restore work incentives, after taking into account work expenses. In my view it is not.

6   RECOMMENDATIONS

Integration is no panacea and the early BIG schemes needed refinement, although none remotely resembled the BIG scheme described in Professor Minford's paper (Chapter 4 in this volume), which is an FBI or Social Dividend. In this section I will start by describing a modified BIG scheme called *Basic Income 2000*, and conclude with some suggestions for transition towards it.

Basic Income 2000 (BI 2000)

The emphasis is on work incentives. All (or almost all) existing Income Tax allowances/reliefs are phased out. In return the new Income Tax is a flat-rate 35 per cent. The revenues from it are hypothecated to the Transfer Income Account, so the Basic Incomes are automatically linked to GNP through the Income Tax base. The Basic Incomes are credited monthly through the banking system, and withdrawn from those who do not need them through the new Income Tax afterwards. Unlike either BIG schemes there are Income

Tax reliefs for earned income and greatly increased emphasis on childcare for working mothers (provision and tax reliefs). Unlike the Basic Incomes, the Cash and Care benefits require proof of need and can be made conditional on participation in locally operated income and work guarantees. Changes to the laws of liability to maintain are also recommended.

Earned-income Tax Discounts (TDS)

These are non-convertible tax credits. Pay As You Earn is collected by employers at 35 per cent of payroll and the Tax Discounts are credited to each person's Basic Income bank account by the Transfer Income Account on receipt of the PAYE. Figure 3.13 shows how the Tax Discount helps fill the gap between the PBIs and the poverty line, thereby reducing the number of people needing Cash and Care benefits. The graph refers to a single person in 1985–6, but the figures are illustrative. The PBI is £24, rent and rates sum to £19 and the tax rate is 40 per cent. The Tax Discount equals 40 per cent of earnings up to a maximum of 40 per cent of the difference between the assumed poverty line (£60) and the PBI (£24), i.e. £14.40. Net income (line GCAB) starts parallel to the 45° line, but at earnings of £60 a week Income Tax cuts in at 40 per cent. The tax break-even point (A) goes over to the right. At first glance it looks as though there is benefit leakage to people with incomes above the poverty line. But the overspill is a tax relief, not a benefit.

Tax-free Childcare Vouchers

All lone parents and second earners in two-parent families would be able to put their work-related childminding costs against Income Tax, on proof of payment to a registered nursery or childminder, and up to fixed ceilings. Like any tax allowance, a childcare Tax Discounts is valueless to parents without the income to set against it. The best solution would be tax-free childcare vouchers (cf. luncheon vouchers), provided by the employer as part of the wage agreement, and redeemable at registered nurseries, childminders, etc. The National Childminding Association, in conjunction with Mercer Fraser, has recently launched a system of *childcare cheques*, but they are not tax-free.

More Childcare Provision

The abolition of earnings rules, the reintroduction of tax reliefs for workplace nurseries and the introduction of childcare vouchers would

Figure 3.13   Basic Income 2000

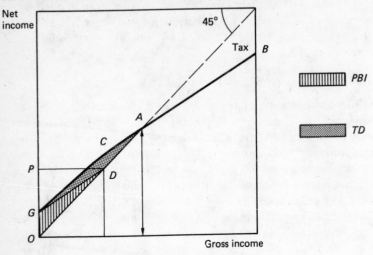

Basic Income 2000: Partial Basic Income plus tax discount £14.40

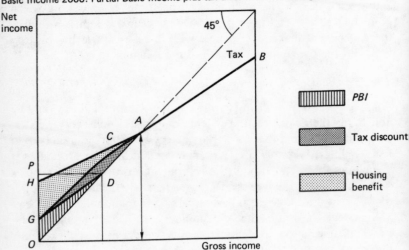

Basic Income 2000: Partial Basic Income plus tax discount and housing benefit encourage more provision. Cash and Care departments should support local initiatives, by providing premises and some finance.

BI Amounts

Table 3.8 gives an indication of the target Basic Income amounts. The full adult Partial Basic Income can be payable at age 16, or later. Either way every 16–17 year old is entitled to the same amount, whether they stay on at school, do vocational training, or take a job. And the first slice of earnings or training allowance is tax-free. The costings take into account demographic change between now and the year 2000. The PBI+ supplement for people aged 65 or over is £65. Whether Partial Basic Income supplements shown could in practice be financed by a 35 per cent tax rate depends on how many of the *non*-personal Income Tax allowances can be phased out between now and the year 2000, on what happens to the State Earnings Related Pension Scheme, and on economic growth. If State Earnings Related Pension Scheme and the private pension tax reliefs are retained the Partial Basic Income old age and disability supplements will have to be much smaller than those in Table 3.8.

Table 3.8   Basic Income 2000: gross costs by year 2000 of illustrative BIs (1985 prices)

	Population (m)	Year 2000–1 weekly BI rate (£ week)	Annual cost (£m)
(1) Partial BIs			
Adult PBI	44.71	26.00	60,448
Children/young people aged:			
0–10	8.91	15.00	6950
11–15	3.80	18.50	3656
16–17	1.43	21.50	1599
(2) PBI supplements			
Expectant mothers*	0.83	15.00	324
Widows/widowers*	0.33	26.00	223
Age 65 or over	9.19	39.00	18,637
Disability	1.0?	39.00	2028
Carers	0.5?	39.00	1014
(3) Disability costs allowance	3.0?	variable	4000
Total cost of BIs			**98,879**

Note:
*   For 26 weeks only.

Look back now to Figure 3.2, and observe the effects of BI 2000 on tax incidence. By comparison with the existing system the figures show a significant redistribution in favour of the lower paid. For families with children this change would be more pronounced.

BIG Phase 1

An interesting development in recent years has been the renewed interest in small, transitional Basic Income schemes instead of 'Big Bang' ones. The 1972 Tax-Credit Proposals resemble a Transitional Basic Income scheme, the main difference being the unit of assessment, which would have remained the single person or married couple, as under existing law. Thanks to computerization and independent taxation, this is no longer necessary.

The main economic stumbling block with the 1972 scheme was cost, but this is avoidable provided the BIs are *deducted* from existing benefit entitlements instead of being *added* to them. During Autumn 1987 and Spring 1988 several Transitional Basic Income schemes were costed at LSE, using Tony Atkinson's and Holly Sutherland's TAXMOD (their chapter refers). One of the advantages of PBIs and TBIs is their flexibility. Policy proposals can be made to reflect the priorities of the government of the day, and can be adapted when there is a change of government.

BIG Phase 1 was worked out as stage one of a transition towards *Basic Income 2000*, the objectives being threefold:

- To prepare the way for future change.
- To reduce dependence on Income Support and Family Credit.
- To make the tax and benefit systems more symmetrical.

From the incentive point of view the second of these objectives is the most important, the others are instruments. Reduced dependence on Income Support gets priority, because of the way Income Support excludes unemployed people and lone parents from the labour market. Family Credit is the second target, because of its poverty trap effects. Housing benefit remains unchanged until BIG Phase 2.

The idea behind the proposal is very simple. Escape the present vicious circle of ever-increasing benefit dependency, and enter a virtuous circle, by giving every man, woman and child a small

Figure 3.14   BIG phase 1 options for the unemployed:
(TBIs as a proportion of IS, 1988–9)

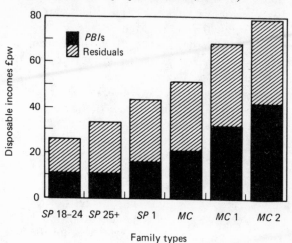

Family types

Source: Parker (1989) Figure 20.1.
Notes:
*SP*1 includes one-parent benefit (child under 5)
*MC*1 and *MC*2 children are under 11.

Transitional Basic Income (instead of existing personal Income Tax
allowances and Child Benefit). Let those who are out of work choose
whether to top up their Transitional Basic Incomes with Income
Support (and red tape) *or* stick with their Transitional Basic Income,
earned-income tax reliefs (and residual Family Credit/Housing
Benefit), using them as platforms on which to build through part-time
work. Assuming that some at least choose the second option, use the
Income Support savings/increased tax revenues to increase the TBIs
next time around, thus tilting the balance even more strongly against
benefit dependency.

For those caught in the unemployment trap the effect of BIG Phase
1 is small but significant (Figure 3.14). Income Support immediately
becomes a smaller part of the total benefit package. There is no
change to overall entitlement, but henceforth only about half carries
an earnings rule, or an availability for work rule.

For most people (those in paid work) the Transitional Basic
Incomes are tax (or child benefit) offsets. For those receiving NI
benefits or Income Support they are benefit offsets. Additionally,

instead of wife's earned income allowance *everybody* (men and women, married or single) is allowed to earn £20 a week tax-free (in the form of a non-convertible tax credit). This makes life easier for the Inland Revenue (who would have the greatest difficulty in collecting Income Tax from the first £1 of earned income), enhances work incentives and makes the system symmetrical (Figure 3.4).

The Transitional Basic Incomes in Figure 3.14 are £10.50 a week for each man, woman and child. Unification of NI contribution with income tax is left to BIG phase 2. This scheme would have been revenue neutral in 1988–9 provided the starting rate of Income Tax had been held at 27 per cent, the top rate of tax had been reduced to 45 per cent (instead of 40 per cent), and tax relief for mortgage interest and superannuation had been restricted to 27 per cent. The costings are in Table 3.9 at the end of this Chapter. They include £803 million for childcare. One-parent benefit is restricted to lone parents with children under 5, but all lone parents in paid work and all second-earner parents may set up to £38.50 pw for the first child and up to £23.10 for each successive child against Income Tax, on proof of payment to a registered nursery or childminder. The earned-income Tax Discount is worth £5.40 pw, and the childcare Tax Discount a maximum of £10.40 pw for first children and £6.24 pw for successive children.

The 1988–9 Budget with its huge tax cuts was a marvellous opportunity for changes that would lift the lower paid out of net tax. Table 3.10 at the end of this Chapter shows how little it achieved for people with low earnings potential, and how much more could have been achieved through BIG Phase 1. At earnings of £150 a week the gain for single-wage couples with two children would have been £13 a week (instead of £3 as a result of Mr Lawson's changes). The beneficial effects of the childcare tax reliefs are clearly visible, although at £50 pw the mother pays too little tax to be able to benefit in full. (Childcare vouchers would be better.) A lone mother with two children under five and a wage of £100 would have been £17 pw better off, and most of the extra would not count against Family Credit. Provided that good childcare facilities can be made available, the incentive for lone parents to take paid work increases enormously.

By comparison with 1987–88, BIG Phase 1 produces gains for most people, which is not surprising considering the scale of Mr Lawson's tax cuts. By comparison with 1988–9 people in the middle of the earnings distribution would lose, but not by comparison with 1987–8. Two-earner couples without children lose most. Two-earner couples with children tend to gain, mainly because of the childcare tax reliefs (see Table 3.11).

7 CONCLUSION

The purpose of this chapter has not been to try and 'sell' any particular scheme, but to recommend that partial integration be taken seriously. Basic Income is not the same as Negative Income Tax, and there are substantive differences between Full Basic Income, Partial Basic Income and Transitional Basic Income. The best way to restore incentives for people with low earnings potential may well be through a partial integration strategy with two components – one integrated and automated, the other combining cash help with job creation, training, childcare and so forth. But a Cash & Care strategy cannot succeed without the BIs, because good case work depends on a small case load.

Although the outlook for further tax cuts is gloomy at present, a standard Income Tax rate of 20 per cent remains government policy 'when circumstances permit'. From the point of view of incentives, cutting the basic Income Tax rate is not the best way to target resources. Moreover a tax rate below 35 per cent (including NIC) is unlikely to solve the twin problems of poverty and incentives, whether through a partially integrated system or through the existing multifarious systems.

Finally a few words about the TUC's proposals in this volume. Partial integration, it seems to me, fits remarkably well with their three-point strategy for reform of taxes and benefits, active labour market policies and the introduction of a national minimum wage. Basic Income is the only tax-benefit reform option currently available that faces up to the limitations of social insurance in post-industrial economies, whilst avoiding the poverty-trap effects of a residual welfare state. Partial Basic Income – unlike Full Basic Income – is a very flexible mechanism. Given, however, that Partial Basic Income is by definition not enough to live on, active labour market policies are a logical and necessary accompaniment, otherwise too many people would have to top up their Partial Basic Incomes with Cash & Care benefits.

The question of a national minimum wage is more complicated. At present, despite wild claims, nobody knows what effects a Basic Income would have on wages, except that the effects would depend

Table 3.9   BIG phase 1 costings

	Estimated revenue loss (−) or gain (+), projected October 1988 incomes	
	Itemised	Cumulative
1. Partial basic incomes (PBIs) of £10.50 pw/£546 pa for each adult, from age 18, replace all the personal *IT* allowances (including age allowance); the PBIs are deducted £ for £ from existing NI benefits and count as a resource for *IS*; residual NI benefits and IS become tax-free; *IVB* taxable like other benefits; abolition of pensioner earnings rule; starting rate of tax is 27 per cent; tax rate is 40 per cent on incomes (excluding BIs) above £21,905 pa/£421.25 pw; tax rate is 45 per cent on incomes (excluding BIs) above £24,405 pa/£469.33 pw		+10,047
2. Independent taxation of husband and wife	− 420	+ 9627
3. New age allowance of £1,040 pa/£20 pw per person, with upper limit £8,460 pa/£162.70 pw; married couples (either aged 65+) can choose joint taxation	−1082	+ 8545
4. First £20 pw of earned income becomes tax-free; fixed amount tax discount of £5.40 pw	−6466	+ 2079
5. Child benefit becomes child PBI and goes up to £10.50; the extra £3.25 is deducted £ for £ from family credit and counts as a resource for *IS*. Net cost	−1793	+ 286
6. Mortgage interest and superannuation *IT* reliefs restricted to 27 per cent	+ 397	+ 683
7. Abolition of contracted-out NI contribution	+1914	+ 2597
8. PBI supplement of about £4 for each person aged 65+ in receipt of NI retirement pension or *IS* with pensioner premium, each *IVB* claimant, each *SDA* claimant and each *ICA* claimant. Net cost	−1914	+ 683
9. One-parent benefit restricted to children under 5	+ 120	+ 803
10. Work-related childcare tax reliefs and increased childcare provision	− 803	NIL
OVERALL GROSS REVENUE GAIN/LOSS		NIL

Notes:
IS = Income Support.
IT = Income Tax.
IVB = Invalidity Benefit.
SDA = Severe Disability Allowance.
ICA = Invalid Care Allowance.

Sources: Parker (1989) Table 20.2.
TAXMOD, London School of Economics.

Table 3.10   BIG phase 1: net incomes of non-mortgagors earning up to £200 per week, 1988 prices and incomes

	Net incomes from gross weekly earnings of:			
	£50	£100	£150	£200
1 Single person				
1987–8	47	77	109	141
1988–9	48	81	112	145
1988–9, *BP*1	50	82	112	144
2 Single-wage *MC*				
1987–8	48	84	116	148
1988–9	48	88	119	152
1988–9, *BP*1	60	92	122	154
3 Two-wage *MC*				
1987–9	–	95	130	160
1988–9	–	95	135	168
1988–9, *BP*1	–	100	132	164
4 Single-wage *MC* + 2 children				
1987–8	62	98	130	162
1988–9	62	102	133	166
1988–9, *BP*1	81	113	143	175
5 Two-wage *MC* + 2 children				
1987–8	–	110	145	175
1988–9	–	110	150	183
1988–9, *BP*1 (no childcare costs)	–	121	153	185
1988–9, *BP*1 (max. childcare tax relief)	–	129	170	202
6 *SP* + 2 children under five				
1987–8	67	103	135	167
1988–9	67	107	138	171
1988–9, *BP*1 (no childcare costs)	76	108	138	170
1988–9, *BP*1 (max. childcare tax relief)	84	124	154	186
7 *SP* + 2 children over five				
1987–8	67	103	135	167
1988–9	67	107	138	171
1988–9, *BP*1 (no childcare costs)	71	103	133	165
1988–9, *BP*1 (max. childcare tax relief)	79	119	149	181

Assumptions: In the case of two-wage married couples, the combined earnings come to the totals shown. On combined earnings of £100, each spouse earns £50, on combined earnings of £150–£500 the wife earns £100, and on combined earnings above £500 the wife earns £200.

Notes:
*BP*1 = BIG PHASE 1.
MC   = Married couple.
Source: Parker (1989) Table 20.3.

Effects of the Tax and Benefit Systems

Table 3.11   BIG phase 1: net incomes of mortgagors earning between £200 and £1000 per week, 1988 prices and incomes

	Net incomes from gross weekly earnings of:					
	£150	£200	£300	£400	£500	£1000
1 Single person						
1987–8	119	156	221	294	360	596
1988–9	121	159	225	300	371	671
1988–9, BP1	122	159	223	296	357	632
2 Single-wage MC						
1987–8	126	163	228	301	370	612
1988–9	128	166	232	307	382	683
1988–89 BP1	133	170	234	307	368	643
3 Two-wage MC						
1987–8	–	176	240	304	377	652
1988–9	–	183	247	313	387	696
1988–9, BP1	–	179	241	305	378	666
4 Single-wage MC + 2 children						
1987–8	140	178	242	315	385	627
1988–9	143	181	247	321	396	697
1988–9, BP1	154	191	255	328	389	664
5 Two-wage MC + 2 children						
1987–8	–	190	254	319	392	667
1988–9	–	197	261	327	402	710
1988–9, BP1 (no childcare costs)	–	200	262	326	399	687
1988–9, BP1 (max. childcare TD)	–	217	279	343	416	704
6 SP + 2 children under five						
1987–8	145	177	–	–	–	–
1988–9	147	180	–	–	–	–
1988–9, BP1 (no childcare costs)	148	180	–	–	–	–
1988–9, BP1 (max. childcare TD)	165	197	–	–	–	–
7 SP + 2 children over five						
1987–8	145	177	–	–	–	–
1988–9	147	180	–	–	–	–
1988–9, BP1 (no childcare costs)	143	180	–	–	–	–
1988–9, BP1 (max. childcare TD)	160	192	–	–	–	–

Assumptions: Mortgage is assumed to be £20,000 at earnings of £150 and for the lone parent at earnings of £150 and £200. Otherwise mortgage is assumed to be £30,000. Interest rate 10 per cent. Division of earnings for two-wage couples, as in Parker (1989) Table 20.3.

Note: BP1 = BIG PHASE 1.
MC = Married couple.
TD = Tax discount.
Source: Parker (1989) Table 20.4.

very much on the BI amounts and would almost certainly differ between men and women. Basic Income neither precludes nor requires a national minimum wage, which is essentially about trade offs. If the priority is to improve work incentives, then the case for minimum wage legislation is very strong, since without it more people would need Cash & Care benefits, with their high marginal tax rates. Moreover this argument applies just as strongly to the existing social security system as to a Basic Income system. If, on the other hand, the priority is to 'price people into jobs' (no matter how low paid and uneconomic) then a national minimum wage would obviously impede this process.

References

Department of Health and Social Security (DHSS) (1982) *DHSS Cohort Study of Unemployment*, DHSS working paper, 1.

European Commission (1988) *Caring for Children: Services and Policies for Childcare and Equal Opportunities in the United Kingdom*, Report for the European Commission's Childcare Network (Brussels: Commission of the EC).

Friedman, M. (1962) *Capitalism and Freedom* (Chicago: Chicago University Press).

Minford, P. *et al.* (1983) *Unemployment: Cause and Cure* Oxford: (Martin Robertson) (2nd edn. 1985, Basil Blackwell).

Parker, H. (1989) *Instead of the Dole: An Enquiry into Integration of the Tax and Benefit Systems After 1990* (London: Routledge).

Rhys Williams, B. (1989), in Parker, H. (ed.), *Stepping Stones to Independence: National Insurance After 1990* (Aberdeen: Aberdeen University Press).

4 The Poverty Trap After the Fowler Reforms[1]

Patrick Minford

What is the aim of income-support systems? I shall take it that, in the eyes of the voter who pays for them and whose judgement is therefore paramount, the aim is to help the poor without damaging incentives more than necessary. That there is a trade-off between poverty-relief and incentives seems unavoidable; the relevant question is how to improve it and where to be located along that best trade-off. The method used in this chapter for assessing this trade-off is to compute efficiency losses of various proposals, assuming that they are all constrained to provide a minimum living standard to those in need. No account otherwise is taken of distributional aspects: it is assumed that there is no desire to reduce inequality for its own sake, over and above the provision of such minimum help. Efficiency losses are computed in the usual manner of public finance by assessing the income-compensated effects on supply and the consequent 'welfare triangles'. Given that they are all subject to the constraint of providing the same minimum support (the 'safety net'), the proposals are judged purely by their efficiency or welfare loss.

Many people feel strongly about distributional aspects, treated in this particular way here. No claim is made here that this treatment is necessarily right, morally for example. The reason the assumption is chosen is that it appears relevant to policy-makers because it is close to values espoused by voters at the present time. Obviously such a claim is hard to test except by revealed political preference at elections: but there is no evidence that the current level of social support through benefits, essentially unchanged now for a decade in real terms, is far enough away from what voters want as to constitute an electoral liability for the government. All proposals are subject to the same revenue constraint also; in the present context this is given by the probable availability of a budget surplus to distribute in various ways. But this of course in no way alters the ranking of the proposals which is what interests us.

1   THE PRESENT SYSTEM OF TAX AND BENEFIT

The present system is after the Fowler reforms close to a negative income tax. The main difference is administrative; people in work have to claim from the Department of Social Security (DSS) instead of collecting automatically from the Inland Revenue. Supplementary benefit (now Income Support) effectively sets a minimum income level which could be seen as a further difference; hence the marginal tax rate becomes 100 per cent at this level.

The current situation is depicted, for a family man with two children and a non-working wife, in Figure 4.1. Fowler improved incentives for families, both to take work (the unemployment trap) and to take better-paid work (the poverty trap); and it is for families that these incentives are at least on paper the poorest. Nevertheless, existing marginal rates for these remain uncomfortably high over various ranges, as Figure 4.1 clearly shows.

I begin by considering reform of the unemployment trap. This seems to be a relatively easy problem in principle, if not necessarily in political practice. Then I turn to possible reforms of the poverty trap.

Figure 4.1   The relationship of net income to gross earnings, 1988/9; married man, 2 children, non-working wife

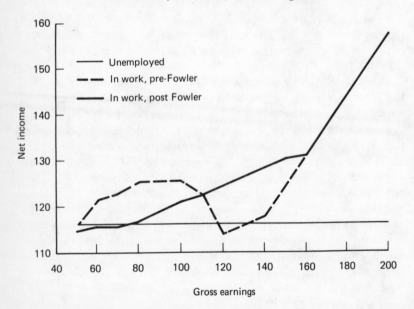

I begin with a critical review of the Basic Income Guarantee proposal. Then I set out my own gradualist proposal.

My assumption in considering poverty trap reform is that the Chancellor has a choice of various routes through which to cut taxes over the next five years; the basic issue is what priority to give to raising thresholds, cutting the standard rate, or cutting the withdrawal rate for benefit in the poverty trap. Hence the background to the discussion of tax structure is one of an improving government revenue constraint.

2   REFORM OF THE UNEMPLOYMENT TRAP

Workfare – that ugly but convenient American neologism meaning working for benefits – is a way of preserving the support level for the unemployed while ensuring that they take any 'approved' opportunity for work; if they refuse it they lose benefit, so the effective marginal tax rate on work becomes zero (because if they do not take the work they technically get nothing from the state, so nothing is taken away when they work).

Workfare is close to the Beveridge rules in our system, so little applied in practice; it also is similar to the Swedish system, and is widely used in the USA, apparently with some success (Burton, 1986). Given that there is little scope at present for other changes in the tax-benefit system, it seems to me to be a highly promising avenue for getting the long-term unemployed into work. Restart has begun along this route and has been useful in its effect. Politically, the response to Restart has been encouraging; and the step of making the Youth Training Scheme an approved scheme has met with general popular approval. I would like to see the new unified scheme become a similarly approved one, or if not to ensure that benefit officers make refusal of a place on it a cause for action on benefit entitlement.

The ingenious idea of the Action credit (Ashby, 1988) has recently been put forward, whereby the unemployed may work part-time without losing benefit and put the proceeds into a saving account, to be released when they get a full-time job. For the unemployed, this quite clearly creates an increased incentive to work legitimately part-time and thence to take a full-time job.

There are two problems. First, this incentive may not be sufficient to dominate the alternative of benefits plus work on the side, especially since the income is not received until the full-time job is obtained.

Second, and more important – since the first problem does not stop Action credit from being at least a marginal improvement – the position of the short-term unemployed must be considered. They now would have an enhanced incentive to stay longer on the dole, since the benefit package is augmented by the part-time work return; it could become highly attractive to qualify for this programme by becoming long-term unemployed. Thus could a subsidy to the long-term unemployed condition produce more long-term unemployed.

This second problem seems too potentially worrying for this idea to be adopted; even as a temporary, 'unrepeatable' scheme for today's long-term unemployed only, it is dangerous. For the temporary scheme of yesterday has a way of acquiring long life; look at the 'temporary employment subsidy'!

Meanwhile, workfare will push the long-term unemployed back into the labour market, while maintaining their living standards at the Supplementary Benefit/Income Support rate. Some, one hopes many, will opt instead to take non-workfare jobs and claim Family Income Supplement (now Family Credit). Either way the reintegration of the long-term unemployed into the labour market will at last occur, as intended by law and endorsed by popular morality. As a footnote to this discussion, the treatment of those who take up Unemployment and Supplementary Benefit even though they intend to work and have been working for most of the year could be reconsidered. Clearly, benefit is not intended to be drawn by people who are deliberately engaging in regular spells of unemployment; yet under the present rules and practices such behaviour is not necessarily prevented. The questionnaires filled out as a condition of benefit should test for this behaviour, and it should be penalized. Otherwise, we have here another form of the (part-year) unemployment trap.

3   REFORM OF THE POVERTY TRAP

The Basic Income Guarantee (BIG)

Basic Income Guarantee comes in varying sizes (Parker, 1989, discusses a large selection of schemes). The smallest award a modest fixed income to all including the unemployed; all further income is to be acquired by work. Such schemes amount to a cut in unemployment benefits and a consolidation of existing child benefits into the Basic Income Guarantee. I in effect put forward such a proposal in my '70% benefit cap' notion (Minford, 1983, 1985); but it did not get a rapturous welcome, because of the widespread desire to underpin the living standard of the unemployed, who are seen – often no doubt rightly – as victims of misfortune, even if they could adjust more rapidly by finding new work. So small Basic Income Guarantees will not get far for the present at least.

Large Basic Income Guarantees take on board the constraint that the Basic Income Guarantee must be no less than the Supplementary Benefit rate. These constitute a massive negative poll tax to the whole population. This requires a substantial marginal tax rate on that whole population to finance it, even assuming no adverse supply effects. But adverse supply effects there will surely be for two reasons.

First, a jump in the standard rate by 10 percentage points or more (costings are uncertain and differ) would have a substitution effect for sure – that is an effect due to the change in the relative price of leisure, ignoring the effect of lower net income (Brown *et al*. 1987, for example set the substitution elasticity at around 0.15 and their number is fairly typical: Minford and Ashton, 1989, have 0.13 for the average employed male; see Bowen *et al*. Chapter 1 in this volume). Though small for each household it would when spread across all be a significant slice of Gross Domestic Product. True, among low-income groups the marginal tax rates would fall to the standard rate, which would produce some compensating substitution or relative price effects among them; but though welcome, this would be unlikely to produce as much in value as the effect on the average and higher paid, because the latter are much more productive and numerous.

Second, there would be a negative income effect on work for those on low incomes – see Figure 4.2. This is the effect on leisure due to the change in net income; here net income would be raised for this group by the payment of a Basic Income Guarantee – the 'negative poll tax' effect – and so this group's demand for leisure would rise and their work effort fall. For the majority on middle incomes the income effect should be small; but for the part-timers on such pay rates it will be seriously negative. For the higher earners the income effect would be positive but this has to be set against the powerful substitution effect.

Figure 4.2 sets out the qualitative possibilities if the tax needed is costed assuming no supply effects. While the net effect on supply of the higher and lower paid is ambiguous because income and substitution effects go in opposite directions, that on the majority is negative because of substitution with negligible income effects. So there are

Figure 4.2   Basic Income Guarantee (BIG)
   a   High income; b   Average income; c   Low income.

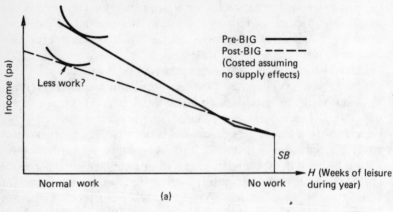

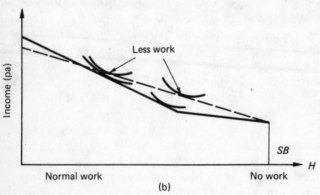

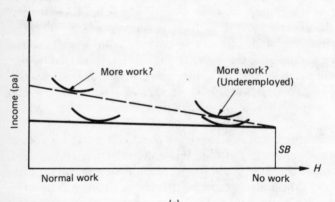

clear dangers of serious negative effects on output. These are examined more formally in the Appendix to this chapter.

These would not only be damaging to the economy in themselves (besides output loss, remember that the pure efficiency losses relate to substitution effects, all negative except for the minority of less productive low paid). They would also drive up the necessary standard rate of tax. Politically, the implied rate looks too high to be accepted by the floating voter, who would be unwilling to pay the price for such redistribution.

Basic Income Guarantee is in short a radical gamble that the reduction of the marginal tax rates at the bottom of the pay scale would beneficially compensate for the damage done higher up by the increased marginal rates needed to pay. Politically unacceptable, it would also be economically dangerous.

Can monitoring produce a 'partial Basic Income Guarantee'? Basic Income Guarantee lowers the marginal tax rate for those in the poverty trap, while raising it for those beyond it. However, Hermione Parker now proposes a 'partial Basic Income Guarantee' (Parker, 1989; and Chapter 3 in this volume) under which a certain payment would be made unconditionally as in Basic Income Guarantee, but it would be less than current benefits. Extra payments would be made conditionally (called 'cash & care') by local benefit officers, who would assess 'need'. This proposal is intended to square the circle: basic benefits are cut as in small Basic Income Guarantees, to keep down costs, and yet benefits are provided at current levels to the poor employed in genuine need.

If this screening process worked as intended, those who could genuinely work harder for more money to support themselves and their family would not get conditional benefits and so would face the general marginal tax rate, so avoiding the poverty trap. Those in genuine need would be helped but being *ex hypothesi* unable to work harder for more money they would not be constrained by the poverty trap; as soon as they could help themselves, conditional benefit would be withdrawn and they would avoid the poverty trap thereby.

There is a parallel with screening the unemployed under Restart and the Beveridge intentions embodied in existing law. There the unemployment trap is avoided in just the same way. But screening of the unemployed and their ability to get a job is clearly much easier than screening the ability to earn more in an existing or alternative job. The former requires evidence of unsuccessful job applications and interviews, as widely practised in Switzerland, Sweden and now increasingly in the UK. The latter requires little short of a complete 'appraisal' of the employee by one or more employers. Its practicality is doubtful and its cost would certainly be considerable. A scheme, such as Parker's partial Basic Income Guarantee, which relies on this for its effectiveness, is therefore flawed. But screening may nevertheless be a useful adjunct to a practicable scheme, by reducing the impact of the poverty trap.

A Gradualist Proposal

The problem with Basic Income Guarantee can be summarized by looking at Figure 4.3, which is a reworking of Figure 4.1. For a typical family man there are two critical points, assuming that he works. There is the minimum support rate, which he gets however low his income sinks; this is the intercept of the net income line with the left hand axis – amount b. Then there is the point at which he loses all benefits in work (benefit withdrawal is complete), and his marginal tax rate becomes the standard rate plus national insurance. This is the kinked point on his net income line, c, along the horizontal axis. BIG proposes to replace the existing line with a straight line going through point b. But necessarily, as Figure 4.3 makes clear, this can be achieved only by lowering the slope of the line for those currently on

Figure 4.3   Structure of tax reform proposals

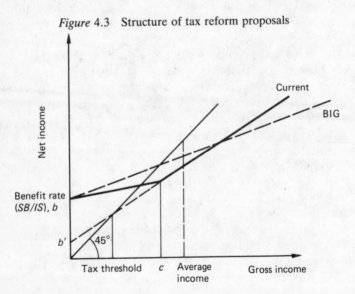

standard rate. This is necessary to pay for the increased support for those in the poverty trap and those currently outside it who will benefit from the lower withdrawal rate. One way to lower the marginal tax rate in the poverty trap without raising it elsewhere is to reduce the minimum support level, b. This is illustrated by the line running through point b'. (Its marginal tax rate would in fact be slightly less than the current standard rate plus National Insurance because the taxpayer pays less in poverty support; but this is not drawn for simplicity.) This proposal would be unacceptable because the safety net principle would be violated, given that current benefit rates are generally believed to be approximately right to sustain families in normal health.

However, the safety net principle is designed to relieve 'absolute poverty'. That is, while living necessities may change over time as society changes and becomes richer, the amount set to maintain health will not vary proportionately with average income; it will probably rise little and over a five-year period it could be regarded as fixed in real terms.

Now suppose b is fixed in real terms (i.e. benefits are indexed to prices) while the economy grows and average real income rises. Suppose, too, that tax thresholds are indexed to prices. Then over time the numbers of households in the poverty trap will fall, but more significantly the numbers just above it will fall fast too. This means that not only will the poverty trap be a less serious problem because it affects less people. Also, it will become worthwhile to repeat the Fowler-style reduction in the withdrawal rate, because less people will be drawn into the trap compared with the beneficial effect of higher incentives on those within it. The possible arithmetic of when it pays to lower the withdrawal rate is worked out in the Appendix to this chapter. But a possible rule of thumb would be to accept the Fowler judgement that it was right to lower the withdrawal rate at the expense of roughly doubling the number of families in the poverty trap to its current 450,000. The Appendix suggests that this could well have been about right.

The reasoning is that any further reduction in withdrawal rate beyond the Fowler point would increase numbers in the trap too much relative to the benefit in better incentives for those already in it. However, if the calculation is done for an increase in the withdrawal rate to pre-Fowler levels, welfare falls slightly, implying that the current number is close to an 'optimum' one (given the constraints on policy choice from fixing the benefit at b) – the best of a bad job. This is a rough judgement given the imprecision of our estimates; but underlying it is the steep increase in population density just above the group currently in the trap (illustrated in Figure 4.4 (b)), and it will therefore generally pay to prevent the trap pulling these extra large numbers in. If this notion is accepted, then it would follow that as the numbers in the trap fall with rising incomes the withdrawal rate should be continuously lowered to maintain those numbers.

My gradualist proposal is then to lower the withdrawal rate annually for those in the poverty trap as average real income rises. In effect, this means that point b would be indexed to prices while point c would be indexed to wages. Thus the marginal tax rate in the poverty trap would fall each year by approximately the rate of real wage growth, times b/c (about 0.7 currently on average). At current productivity growth of 4 per cent a year, this would cut the rate by around 11 percentage points over the next five years. But there is a further source of cuts in the withdrawal rate. This is income tax cuts. It is shown in the Appendix that standard rate cuts dominate threshold rises, because the former give a stronger incentive boost. Suppose then that the standard rate is cut by 5 more points over the next five years. We must calculate the consequential rise in net income of someone at point c, receiving no benefit. Typically, this is now about 2 per cent for a 5 per cent cut in standard rate. The withdrawal rate can now be cut by 2 per cent because benefit income can be higher up to point c .

The mechanism of these adjustments to the withdrawal rate is illustrated in Figure 4.4. The formula for the withdrawal rate is [$c(1-t)$ -b]/c or 1-t -(b/c) where t is the average tax rate paid by someone at point c (the point at which benefits have been totally withdrawn), and b is the minimum support level of benefit. Hence the change in the withdrawal rate is -(change in t) +b/c(the proportional change in c). Tax cuts could well reach 10p – making a standard rate of 15p – given the present fiscal outlook. If so then the total cut in the withdrawal rate would reach a worthwhile 15 percentage points over the next five years.

This may seem slow progress. But the problem with faster progress is that it would draw too many new people into the trap, at a cost in efficiency greater than the gain from better incentives for those in the trap already. Incrementalism appears to be inevitable from an efficiency viewpoint. Would such slow progress provoke social unrest? This is a fear of some, who feel that those in the poverty trap could strengthen the tendencies towards production of an 'under-

Figure 4.4 Changing the withdrawal rate as net incomes rise
a The changing withdrawal rate
b The shifting population density function over gross income.

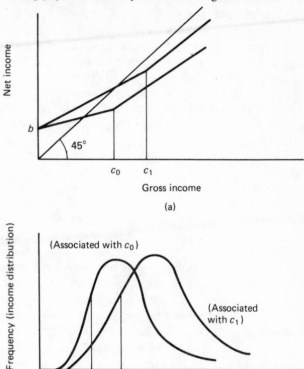

(a)

(b)

class'. Yet as far as this aspect goes, monitoring must have a role to play. In the giving of unemployment benefit the policing of moral hazard is important not only for efficiency reasons but also for reasons of social behaviour (idleness and the black economy must breed underclass attitudes). So in the giving of in-work benefits there is a case for monitoring that the receivers are making reasonable efforts to maximize their own sources of income.

This could act as a check on underclass tendencies, as well as improving the incentives within the poverty trap. As with unemployment benefit, the fact that the taxpayer gives must entitle him to monitor that it is given to those in true need and not to those who could help themselves. Monitoring or 'screening' of this type would in terms of Figure 4.3 have the effect of cutting the numbers subject to the poverty trap since anyone found to be capable of supporting themselves would lose in-work benefit eligibility. If screening was perfect, as noted above in the discussion of Parker's partial Basic Income Guarantee, then the poverty trap would disappear, since those capable of self-support would pay the standard rate of tax, not receiving benefit, while for those not capable and so receiving benefit the question of incentives would not arise. Of course screening of this sort can never be more than modestly effective, as argued earlier. But it could produce a useful alleviation.

4 CONCLUSION

Incremental progress appears to be by now both politically possible and capable of improving incentives at the bottom while not sacrificing those higher up. Under this approach high marginal tax rates will remain for the employed in the poverty trap for some time to come, but not for the unemployed if workfare is introduced. The cost to the economy of these high rates for low-paid workers is probably quite small, as the numbers involved are small and their productivity is low; even though their substitution effect may outweigh their income effect, the value lost is modest. To attempt to retrieve it by Basic Income Guarantee risks losing far more resources from substitution higher up the scale; and the redistribution involved would be unlikely to please the voters.

The proposal made here is to maintain the minimum support levels constant in real terms and to lower the withdrawal rate in the poverty trap so as to keep the numbers in the trap constant. (To lower the numbers in the trap would mean an undesirably higher withdrawal rate, and to lower the withdrawal rate faster would raise numbers undesirably.) This implies that the withdrawal rate can be reduced by the rate of growth of real wages plus the per cent effect of tax cuts on the net income of the marginal man outside the trap. To strengthen incentives in the trap and to help counter the development of an underclass culture, monitoring of efforts made to maximize private income would be advisable.

Appendix: The Arithmetic of Poverty Trap Reform

The proposal made here is incrementally to cut the safety net level of support relative to average income, by indexing it to prices not wages for an indefinite period. I assume that cutting the support level in real terms is not popularly desired. In terms of Figure 4.1, our illustrative starting point, it would steepen the net income curve in the lower ranges without flattening it higher up – unlike BIG. I also propose a tough work-testing/workfare scheme that de facto eliminates the 'incentive' to be unemployed; BIG schemes aim to tackle incentives of the unemployed without this.

Let us examine the argument arithmetically, using some recent estimates of labour supply responses. Clearly, strong value-judgments are involved in redistribution. But let us, in normal public finance manner, leave distribution effects on one side, at least for a start, and measure incentive effects only – i.e. substitution effects and consequent welfare loss. (To this measure we may perhaps add a cruder one, that of total work effort produced or lost; this measures effects on the measured GNP rather than welfare in money metric form.) These measures give us something to put in the balance for those who wish to redistribute as for those who are content to provide an absolute safety net.

Table 4.1 shows the price elasticities (substitution effect only) for various groups culled from my GHS study with Paul Ashton (Minford and Ashton, 1989). The weights are the share in value-added of each group. One way to proceed would be to take different schemes of tax reform and compute welfare losses.

A more transparent method is to proceed from the optimal tax end. If we assume no cross-elasticities of supply, which seems quite reasonable here since relativities between occupations at the same general pay level will not

Table 4.1   Elasticities and weights in GDP

	Elasticity		Weight
	Substitution	Income	
Employed			
– Top rate	0.50	−0.45	0.12
– Standard rate	0.13	−0.16	0.86
– Poverty trap	0.40	−0.39	0.01
Unemployed	0.80	−0.65	0.01
Weighted average	0.13	−0.20	1.00

Source: Minford and Ashton (1989).

be disturbed, then we can make use of the Ramsey reasoning (Ramsey, 1927). Welfare costs from a marginal tax rate, t_i, on the ith person equal $e_i V_i t_i^2$ where e_i is the elasticity of supply and V_i is the value-added by the person. Minimizing welfare costs subject to the revenue constraint yields the well-known Ramsey formula that the ratio of the tax rates of two groups should equal the inverse ratio of their elasticities: $t_i/t_j = e_j/e_i$. The GHS evidence suggests that for those with normal marginal tax rates elasticities are both fairly low and similar; elasticities rise with the marginal tax rate. If so, then the optimal marginal tax rate will be equal, since at equality elasticities will be roughly equal too. But the Ramsey rule also sets benefits and thresholds to zero since this minimizes the marginal tax rate.

This clearly gives us an (impractical) ideal. Note that equal tax rates can be achieved either by BIG or by my proposals. However, under mine the proposed marginal rate is the result of levelling down to the standard rate. Under BIG, the rate is much higher, representing a lowering for those in the poverty trap but a substantial rise for the millions more outside it. Obviously the welfare costs of BIG are higher. How much higher depends on the exact proposals, not pursued further here.

A last interesting question is how total welfare costs of these proposals compare with the present situation, which though not ultimately optimal may yet be the best feasible option for now. Obviously my proposals offer lower welfare cost, but since cutting benefits in real absolute terms is not suggested to be feasible, or desirable on safety net grounds, no progress in that direction is immediately possible. As for BIG, very rough calculations on a thorough-going and generous scheme – Table 4.2 – suggest a rise in welfare costs, since though elasticities are higher among the unemployed and low-paid their numbers and value-added are very low relative to those of the standard rate taxpayers whose incentives are worsened. Notice that Table 4.2 also suggests there would be a fall in work effort under BIG, compared with now.

The question remains of whether there is any other incrementalism that could help matters temporarily, while retaining the levelling-down aim. Here we note the fact that those in work in the poverty trap face much higher marginal rates than those just outside it on standard rate; they also seem to have higher elasticities. This might suggest that, as taxes are cut, priority (over standard rate cuts) can be given to raising thresholds especially for those in the poverty trap, since this will take households out of the trap and put them on the standard rate portion of their budget line. It was for this reason that I was anxious to see Nigel Lawson when Chancellor retain his 1987 Green Paper proposals on transferable allowances, which would have taken many families out of the trap. In fact, what follows shows that while the Green Paper proposals would have reduced welfare costs, this would not be true of a general rise in thresholds, because these would transfer too few out of the poverty trap relative to the worsening of incentives for those on standard rate. Over such a general rise in thresholds standard rate cuts should have precedence.

The possibility of increasing the taper, as Norman Fowler effectively did in his reforms, can also be considered. This has the difficulty that it puts more people into the trap, while reducing the marginal rate for those already in it. The balance of costs depends on how many are in each category. At present

Table 4.2 Possible welfare costs of BIG (assuming 50 per cent equal marginal tax rate, current benefit rates) compared with present situation

Working people	Unemployed	In poverty trap	High income (top 5%)	Others employed	Weighted total
Weight in current GDP (Source: Table 4.1)	0.01	0.01	0.12	0.86	1.00
% Change in net marginal wage	+230.00[1]	+230.00[2]	−17.00[3]	−33.00[4]	−25.80
Substitution elasticity (Source: Table 4.1)	0.80	0.40	0.50	0.13	0.11
Substitution effect on hours (%)	+184.00	+92.00	−8.50	−4.29	−1.96 (−3.80)[5]
Weighted substitution effect on GDP (%)	+1.84	+0.92	−1.02	−3.70	
Welfare change (% of GDP)	+0.92	+0.46	−0.51	−1.85	−0.98 (−1.90)[5]

Notes:
1 Assumes replacement ratio of 85 per cent currently.
2 Assumes withdrawal rate of 85 per cent currently
3 50 per cent v. current 40 per cent.
4 50 per cent v. current 25 per cent.
5 Figures in parentheses show effects excluding the unemployed (i.e. assuming that worktest/workfare became operative under the current system).

135

the balance looks unfavourable, as there are large numbers just outside the trap, and only some 450000 in it. But this could change back with fast-growing incomes. This arithmetic is set out with a little algebra in what follows.

Let there be two groups of households: i employed at standard rate (t_i), j employed in the poverty trap (tax, i.e. withdrawal, rate t_j). Elasticity of hours $= e$. Number of households $= n$. Value-added per household at zero tax rates $= V$. Benefit rate $= b$. Tax threshold $= a/t_i$. Total revenue to be raised $= R$.

Optimal Tax

Revenue constraint is $R = (- b + t_j V_j - t_j^2 V_j e_j)\, n_j + (\, t_i V_i - t_i^2 V_i e_i - a)\, n_i,$ where the terms with squared tax rates allow for the effect of rising tax rates on the tax bases, V_j and V_i respectively.

Loss function is $C = 0.5\,(\, t_i^2\, V_i n_i e_i + t_j^2 V_j n_j e_j\,)$.

Minimizing the Lagrangian, $L = C + pR$, with respect to t_i, t_j yields:

$$0 = dL/dt_i = V_i n_i\,(t_i e_i + p[1 - 2\, t_i e_i])$$
$$+\ dn_i/dt_i \{0.5\,[t_i^{\ 2} V_i e_i - t_j^2 V_j e_j]$$
$$+\ p\,[\, b - t_j V_j + t_j^2\, V_j e_j + t_i V_i - t_i^2\, V_i e_i - a]\}$$
$$0 = dL/dt_j = V_j n_j,\,(t_j e_j + p[1 - 2\, t_j e_j])$$
$$+\ dn_j/dt_j\,(0.5\,[t_i^{\ 2} V_i e_i - t_j^2 V_j e_j]$$
$$+\ p\,[\, b - t_j V_j + t_j^2\, V_j e_j + t_i V_i t_i^2 V_i e_i - a]\}$$

Note that $dn_i/dt_s = -dn_j/dt_s\ (s = i, j)$.

In the region between the optimum and zero tax rates, the arc elasticities are likely to be similar and close to those estimated for our average employed person. The terms dn_i/dt_s are the effects on the numbers of households in the poverty trap – see Figure 4.3: a = b = o minimizes C with respect to a, b. $dn_i = o$, since people cannot claim benefits and n_i, n_j are fixed groups.

Hence, for $e_s = e$

$$t_i e/(1 - 2t_i e) = p = t_j e/(1 - 2t_j e)$$

so that $t_i = t_j$.

Incremental Change From the Current Situation

Let e_s be as estimated for current tax rates. Suppose b and R are constrained. Then varying a or t_j implies a corresponding variation in the standard rate t_i.

Inspection of Figure 4.3 shows that raising tax thresholds and so a, must reduce numbers in the poverty trap until the threshold, a/t_i, reaches the point where the poverty trap segment crosses the 45° line.

Lowering t_j will raise numbers in the poverty trap while lowering the marginal rate on those within it.

Changing t_i will have a negligible impact on numbers in the poverty trap $(dn_i/dt_i = 0)$ but will change incentives for others of course.

(I)   Varying t_j

From the revenue constraint we have

$$dt_j \{n_j V_j (1 - 2t_j e_j)$$
$$+ dn_j/dt_j [b - t_j V_j + t_j^2 V_j e_j + t_i V_i - t_i^2 V_i e_i - a]\}$$
$$= -dt_i (n_i V_i (1 - 2t_i e_i))$$

And $dC/dt_j = t_j V_j n_j e_j + 0.5 (t_i^2 V_i e_i - t_j^2 V_j e_j) dn_i /dt_j + dC/dt_i . dt_i/dt_j$

Our estimates are: $e_j = 0.2$, $e_i - 0.07$ (based on Minford and Ashton, 1989); and (based on official statistics and Liverpool calculations)

$V_i = 200$, $V_j = 100$, $b = 110$, $a = 15$ (all in £ per week, 1987 prices)
$n_j = 0.45$, $n_i = 22$, dn_i/dt_j (for a cut in t_j) = 2.5 (all in millions)
$t_i = 0.25$ and $t_j = 0.85$

(a) A cut in t_j – increasing numbers in the poverty trap but lowering the withdrawal rate further as in the Fowler reforms:
In this case we estimate $dC/dt_j = -26.0$ (£ million per week), implying that further cuts in the withdrawal rate would reduce welfare; for example, a reduction of 0.05 would cause an increase in welfare costs of $0.05 \times 26.0 \times 52 = £68$ million per year.
(b) Returning to pre-Fowler levels:
For a rise in t_j (back to pre-Fowler levels) dn_i/dt_j is much smaller (about 0.7) so that $dC/dt_j = +3.5$, implying that a return to pre-Fowler levels would raise welfare costs. The optimum therefore must lie somewhere between current and pre-Fowler levels. Since dn_i/dt_j falls steeply as we move away from the current level back towards pre-Fowler, this optimum is likely to lie close to the current level.

(ii) Varying a

Revenue constraint:

$$da\{dn_i/da [b - t_j V_j + t_j^2 V_j e_j + t_i V_i - t_i^2 V_i e_i - a] - n_i\}$$
$$= -dt_i \{n_i V_i (1 - 2t_i e_i)\}$$

And

$$dC/da = 0.5 (t_i^2 V_i e_i - t_j^2 V_j e_j) . dn_i/d_a + dC/dt_i . dt_i/da$$

Hence, given also $dn_i/da = .02$, we obtain $dC/da = 0.4$ (£ million per week), indicating that raising tax thresholds would slightly raise welfare costs because of the corresponding rise in the standard rate. In other words, priority should be given in tax cuts to lowering the standard rate rather than raising general thresholds. This particular result is however rather sensitive to the assumptions. Also, if the rise in tax thresholds were concentrated on married couples as in the Green Paper proposals, then dn_i/da would be much higher (about 0.3) and dC/da would turn negative. In any case, the sums are finely balanced.

Note

1.   I am grateful to Paul Ashton for assistance and comments on the calculations in this chapter; I remain responsible for errors.

References

Ashby, Peter (1988) ' *Proposal for the Action Credit*' (Windsor: St George's House).
Brown, Charles V., Levin, E. J., Rosa, P. J., Ruffell, R. J. and Ulph, D. T. (1987) *Taxation and Family Labour Supply*. Final Report of HM Treasury Project. (Department of Economics, University of Sterling).
Burton, John (1986) *Workfare*, Institute for Employment Research, Buckingham University.
Minford, Patrick and Paul Ashton (1989) 'The poverty trap and the Laffer curve – what can the GHS tell us?' CEPR discussion paper, revised December 1989 (London).
Minford, Patrick *et al.* (1983) *Unemployment: Cause and Cure* (Oxford: Martin Robertson) now (Oxford: Basil Blackwell, 1983, 2nd edn, 1985).
Parker, Hermione (1989) *Instead of the Dole: An Enquiry into Integration of the Tax and Benefit Systems After 1990* (London: Routledge).
Ramsey, F. P. (1927) 'A contribution to the theory of taxation', *Economic Journal*, 37: 47–61.

5 Training for the Low-paid'

Ewart Keep

Talking down pay is a relic of the bad old days of the 1970s . . . there's nothing morally attractive about low pay. What we want is a high wage/high performance economy, John Banham, director-general of the CBI, interview on the 'World at One', BBC Radio 4 (24 July 1989).

This nation's people are its most precious resource. Our companies and organisations, of whatever size and in whatever business, must recognise the need to invest in people to give them the skills of the future. Effective investment in training is crucial to business success, Rt Hon Margaret Thatcher, Prime Minister (quoted by Roberts, 1989).

It is no longer technologies and raw materials which make all the difference between companies that succeed and those that do not. It is people who work for those companies, their skills and capabilities. They are the *key* to providing quality, customer service and the prompt delivery of goods and services, Rt Hon Norman Fowler, Secretary of State for Employment, HRD Week Conference (1988).

Customers are becoming increasingly insistent on value for money, both in the quality of goods and in higher levels of service . . . the key to operational excellence is properly motivated staff, and Kingfisher is fully committed to supporting and developing its people, Geoffrey Mulcahy, chief executive, Kingfisher plc (Woolworths, B&Q, Superdrug, etc.) (*Report and Accounts 1988/89*).

There is a widespread belief, reflected in the above quotations, that training is the key to achieving major improvements in the productivity and competitiveness of British enterprises and that, in terms of national economies, high skills and high wages are linked in a virtuous circle of cause and effect. As a result of the widespread acceptance of this belief, the last decade has witnessed increasing attention being paid to improving Britain's overall levels of provision of vocational education and training (VET). Indeed, in a recent report the CBI suggested that in view of the progress made in this area by our major overseas competitors, 'nothing short of a revolution – in expectations, standards, responsiveness and delivery of education and training will suffice' (1989, p. 10).

This chapter takes as its starting point the policy debate that arises from these beliefs, and focuses attention on the contribution that improved training might make towards both increasing the competitiveness and efficiency of the low-pay sectors of the UK economy, and in helping solve the long-standing problem of low pay. It also seeks to examine what avenues are currently available to upgrade the skills, knowledge and competence of those working in areas of low pay, and how they might be expanded.

The chapter begins by highlighting a number of basic features in the UK economy that need to be borne in mind when considering the issues of low pay and training. The next section very briefly outlines the incidence of low pay, and describes the scale of the training problem in the low-pay sectors of the UK economy. The reasons that underlie this poor performance, their linkage within a 'low skills equilibrium', and the relationship between training, product market strategies, and work organization, are explored. Current policies aimed at dealing with the problem are examined, and the chapter then looks at other pressures for change, including demographics and the tightening of UK labour markets. A range of possible future strategies to speed up the rate of change are discussed, covering policies targeted at employers, individuals, and the provision of initial vocational education and training. The chapter concludes with an assessment of the prospects for future progress and their overall importance to UK economic performance.

1 BACKGROUND

At the outset, it is worth emphasizing three points, against which any consideration of the role improved training provision could make towards helping solve the problem of low pay in the UK needs to be set. Firstly, Britain as a whole can be characterized as a low-wage economy. When the social, non-wage costs of employment (national insurance, holiday pay, sickness pay, training costs, etc.) are included in the calculation of employers' total labour costs, the UK in 1986 had the lowest total labour costs of any advanced industrial economy (Nolan, 1988, p. 3). The reason that the UK economy is not more successful, given this apparent advantage, is that generally low wages have existed side-by-side with extremely low levels of productivity, with the result that UK employers' unit labour costs are very high by comparison with those in other advanced industrialized countries (Nolan, 1989, p. 84).

A second point is that the provision of training by British employers is, in aggregate, poor by international standards at all levels and within most industries. As studies such as *Competence and Competition* (MSC/NEDO, 1984), the work of the National Institute for Economic and Social Research (NIESR) and the Handy Report (MSC/NEDO/BIM, 1987) have shown, the UK labour force as a whole is poorly educated and trained by comparison with countries like West Germany, the USA and Japan. These deficiencies extend through all strata of employment, from operative, through skilled workers, technicians and supervisors, right up to senior management. Problems of inadequate levels of vocational education and training (VET) are thus by no means simply confined to low-pay sectors or to workers receiving low levels of remuneration. It is rather the case that, in areas of low pay, training tends to be below average compared to a general UK level of performance that is already below average in international terms

As a result, therefore, it is in some senses not easy to distinguish training policies that ought to be aimed solely at low-pay sectors and occupations. As is argued at greater length below, while there are some VET policies that might be targeted at certain specific areas of low pay, many of the initiatives being suggested are equally applicable across the whole economy.

One final background feature remains to be emphasized; both low pay and inadequate provision of vocational education and training are weaknesses of long standing within the British economy, and the longevity and persistence of these difficulties indicates that their underlying causes are deep-seated. Hence, their resolution is unlikely to prove simple to achieve. Each is, in its own right, a complex and multi-faceted problem, and as this chapter will seek to demonstrate, simple solutions are not readily available. With this caveat in mind, we can turn to examine the scale of inadequate training for the low-paid.

2 THE SCALE OF THE PROBLEM

It is not the intention to try to provide a detailed analysis of the incidence of low pay within the UK economy. There may, however, be value in very briefly outlining certain of the overall features of distribution.

The incidence of low pay is heavily concentrated in certain sectors of the economy: agriculture; food, drink and tobacco; textiles; clothing and footwear; timber and furniture; the distributive trades; professional and scientific services (education and the health service); and miscellaneous services (hotels, catering, hairdressing and laundries). As Pond (1983, p. 186) indicates, two industrial sectors – the distributive trades and miscellaneous services, together account for one-third of all low-paid men and women, despite the fact that these two sectors employ less than a sixth of the total national labour force. Size of firm often influences the incidence of low pay, with small firms showing a general tendency to offer lower pay to their employees than larger companies within the same sector (Bosworth, 1989, pp. 60–4).

To look at the pattern of low pay from another perspective, Smail (1987, p. 8) provides a ranking of what were, in April 1986, the ten worst-paid full-time jobs for men and women. The least well-remunerated jobs for women were: shop checkout assistants, hairdressers, shop assistants, barmaids, waitresses, other cleaners, sewing machinists (textiles), receptionists, chefs/cooks, and packers and canners. For male workers, the list was as follows: general farmworkers, barmen, hospital porters, caretakers, butchers, salesmen/ shop assistants, bakers, goods porters, craftsmen's mates, and general labourers.

Low pay is heavily concentrated, not only in certain industries and occupations, but also in terms of different groups within the overall labour force. In general, women workers, part-time workers, and members of ethnic minorities are all more likely to be low-paid. Age also plays an important part in low pay, with older manual workers proving particularly vulnerable (Layard, Piachaud and Stewart, 1978). Of the various factors that mark out these groups, perhaps the most important is gender. Female employment is heavily concentrated in areas such as cleaning, catering, clerical, and retailing jobs, with disproportionately few women in higher paying sectors like engineering or construction.

Unfortunately, information about current levels of vocational education and training activity in the UK is inadequate in a number of respects, and it is difficult to speak with any great degree of certainty about the amount or quality of training that has been, or is currently, available to those in low-paid jobs. Nevertheless, there is a general assumption, which has not been openly challenged by anybody party to the policy debate about training, that the low-paid are on average likely to have received less vocational education and training than those in better-paid occupations, and that the level of qualifications held by low-paid individuals will reflect this. What evidence is available supports these assumptions.

Data from the 1984 Labour Costs Survey indicate a number of industries in which the costs of vocational training as a percentage of total labour costs tends to be low – food, drink and tobacco, textiles, leather goods, clothing, retail distribution, and wholesale distribution (*Employment Gazette*, March 1988, p. 135) – all industries associated with the incidence of low pay. The 1981 Labour Force Survey (*Employment Gazette*, April 1983, p. 162) suggests that half of the unqualified female labour force worked in clerical and related occupations, or in catering, hairdressing and other personal services, all occupations associated with low pay. The 1987 Labour Force Survey (*Employment Gazette*, October 1988, pp. 549–63) indicates that in a number of the service industries associated with low pay, such as distribution, hotels and catering, and transport, there are relatively few workers with degrees, and large numbers of employees who possess no formal qualifications. Moreover, within an individual industry or sector the smaller firms, which will usually be paying lower wages, are also likely to spend less on training per employee than the larger companies (see Bosworth, 1989, pp. 72–5).

Regrettably, the most detailed survey of UK employers' training activities and costs, undertaken for the Training Agency, has yet to be published in full, but outline results show that manual workers and employees in small establishments are generally less likely to receive training (Pell, 1989, p. 10). The survey also reveals that for adults, the likelihood of training is strongly correlated with earnings, and that the amount of training received is higher for those on higher incomes. Those with low incomes (especially those earning below £6000 per annum) received appreciably lower amounts of training than those on higher incomes (Training Commission, 1988, p. 4). It is expected that the full survey data will also confirm that, in industries and sectors characterized by low pay, both the frequency and duration of training is lower than elsewhere.

Beyond these general statements about levels of training available to the low-paid, there may be value in examining the example of one of the largest low-pay sectors, tourism and leisure, which covers hotels and much of the catering industry. In contrast to some of the and much of the catering industry. In contrast to some of the manufacturing industries characterized by low pay, which are arguably declining areas of activity with an uncertain long-term future (for example clothing, and furniture manufacture), hotels, catering and tourism have been identified by government and bodies such as the English Tourist Board as major areas for future job creation (Parsons, 1987, pp. 344–5).

A study of 400 companies within the tourism and leisure sector (Metcalf, 1988) indicated a distinctive employment structure in which most jobs were characterised by young recruits, no promotion and high turnover (1988, p. 89), and concluded that 'careers in the tourism and leisure industry appear to be restricted, in the main, to managers and professionals and to qualified chefs, with little opportunity for lower grade staff to work their way up' (1988, p. 92). In 1981 over half of the employees in the hotel and catering industry were semi-skilled and unskilled operatives, and 'many of the manual and clerical occupations continue to offer widespread opportunities for both mature entrants and school leavers with few or no academic qualifications' (Parsons, 1987, p. 343). Part-time female employment is characteristic of many parts of the leisure and tourism sectors (Parsons, 1987) and turnover rates among staff are high. For example, within the hotel sector rates of 100 per cent are not unusual (*Employment Gazette*, February 1989, p. 88).

Levels of training in the tourism and leisure sector are generally low. Metcalf's study showed that beyond basic induction training there was little on offer. Training for externally recognized qualifications (ERQs) was extremely limited, with perhaps 3 per cent of employees undergoing training at any time. What training there was tended to be concentrated among the larger employers (Metcalf 1988, p. 92). Moreover, 'training for managers and professionals, other than for trainees, was found in very few organisations' (1988, p. 92).

As has been mentioned above, British levels of vocational education and training in most sectors of the economy are poor by international standards. A number of studies conducted by the National Institute for Economic and Social Research have made clear the degree to which British low-pay sectors trail their counterparts in France and West Germany in terms of the training they provide their employees. These studies have covered clerical occupations (Steedman, 1987), retail sales (Jarvis and Prais, 1989), furniture manufacture (Steedman and Wagner, 1987) and clothing manufacture (Steedman and Wagner, 1989).

The results of the comparative study of kitchen furniture manufacture in Britain and West Germany (Steedman and Wagner, 1987) are fairly typical. The study revealed that whereas 90 per cent of the West German shopfloor employees had undergone a three-year apprenticeship, in Britain less than 10 per cent had craft qualifications (1987, pp. 91–2). The German firms were also training five times as many craft apprentices as their British counterparts (1987, p. 92).

It is important to recognize that the British situation is not static. Changes are taking place in the skills and qualifications of the workforce in low-pay sectors. For example, within 'other occupations excluding agriculture' (a group covering unskilled male labourers and female cleaners and domestics), there is 'clear evidence of the "filtering" down of qualifications, as a result of relatively well qualified new entrants replacing less well qualified older workers retiring from work' (*Institute of Employment Research Bulletin*, 3, 1989, p. 6). This is partly a reflection of the gradual rise over time in the average levels of qualification being achieved by the cohorts of young people moving through the secondary education system.

The most important change in skill supply and training within many low pay occupations and industries, however, has been the arrival of the Youth Training Scheme (YTS). One of the Youth Training Scheme's major achievements has been to extend training into many areas, usually characterized by low pay, where previously there had been no structured period of vocational training available to young employees. These include health and community care, administrative and clerical, retailing, and hotels and catering. Witherspoon (1987) calculated that in November 1985 as many as 62 per cent of all Youth Training Scheme trainees were to be found in occupations which in the past had been without strong initial training arrangements. Moreover, in a much smaller number of low-pay areas where there has been a long-standing tradition of initial training for young employees, most notably hairdressing, the Youth Training Scheme has offered public funding support for employers' training efforts, as well as promoting greater uniformity of standards.

Nevertheless, despite initiatives such as the Youth Training Scheme low-pay sectors remain characterised by low levels of vocational education and training among the workforce. The question that logically arises from this situation is, why should low levels of education and training be associated with the incidence of low pay. Section 3 addresses this issue.

3   REASONS FOR THIS LACK OF TRAINING

Traditionally, much of the debate about the causes of low pay and its relationship with poor levels of investment in skills has centred on arguments about the degree to which levels of pay reflect the inefficiencies and low productivity of the 'low quality' of labour being employed. The view that low labour quality (in terms of educational qualifications, skills and experience) on the part of the individuals employed is the cause of low pay has been disputed by those who suggest that labour market segmentation, with a division of employment into primary and secondary sectors, is the main mechanism that determines the pay and training opportunities available to workers. Segmentation theory (Piore, 1971) suggests that the divide between primary and secondary employment will be determined by structural characteristics within industry. One example of a structural characteristic associated with low pay and low skills is the absence of either strong internal or occupational labour markets.

Labour Market Segmentation

While not wishing to discuss the segmentationist approach in detail, it is worth emphasizing that research undertaken on a number of UK low-pay sectors (Craig *et al.*, 1982) appears to bear out the importance of labour market segmentation as an underlying cause of low pay. Craig *et al.* identify a number of structural characteristics that are often associated with low-pay industries; including the prevalence of small companies, the use of old technology, labour intensive work organization, unstable product markets, high levels of competition, and weak or non-existent unionization. In particular, the characteristics of the product market were found to be important in determining the division of employment into primary and secondary areas (1982, p. 82).

Moreover, the case studies tended to show that in many instances definitions of skill and status reflected social or historical construction, rather than any objective assessment of the activities undertaken. In a number of the industries studied, the degree of manual expertise, dexterity and concentration that was required of workers was high, though formal qualifications were lacking, but these jobs were viewed by management as 'unskilled' because they were undertaken by workers whose social status was low. Of all the factors influencing status, gender was found to be the most important (1982, p. 84). Thus Craig *et al.* concluded that 'jobs are regarded as unskilled because they are feminized and not feminized because they are unskilled' (1982, p. 77).

These case study findings are important as they indicate some of the difficulties that confront any attempt to upgrade skill formation in low-pay industries. If management's definition of skills and skill requirements tends to be subjective and derived from class and status, rather than being objective and task-related, then it may be difficult to persuade them of the need to afford greater training to people who occupy jobs whose traditional social and occupational status is low.

Weak Investment in New Technology

There are a variety of other causal factors that warrant consideration. One problem frequently mentioned in connection with low-pay/low-skills industries is their failure either to upgrade production and skill requirements through investment in new technology or, if new technology is acquired, to utilize it to its maximum potential. Evidence from the National Institute for Economic and Social Research comparative study in the furniture industry (Steedman and Wagner, 1987) confirms that the British companies were often slower to adopt new production technology and were far less adventurous in its usage than were their West German counterparts. One of the major reasons for this contrast appeared to rest with the general lack of technical expertise among British management, which acted as a major brake on the introduction and proper use of new technology (Steedman and Wagner, 1987; Lane, 1988, p. 160). As Brady (1984, p. 112) has commented, 'many managements do not possess the necessary technical skills to assess the feasibility of investing in the new technologies nor do they fully understand the implications for the organisation of work, for manpower requirements and for training needs'.

A further important reason for the failure to place greater emphasis on the investment in new technology and re-skilling of the workforce is the disincentive posed by low wage levels. Because wages are low, they reduce the incentive to invest in new technology and training, by limiting the rate of return that can be achieved through any resultant reductions in manning levels.

Instability of Employment

In sectors such as hotels and catering, casualization of the workforce and the associated high levels of labour turnover discourage employers from investing in the training of workers whose association with the company is only transitory. Added to this, the absence in many low pay sector firms of a well-established internal labour market which might help bind more experienced workers to the firm means that companies 'tend to be forced towards . . . relatively low cost/low quality' (Bosworth, 1989, p. 77) production. This occurs because the expense of using more formal recruitment and selection systems in conditions of high labour turnover are too great, and companies therefore tend to rely upon informal, low-cost methods which are more appropriate to obtaining lower skill levels.

The Low Skills Equilibrium

In overall terms, it can be argued that many UK employers, particularly in the low-pay sectors, find themselves caught in a vicious circle of self-reinforcing factors that perpetuate what Finegold and Soskice (1988) have dubbed a 'low skills equilibrium'. One example of the interaction of these mutually reinforcing factors is the limitations imposed on competitive strategy by lack of skill. These limitations are reflected at the level of both the company and the national economy. As Sharp and Shepherd (1987) emphasize:

> The United Kingdom is concentrating on low value-added goods at the lower end of the market spectrum while its European partners have tended to specialise increasingly on high value-added goods. (1987, p. 143).

This point is underlined by a survey sponsored by the British Institute of Management (BIM) (New and Myers, 1986), which identified an important difference in competitive strategy between UK managers and their counterparts in Europe and the USA. Whereas overseas managers ranked the ability to produce high performance products over the ability to produce at low cost, British managers tended to reverse this order of priority.

Dependency upon these low-cost competitive strategies then feed back into the causal matrix by undermining the need for higher skills. The strength of this inter-relationship is brought out in the two

National Institute for Economic and Social Research international matched plant studies referred to above (Steedman and Wagner, 1987, 1989). In both the kitchen furniture and clothing industries the British companies were operating at the bottom end of the market, producing large batches of standardized, low quality, low value-added product lines. Their West German rivals were operating at the quality end of the market, using the techniques of flexible specialization to produce smaller batches of customized, high value-added products. Steedman and Wagner conclude (1989, pp.52–3) that the main reason that British companies were not able to adopt a similar strategy was the non-availability of the requisite skills to sustain this style of product among the British workforce.

The result is that British employers may often be providing their workforce with levels of vocational education and training which are more or less appropriate to the product market strategies they are following, and which reflect the levels of service they currently aim to provide. As Craig *et al.* point out, 'in many jobs there is little scope for utilising improved "quality" in the workforce without reorganization of job structures or changes in technique' (1982, p. 76). The problem is thus not one of companies perceiving a need for training that they are unable to meet, but rather a lack of any genuine widespread demand for higher levels of skill and knowledge. As is discussed below, in order to change these perceptions, the nature of competitive strategies and work organization need to change.

Some evidence for the existence of this kind of low skills equilibrium in British low pay sectors comes from current attempts to upgrade the overall skill levels of the workforce through the Youth Training Scheme. When the advent of the two-year Youth Training Scheme was announced, many companies, particularly in sectors such as retailing, saw little point in extending the period of training and work experience (Pointing, 1986, p. 2). The National Institute for Economic and Social Research studies of clerical and retail training (Steedman, 1987; Jarvis and Prais, 1989), and of the West German and British clothing industries (Steedman and Wagner, 1989), indicate that by international standards the British Youth Training Scheme trainees in these classic areas of low-paid, female employment were achieving very low levels of skill and qualification. Steedman's work on clerical training in the UK and France indicated that the British Youth Training Scheme trainees were being offered training at a level which French employers planned to eliminate 'as being too low . . . to be useful to industry' (1987, p. 22).

Despite the work of the National Council for Vocational Qualifications (NCVQ), the available evidence suggests that British employers continue to specify very low levels of skill requirement. In the clothing industry, a National Council for Vocational Qualifications-validated Youth Training Scheme provided trainees, after two years, with skills most of which their West German equivalents were expected to master within two months (Steedman and Wagner, 1989, p. 48). A depressingly similar picture emerged from comparisons of the levels of vocational qualifications being sought by retail employers in Britain, France and West Germany (Jarvis and Prais, 1989). Thus attempts to increase the supply of higher level skills in UK low pay sectors have run into the difficulty of an underlying lack of demand from employers.

Although Britain would appear, for the moment at least, to be trapped in a low skills equilibrium, there are countries, such as West Germany, where the causal cycle runs in the opposite direction to the UK. A brief examination of this very different national scene may help illuminate the characteristics that underpin an economy in which there is a successful relationship between high levels of training and high value-added product market strategies.

The West German Example

Research on West German training (Streeck, 1985; Lane, 1988) suggests that, unlike the UK, West Germany possesses a variety of structural factors which help promote a virtuous circle, encouraging both training and 'upmarket industrial adjustment' (Streeck, 1985; p. 10). Among the factors contributing to this virtuous circle were product market strategies aimed at high-quality goods and services; strong trade unions with the power to remove the options of low pay and easy recourse to the external labour market, thereby fostering the development of strong internal labour markets; a flexible 'socio-technical system of work organisation'; and a system of industrial training that operates independently of market forces and which provides 'a pool of excess skills' (Streeck, 1985, p. 10). One indication of the strength of skills training through the 'dual system', is the fact that it covers industries and occupations which in the UK offer little if anything in the way of formal training. Research by the National Institute for Economic and Social Research has highlighted these differences in areas such as retailing, clothing manufacture, and clerical work.

The contrast between our country and West Germany also strongly underlines the important influence over training and personnel policies exercised by two very different models of work organization. The first of these – traditional Tayloristic work organization – is based upon a largely de-skilled, often casualized workforce, organized in and governed by rigid hierarchies, which is engaged in a series of routine tasks often associated with the mass production of standardized products or services. The second, and very different model, has been termed 'flexible specialization' or 'responsible autonomy', and is founded upon a strategy of utilizing a skilled, polyvalent workforce to produce high value, custom-made products. Work patterns are based on:

> A strategy which allows workers a reasonable scope in utilising their skills and trusting them to use them responsibly ... this form of work organisation implies a structure of control which minimises task control and instead exerts ideological control. The control process utilises an ideology inculcated during the training process ... the ideology is based on the idea of a professional community in which superiors are respected as 'experts' rather than as puni-tive controllers, and a common task orientation dwells on unity of purpose and de-emphasises hierarchical divisions (Lane, 1988, p. 144).

A study by Lane (1988) which compared the adoption of these two models of work organization in Britain and West Germany, suggested that West German employers were making more consistent progress towards flexible specialisation than were their UK counterparts, who appeared to be locked into a 'very half-hearted and inconsistent form' of Taylorism (1988, p. 146).

Styles of Personnel Management

As the description above outlines, the type of high-quality production characterized by flexible specialization relies upon the ready availa-bility of skilled labour, as well as upon the broader motivation benefits that accrue from a particular form of training. It also requires personnel management and industrial relations policies very different from those associated with Taylorism. In the UK this new style of personnel management is usually termed human resource manage-ment (HRM) or human resource development (HRD), and can often be associated with increased efforts in employee communication and involvement, more sophisticated reward systems, new styles of supervisory management, and a commitment to learning and development. It is this style of personnel management that has been linked with the limited number of UK-based companies that are seen as exemplars of both good training practice and high-quality product market strategies, such as IBM, British Airways, British Steel, Jaguar Cars, and Marks and Spencer.

A major series of case studies undertaken for the Training Agency on training organization in UK companies (Pettigrew, Sparrow and Hendry, 1988) indicated that successful training was usually associated with the existence of this type of human resource management/ human resource development policy. A further requirement for successful training was that 'the systems to identify training need (appraisal, the use of performance records, annual organisation and manpower reviews, structured models for skill development) have to be imbedded in the organisation, and backed by top management' (Pettigrew, Sparrow and Hendry, 1988, p. 30).

Unfortunately, nothing that is known about management or training practice in British low-pay sectors suggests that the sorts of complex work organization and personnel systems alluded to above exist to any very wide extent. The evidence available in fact suggests that even large, sophisticated UK companies have found it difficult to create and sustain successful human resource management systems (see Storey, 1989). It seems reasonable to assume that the difficulties are likely to be even greater among smaller employers in low-pay sectors. Indeed, it can be argued that in the case of many of the low-paid, their employers view them not as a resource to be developed and nurtured but as a commodity to be bought and disposed of at will, or as a cost to be contained.

As the foregoing has outlined, the matrix of inter-related factors that underlie a weak investment in skill formation in low-pay sectors is extremely complex; embracing the influence of status on definitions of skill, product market choice, work organization, the structuring of the employment relationship, and a variety of other structural factors. The overall result is the creation of a self-sustaining vicious circle. The problem that this poses for policy-makers is how to produce pressures and incentives that will encourage a far greater number of employers to adopt product market and associated work organization and human resource management strategies that will enable their companies, and indeed the economy in general, to reach a level at which a virtuous circle of high levels of training and high wages can be supported by high productivity, and high value-added production.

4 PRESENT POLICIES

Having looked at the scale, nature and causes of the problem, an examination of the policies currently in place to deal with it would seem logical. In broad terms it can be suggested that the inherent problem with current policies towards the issue of training for the low paid is that they encompass two not entirely compatible visions of future labour market development.

Ministers have on numerous occasions sought to emphasize the need for British employers to achieve across-the-board improvements in the training and development of the national workforce. The quotations given at the start of the paper are typical of these pronouncements. As the white paper *Training for Employment* (Cm 316, 1988) suggested, 'Britain needs a strategy of training through life: a process through which the skills and qualifications of the workforce are continuously broadened and upgraded' (1988, p. 19). Within the same document, the government also stressed its view that in future, 'even where jobs do not demand of workers a high level of technical skills, they will certainly require greater flexibility of approach, greater breadth of experience, and greater capacity to take responsibility' (1988, p. 19).

Ministers have also made plain their belief that the onset of increasing international competition, whether coming from within a post-1992 Single European Market (Roberts, 1989, p. 8), or from the developing countries of the Far East and the Pacific Ocean (*Lifeskills News*, June 1988, p. 6), will make it imperative for British employers to enhance the skills of those they employ. The then Secretary of State for Employment, Norman Fowler, commented: 'our ability to compete in international markets will depend on the skills of our workforce. Training will be a crucial factor in determining whether our companies remain competitive and seize the opportunities which will become available' (*Financial Times*, 28 November 1988, p. 31). Thus attempts to improve the supply of training appear to spring from the vision of an economy based on high levels of productivity, the supply of high quality goods and services, and competitive strategies aimed more at non-price factors in competition.

The government-sponsored National Quality Campaign is illustrative of this strategy, placing emphasis on the need for firms to see quality of goods and services as a key element in their competitive strategies. The minister responsible for the campaign pointed out that the government believed that half of all buying decisions were made on non-price factors (Kennedy, 1987, p. 46). The National Economic Development Office's 'People – the Key to Success' initiative is another good example of this approach, as are the many attempts made by the Manpower Services Commission/Training Agency to alert British employers to the need to improve both the quantity and quality of their training and development activities. Current policies also aim to improve the supply of training through measures, such as the Youth Training Scheme; Employment Training (ET) for the adult unemployed; the Professional, Industrial and Commercial Updating Programme (PICKUP); the introduction of a network of local, employer-controlled Training and Enterprise Councils (TECs); and the Business Growth Through Training (BGT) initiative (Hillier, 1989), which aims to help employers to develop training that aids the growth of their enterprises.

However, the government is at the same time pursuing a series of policies which appear to embrace a very different perception of the way forward. This strategy covers attempts to de-regulate the UK labour market, to weaken the measure of employment protection afforded to employees, and, through processes such as competitive tendering and the removal of legal safeguards on minimum pay, to encourage greater pay 'flexibility'. Thus the white paper *Employment for the 1990s* (Cm 540, 1988), announced the government's intention to set in train a further review of the wages councils (1988, pp. 26–7) with a view to their possible abolition, on the grounds that they are inhibiting 'business developments on which job creation depends' (1988, p. 27). The aim of removing the protection offered by statutory minimum wages appears to be to encourage the payment of even lower wages in many traditional low-pay sectors, in order partly to enable people to price themselves back into jobs, and also as a means of offering competitive advantage to companies.

It is perhaps open to question how far the design, production and delivery of high-quality goods and services are compatible with policies aimed at securing further reduction in what are already often extremely low wages. In this connection the example of competitive tendering in the health service is instructive. One study (Bach, 1989) of a hospital where cleaning services were contracted out indicated that the results were unsatisfactory, and the service had to be returned in-house, because of poor staff training by the contractors. Moreover, it is interesting to note that the larger cleaning companies competing for NHS contracts which have been put out for tender have now formed what is effectively a wages cartel. One of the reasons for this was that 'large contractors say that the type of cleaning required by the NHS demands a much higher skill and commitment than is normal for their usual office and factory cleaning work. Pay therefore needs to be adequate to attract labour of suitable calibre' (White and Palmer, 1987, p. 47).

Furthermore, attempts in Britain to foster the concept of 'flexibility' have tended to elicit a response in terms of numerical rather than task flexibility, and have been associated with reduced job security, and increased casualization and ad hoc patterns of labour usage (Darling and Lockwood, 1988, pp. 9– 10). As Lane comments:

> Although numerical flexibility can successfully cope with uncertainties in demand of a quantitative type it is doubtful whether a casualised labour force can handle other aspects of market uncertainty, such as frequent product changes or product diversification, and the demand for customised high-quality goods (Lane, 1988, pp. 185–6).

Moreover, the provision by government of 'in-work' benefits arguably provides what the Institute of Personnel Management (IPM) have termed 'a hidden subsidy for inefficient employers' (*IRS Employment Trends*, 434, 21 February 1989, p. 3), thereby weakening the effect of pressures that might otherwise help force companies to improve their efficiency and aim for an upward adjustment in market strategies. Furthermore, state assistance to the employees of companies paying low wages in effect promotes unfair competition with companies efficient enough to be paying wages above the thresholds that would allow their employees to qualify for state support.

Perhaps most importantly of all, current policies offer encouragement to low-pay employers to rely on further depressing wage levels as a strategy for survival, rather than helping them to make the change to more efficient production of high-quality goods and services. Indeed, if the arguments that have been made above are correct, and low wages act as a disincentive to firms to invest in new technology and training by reducing the potential returns available from such investment, then measures further to depress wages can only add to the problem.

It is also worth underlining the fact that attempts to reduce employment protection, lessen the power of trade unions, and further depress pay levels, all run counter to the evidence from West Germany as to the factors that interact to produce the virtuous circle that underpins the production of high-quality goods and services. By weakening the already fairly limited restraints on employers, current UK policies may be making it easier for companies to opt for routes to short-term survival based on low wages, labour intensification and further job segmentation (Darling and Lockwood, 1988), rather than on investing to 'upgrade production facilities and labour force skills' (Nolan, forthcoming).

In summary, current policy reveals the existence of two competing, and arguably mutually incompatible, models of labour market development. On one hand is a vision of policies leading to the creation of a high-skill, and implicitly high-wage, national workforce whose competitive advantage lies in their ability to design, produce and deliver high-quality goods and services. On the other is a labour market model that sees the way forward in terms of an increasingly numerically flexible, casualized workforce, which possesses very limited job protection, and which affords employers a competitive advantage based on price rather than quality.

It may be that the segmentation of the national labour force that the simultaneous pursuit of these two models implies is a policy goal, and that the intention is to create a core national workforce to whom one model of development applies while, beneath this, there at the same time exists a peripheral workforce for whom very different conditions and prospects will pertain. If this type of dualism is the goal of current policies, it has not been made explicit.

5   FORCES FOR CHANGE

The tensions between the two policy models outlined above are thrown into sharper relief by a variety of changes in the national and international economic environment. These changes are likely to have a major influence on the need for British employers, particularly in the low-pay/low-training sectors, to achieve significant improvements in their provision of training and development.

Increased International Competition

The first of these, the creation of a single European market in 1992 and the general expected increase in international competitiveness, has already been mentioned. As Hayes and Fonda have emphasized (1988), the onset of a more turbulent and uncertain business environment will require companies to position themselves to cope with change. One important element in changing the capability of the enterprise to cope with discontinuity will be its system of vocational education and training. As the then Manpower Service Commission's *Youth Training News* (36, February 1987, p. 15) put it, 'the workforce as a whole needs to be able to adapt to, to initiate, and to be confident that it can cope with change'. In addition, increasing world market competition will mean that developed countries will be forced to undertake:

> rapid economic restructuring towards a less price- and more quality-competitive product range . . . producing such products requires a high input of skills. The same is true for product diversification and customization which also help remove production from the pressures of price competition. (Streeck, 1989, pp. 90–1).

Increasing Demand for Higher Quality

Another force that it has been suggested will act as a lever for change is a continued increase in consumer demand for high-quality goods and services. One reflection of this demand is the effort which various UK service organizations have started to devote to customer care training. Probably the best known example is British Airways's 'Putting People First' campaign, but many other organizations, in areas such as banking and retailing, have also recognized that in markets where the basic rival products or services are broadly similar, the only major differentiating factor is 'the people in the organisation that represent the greatest element of the customer's perception' (Davis, 1987, p. 47).

The demand for higher product quality and reliability is moreover expected to encompass both the individual consumer and corporate customers, and an added impetus comes from overseas competition. Japanese companies have, for a long time, had a reputation for paying close attention to quality and 'zero defects' production. Spurred on by this example, many US companies have started to adopt a similar philosophy (Kennedy, 1987, p. 45). In addition to overseas pressure, a more competitive UK environment will make the costs of failures of quality harder to support. In 1978 it was estimated that the overall cost of quality failures to UK industry was of the order of £10 billion, a figure at the time equal to about 10 per cent of Gross National Product, and the Department of Trade and Industry were suggesting in 1987 that quality-related costs accounted for between 5 and 25 per cent of company turnover (Kennedy, 1987, p. 46).

Such pressures have important implications for companies' manpower and training and development strategies, for it is noticeable that those British companies that have decided to adopt a strategy aimed at high quality, such as Jaguar Cars or British Steel, have seen a heavy investment in the education and training of their workpeople as an essential component of the strategy. Put simply, there has been a recognition on the part of management in these companies that high-quality goods and services can be delivered only by a well-motivated, high-quality workforce.

Demographic Change

The third and final major source of pressure for change in low-pay sectors is the onset of demographic changes which are forecast to result in a very much tighter UK labour market in the 1990s. The sharp decline in the overall number of young people entering the labour market in the 1990s means that employers will need to tap a variety of alternative sources of labour if they are not to experience labour shortages. These alternative sources include women returners to the labour market, older workers, members of ethnic minorities, the long-term unemployed, and the disabled (NEDO/TC, 1988). Thus, the government, National Economic Development Office and the Training Agency have all suggested that the decline in the supply of young people offers an opportunity for employers to help bring many who are currently economically inactive into the labour force.

However, the suggestion that organizations should seek to utilize alternative sources of labour supply as a solution to the impending shortfall in the number of young entrants to the labour market carries with it an implicit assumption that organizations either possess, or have the capacity to acquire, the expertise and infrastructure that will support the relatively sophisticated personnel management/human resource management systems needed to tap these sources. The degree to which companies in many low-pay sectors possess or could readily acquire this kind of expertise is open to some doubt.

Changes in the labour market thus arguably represent something of a two-edged sword (CBI, 1989, p. 13). On the one hand, tighter labour markets will make the costs incurred through high levels of labour turnover increasingly difficult to sustain (Lunn, 1989), and may force employers to take the retention, training and re-training of adult workers more seriously, and to recognize the necessity of developing every employee in order to help him or her reach full potential. On the other, there is a very real possibility that tighter labour market conditions and reduced numbers of young workers may simply compound the problems already faced by low-pay sectors. The danger is that more profitable and higher-paying sectors will tend to concentrate their response to a tighter labour market for young people on efforts simply to fish harder in a dwindling pool. As they absorb a greater and greater proportion of young entrants to the labour force, so the risks and difficulties of tapping the alternative sources of supply will be passed on to those who are less able to offer attractive pay and job prospects to the young. Through the possibility of this cascade effect, there is a risk that a disproportionate share of the problems and costs of employing and re-training women re-turners, the long-term unemployed, older workers, and the disabled, will be forced upon precisely those employers whose personnel policies and systems are least able to make them either amenable towards adopting such radical solutions, or able to provide the support structures that will be required to make them work, such as staff nursery provision, disabled access to the workplace, or training facilities.

Furthermore, if the demand for better qualified labour exceeds supply, then those organizations offering lower rates of pay will usually be the least able to secure a share of such labour. The result of this may be that the 'filtering' effect referred to above, whereby overall rises in the educational attainments of young people have meant young people with qualifications moving into areas where the previous, older workforce had been unqualified, will cease. Indeed, with the qualified heading for employers offering higher pay, low-pay sectors and employers are likely to prove attractive only to the most disadvantaged sections within the overall pool of labour. Thus, the 'demographic timebomb' may ultimately have the result of heightening existing problems of labour market segmentation.

Insufficient time has elapsed for it to be possible to offer any definitive judgment as to exactly how, at aggregate levels, employers will react to the problems and opportunities posed by demographic change. Nevertheless, current indications are not particularly encouraging. For example, evidence from a recent study undertaken for the National Economic Development Office suggests that the majority of employers have responded to a tightening youth labour market by simply competing harder for young recruits (NEDO/TA, 1989). Too few employers appeared prepared to consider alternative tapping sources of labour or changes in their employment practices. A survey covering 600 employers in the Crawley area indicated that the most common employer response to labour and skill shortages was an upward adjustment in wages (Pickard, 1989), and 'despite all the talk of the need for women returners, only 2000 workplace nurseries and creches exist' (Devine, 1989:5). Employer discrimination against older workers also remains widespread (Nash, 1989, p. 53; *Personnel Management*, June 1989, p. 103) and is apparently particularly heavily concentrated in the private sector (*Personnel Management*, 1989, p. 103).

Both the Training Agency and the CBI have acknowledged that they believe that tighter youth labour markets pose a serious threat to the Youth Training Scheme, the major change that has happened to training provision in many low-pay sectors in the last decade. As the head of the Youth Training Scheme marketing at the then-Training Commission commented, 'experience suggests that changes in the youth labour market may lead to short-termism. In this situation the risk exists that many young people may side step training; and large numbers of employers will abandon training and resort to inflationary wage bidding' (Goulbourn, 1988, p. 14).

In summary, it can be said that the forces for change that have been discussed above heighten the need to tackle the difficulties posed by the low pay, low productivity, and reliance upon low-cost competition, but do not, in themselves, necessarily offer a sufficient catalyst to transform those areas of the UK economy afflicted with these problems. Indeed, demographic change carries with it the threat of actually significantly worsening the manpower and skill supply position of low-pay sectors. The problem for policy-makers is what further measures might be contemplated to augment, and/or supersede present policies.

6   FUTURE STRATEGIES FOR CHANGE

If the arguments stated above are accepted, it will be apparent that attempts to improve the supply of training and development, on their own, can play only a limited part in solving the underlying structural problems that lead to the assignment of weak priority to training in the low-pay sectors. Success is more probable if attempts to boost the supply of training form part of a broader strategy that embraces simultaneous efforts to tackle limits on the demand for skills. This would entail framing measures to shift companies' competitive strategies away from a cost basis, towards the provision of higher-quality, higher value-added goods and services. A review of the various policy options by means of which such broader changes in industrial organization and strategy might be accomplished lies outside the scope of this chapter. The section below instead attempts to review, from the perspective of government and other national bodies, such as the National Economic Development Office and the Training Agency, the options available in attempting to frame the training-related part of this wider strategy. The treatment does not pretend to be exhaustive, but seeks rather to offer up for discussion a variety of avenues worthy of further exploration.

Staying With Present Policies

The first of these is to carry on with present policies, and to hope that market forces and the other changes in the business environment described above will be sufficient to force an improvement. Leaving aside the potential contradictions between the very different visions of future UK labour market development encompassed within current policies, it is open to question whether the initiatives already in train are, on their own, sufficient to deal with the scale of the challenges that face the national economy in the 1990s (Fonda, 1989; Finegold and Soskice, 1988; Keep and Mayhew, 1988).

One particular difficulty with current training policies, is that they are very clearly based on a belief that the primary responsibility for training decisions rests with the employer and the individual enterprise. Government initiatives exist either to help companies to help themselves, or to tackle unemployment. The danger of relying on self-help is that companies' ability to perceive the need for change, and to manage the process of change, varies enormously. It is possible that, in the long term, the major beneficiaries of government help will tend to be those already best placed and best motivated to help themselves – i.e. larger companies with relatively sophisticated personnel systems, and enterprises operating in existing product markets that demand higher levels of skill. It may be, therefore, that there is a need for a greater emphasis within policy for targeting help and encouragement towards those employers and sectors of the economy which constitute the training 'black spots'.

Depending on the priority that is attached to the need to improve the performance of the low-pay sectors of the UK economy, there are three other possible avenues for policy development that might be explored as a means of targeting additional help in this direction. In many senses the possibilities discussed below are aimed at supplementing and building upon current training initiatives, and the alternatives being proposed need not be regarded as being in any way mutually exclusive.

Targeting Key Groups

Before examining these potential lines for development, one point needs to be emphasized. If there is a need for vocational education and training initiatives targeted at those areas of the economy with the worst training record, there is also a need for a new training provision within these sectors to be aimed at certain key groups.

Firstly, efforts need to be directed at those groups currently most disadvantaged in the labour market – women, ethnic minorities, the disabled, the long-term unemployed, and older workers – among whom low pay is heavily concentrated. This will mean not simply providing them with greater opportunities for training and development, but also using training to break down the barriers that force them into secondary labour markets, and which make them vulnerable to exploitative low pay. For example, as has been suggested earlier, one of the most important examples of these barriers is gender stereotyping, and the designation of certain forms of employment as 'women's work'. Gender divisions in the structure of employment are supported by a 'channeling' effect within education and training (see Cockburn, 1987) which structures choices and expectations early on in people's lives. Greater efforts to address this problem, and to produce education and training that is genuinely non-gender specific would be an important component of helping ease the structural factors that underpin low pay. The record of the Youth Training Scheme to date indicates the difficulty of achieving widespread change in this area (Cockburn, 1987). The Training Agency admits that 'although some progress has been made in providing non-traditional occupational training in individual areas, this has had little effect on the broad occupational groups' (TA, *Youth Training News*, 55, June–July 1989, p. 24).

A second key group towards whom efforts need to be directed is management. The education and training of many British managers is deficient by international standards, and it is managers, more than any other group, who determine the product market, competitive, and training strategies of the enterprise. Thus, unless managers are helped to understand the long-term dangers of strategies based solely on price competition, fundamental change will not take place. Moreover, if managers are themselves poorly educated, and exposed to little in the way of training, they are less likely to find similar deficiencies among their subordinates either unusual or undesirable. Indeed, if managers and owner-managers are in any way aware of the limitations imposed upon them by their own lack of training, then it is possible that they may see attempts to upgrade the skills and knowledge of their subordinates as a threat to their own authority. The lack of adequate levels of managerial education and training are hence major barriers to more general improvements in training, and to the adoption of non-Taylorist styles of work organization based on non-hierarchical, 'expert' leadership.

The Training Agency's new Business Growth through Training (BGT) initiative is a useful start in the direction of improving the business skills of owner-managers and in helping managers to link training to broader business strategies (Hillier, 1989), but the scale of problem to be tackled is massive. Moreover, as a senior Training Agency official admitted, because use of the help that Business Growth Through Training offers is entirely voluntary, 'for it to be successful, employers must be convinced that putting training at the centre of their corporate strategies really will improve business performance . . . this may not always be easy' (Hillier, 1989, p. 223).

Altering Company Training Strategies

Having identified the key groups at whom new training initiatives need to be directed, we can now turn to the policy options available to provide enhanced vocational education and training provision. The first would be to embark on further measures to tackle weaknesses within individual companies. Various additional leverage mechanisms could be adopted by government and other actors to help encourage the process of change in companies' manpower and training policies, and in their perception of their skill needs. A limited number of examples are discussed below.

One possibility would be for the government, both central and local, to designate selected public sector areas of low pay as exemplars of good training practice and to provide model programmes of vocational education and training for the workforces in these areas. This training would need to encompass both the initial training of young employees and the training and re-training of adults. Such training programmes could be combined with other elements of a sophisticated model of human resource management, such as better employee communication and participation, employee involvement in quality initiatives, and the use of more sophisticated selection, recruitment and reward systems. It would also be possible, and arguably beneficial given the tighter labour market that will exist in the 1990s, for these developments also to go hand in hand with attempts to mount model schemes for the employment of under-utilized groups within the pool of available labour, such as ethnic minorities, the disabled, the long-term unemployed, and older workers. In this latter area, some local authorities have already made progress, but more could be done, particularly by central government departments.

The use of the public sector in such a way would demonstrate its commitment to the belief, often expressed by government and by bodies such as the National Economic Development Office and the Training Agency, in the motivational and productivity gains that spring from investment in human capital. It would also strengthen government exhortation by offering an opportunity for the government to be seen to lead by example.

Another area worthy of investigation could be making the award of government contracts or grants to companies (for example in tourism) dependent upon the companies meeting certain basic criteria covering the levels of training provision available to their workforces. While central government has attempted to prevent the use of contract compliance procedures by local authorities, its objection does not appear to be one of principle, as it has been prepared to sanction their use in Northern Ireland in support of attempts to discourage employment discrimination against the minority community. An argument can be made that if companies wish to profit from public monies, it is not unreasonable to require them to be making efforts to implement various aspects of public policy that have been deemed beneficial to their own and the nation's good.

Building on the likely increase in demand for higher-quality goods and services discussed above offers another way forward. Greater efforts could be made by many large British companies to develop positive links with their suppliers. Marks and Spencer are the best-known example of a company that has attempted to extend its quality control procedures back into its suppliers, but it is by no means a totally isolated one. A number of companies, particularly in motor manufacturing, have also offered help with training to some of their suppliers in an attempt to boost the efficiency and quality of the goods and services they receive. A major attempt by bodies such as the National Economic Development Office, the Training Agency, and the CBI to spread this kind of good practice could be valuable.

A further possibility is increasing the pressure brought to bear upon employers to undertake training by trade unions. The government (*Employment for the 1990s*) has suggested that:

Trade unions ... need to accept that their members are more concerned with such issues as training and pensions than they are with defending out-of-date methods of working (1988, p. 17).

A number of trade unions have started to take up this challenge, most notably Manufacturing, Science and Finance (MSF), the Amalgamated Engineering Union (AEU) and the General, Municipal and Boilermakers Union (GMB). John Edmonds, General Secretary of the GMB, has acknowledged the need for a change:

In the past, unions seemed to work towards restricting management's ability to manoeuvre, which has been very much a traditional union role. The thinking is that the more you restrict management the greater freedom is created for individual working people. That simply does not work. We've got to negotiate positive things ... training will be of greatest importance in the coming years (Gurdon, 1989, p. 16).

For their part, MSF have concluded that 'training is the best form of job security' (Webb, 1988, p. 23), and are committed to the negotiation of workplace training agreements with employers. They have proposed that such negotiations could cover the establishment of a joint company/union training committee, the development of regular career planning and counselling services, an emphasis on equal opportunities in training provision, and the confirmation of the right of every employee to training and re-training after a minimum period of service (Webb, 1988, pp. 23–4). The union has also suggested that details of any access the employer is likely to make available to training and re-training should form part of every employee's legal contract of employment.

The major drawback to this approach, at least in many of the sectors and industries characterized by low pay, is the weakness and disorganization of the trade unions. This stems in part from the distinctive structural characteristics of these areas, particularly the difficulties of organizing in industries characterized by large numbers of small employers and by often very high rates of labour turnover. It also reflects the vulnerability of many of those groups within which low pay tends to be concentrated, such as women workers, part-timers, and members of ethnic minorities (Pond, 1983, pp. 202–3).

The difficulties that trade unions have faced in low-pay sectors have meant that, even at the height of their powers, the unions were unable, through free collective bargaining, adequately to protect the most vulnerable workers (Basnett, 1982). Since then, government legislation has sought to weaken the power of the unions. The result is that the pressure that trade unions can bring to bear upon employers in low-pay sectors is often extremely limited, and is unlikely, on its own, to force those employers unwilling to train to change their minds.

The final form of leverage that might be contemplated is statutory underpinning for training provision. At the present the general use of this option has been rejected by government, and Britain, in contrast to many other European countries, now relies entirely upon a voluntary system of training. However, in the past the Manpower Services Commission considered that 'there are a number of areas in which legislation could conceivably play a part in securing better training provision' (MSC, 1981, p. 7), and the eventuality may arise when the issue needs to be considered again. In particular, any further widening of the disparity between best and worst practice in UK training, and between general levels of UK training and those found in the UK's major competitors, would reopen debate about the value of legislation in guaranteeing certain minimum standards of provision and performance in strategically important areas of economic activity (Willis, 1989).

In this connection, it is interesting to note that proposed government legislation on food hygiene would apparently impose some form of statutory duty on employers to train staff whose work includes food handling and preparation. If legislation and the statutory imposition of training are justified in ensuring public health standards, it could be argued that they are also justified in establishing minimum standards of training necessary for the health of the national economy. At the end of the day, a willingness to contemplate the use of legislation depends on an assessment of the balance between the economic costs arising from the incidence of weak and uneven investment in training, and the dangers and costs of state intervention in companies' decision-making processes.

Given the present and likely future problems faced by the UK economy, the need to promote change in companies' attitudes towards training is strong, but the difficulties of doing so should not be under-estimated. A number of large retailers, such as Woolworth's and Tesco's offer examples of companies in a traditional low-pay sector which have moved towards higher-quality, less price-based competition. With such changes have come greater investment in training, and the development of more sophisticated personnel management systems (see TA *Focus on Training*, 12, July 1989). However, the experience of working with smaller employers in the low-pay manufacturing sectors (see for example Fennell, 1989) suggests that it is often difficult for these changes to come from within the enterprise, and that, even with strong external support, it is not easy to reach the stage where they become self-sustaining.

Helping Individual Adults

Having reviewed a number of the measures that could act as levers on companies' training performance, we can turn to the second strategy, which would be to try to help individual adults to improve their qualifications and skills. Experience to date suggests that there is considerable untapped demand for training and re-training opportunities among the adult population. There are already a variety of efforts being made to try to release this latent potential. Examples include the TA's Employment Training scheme for the long-term adult unemployed, the Open College, the Department of Education and Science's REPLAN initiative for the adult unemployed, and the National Council for Vocational Qualifications' attempts to develop a more readily comprehensible and accessible system of vocational qualifications which will provide clear routes for progression. Nevertheless, a great deal more could be done, not just by central government, but also by local education authorities, trade unions, community groups and educational institutions.

One requirement is for the new types of provision in the field of adult education and training. The experiences of the Department of Education and Science's REPLAN project and the curriculum development work of the Further Education Unit (FEU) show the way forward, in terms of making access to courses simpler, in designing provision that is closely tailored to the needs of the client group, and in devising the means of ensuring that the entire community is aware of what is available and how it might be relevant to their needs. One example of what can be achieved is the work undertaken by the Further Education Unit and a number of further education colleges in designing and marketing courses for those working or wishing to work in the leisure and tourism industry (see FEU, 1988). Another is a Training Agency-funded course, set up by the South Glamorgan county council, on new technology, computing and electronic skills for unemployed, unskilled women (see Platt, 1987, p. 7). The major brake on progress at present is the lack of adequate resources to extend the often very limited scale of many of these pilot initiatives.

In seeking to encourage people to invest in their own training, there is also a need to increase the incentives that are available. One possibility would be the provision of tax incentives to employees that paid for their own training. This is an area where Britain compares unfavourably with many other countries (*Transition*, June, 1988, p. 5), with most individual expenditure on training not being tax deductable. Interest in increasing the tax relief available has been expressed by the Department of Education and Science (*Transition*, June 1988, p. 5), but little actual progress in gaining Treasury approval appears to have resulted.

There seems little doubt that there is a considerable under-utilized potential among much of Britain's adult population, but it would be idle to deny that there are major difficulties with relying solely upon strategies targeted at the individual low-paid worker. Individuals' perceptions of the need for and value of training are governed by a variety of factors that go beyond the issue of the availability of appropriate courses and facilities outside the workplace. For example, experiences within the workplace play a major role in structuring people's broader expectations of training. As an Organization for Economic Cooperation and Development (OECD) study of educational leave provision points out:

> when training is defined as vocational if it is relevant to the individual's current or immediately foreseeable occupational position, its scope will broaden according to the interest of the job,

with the consequence that those who already occupy the most interesting positions will be able to benefit from a far wider range of opportunities than the unskilled workers in dead-end jobs (OECD, 1977).

The importance of limited in-work opportunities is emphasised in research conducted for the Training Agency by the Policy Studies Institute (Rigg, 1989), which indicates that the capacity of individuals to see value in obtaining further training is heavily influenced by previous levels of educational qualification and by people's exposure to the recent experience of training. As Rigg points out:

At present, employer-funded training of adults is concentrated heavily on professional and managerial occupations. Members of other occupations, usually possessing lower qualifications, are less likely to receive training from employers and appear to have their capacity to envisage participation in training blunted by lack of exposure to training at work (Rigg, 1989, p. 12)

A further difficulty is that the tendency for low-paid employment often to be insecure, with high levels of labour turnover, means that the willingness of individual employees to fund their own training will be limited (Bosworth, 1989, p. 74).

Even more importantly, as Paul Ryan's study (Chapter 6 in this volume) argues, the problem is not just one of improving the training opportunities available to the low-paid, it is also one of improving the incentives/payback that the utilization of such opportunities for the acquisition of new skills provides. Given that many low pay sectors do not operate well-formed internal labour markets, and offer very limited scope for the advancement of the individual worker, two results may stem from improving individual access to training. The first is that the individual may upgrade his other skills and knowledge, either at his or her own expense, or at the expense of the state or other agency, only to find it impossible to utilize new-found skills to the full within the scope offered by the low-paid employment.

The second, and to some extent consequent result, may be that by upgrading the skills of individuals, training will enable them to leave the low-pay sector and find employment in better remunerated areas of the economy. While this would be of direct benefit to the individuals making this transfer, it has a broader effect of simply cascading occupancy of low-paid jobs onto even more disadvantaged groups in the labour market.

The final objection to an approach centred on helping individual adults to upgrade their skills is that it can be suggested that much of the effort that currently goes into adult education and re-training is essentially remedial in nature. In many cases it is simply attempting to correct earlier disadvantage experienced within the period of initial, compulsory education. This is certainly a line of argument which the recent CBI Task Force on training report endorses (1989, p. 15).

Improving Initial Education and Training

This brings us to the third strategy, which would be to try to tackle the problem of low levels of skill and qualifications before people enter the labour market, through improvements in the general provision of initial education and training, in terms of both quality and duration. The CBI Task Force report *Towards A Skills Revolution* (CBI, 1989), has helped focus renewed attention on what a recent *Financial Times* editorial described as 'the single most obvious flaw in Britain's education system' (20 February 1989). This flaw is our failure to develop a comprehensive and coherent system of education and training provision for the 16–19 age group.

In answer to this problem the CBI Task Force proposed a number of policies, including the establishment of national education and training targets for the 16–19 age group leading to increased participation in post-compulsory education: and the development of a training credits system, under which the government would offer all young people a credit covering the learning costs of reaching two A levels or their equivalent, while employers covered the full wages costs of the trainee. The overall aim would be to end the option of paid employment without training for the under-18s. One of the reasons underlying the CBI's suggested reforms was concern at the fact that the general skill levels of the UK workforce still trail those of our overseas competitors (*Financial Times*, 5 July 1989).

These concerns are well-founded. Most advanced countries have developed, or are developing, the means effectively to withdraw the 16–18 age group from paid employment. The choice is normally between a system based on educational provision, or some form of structured, work-based training. The former solution is represented by countries such as Japan (with 94 per cent of 16–18 year olds in education), the USA (79 per cent), Taiwan (80 per cent), South Korea (85 per cent), and France (58 per cent). In West Germany,

Switzerland and Austria, the choice has been for a comprehensive system of high-quality employer-based apprenticeships.

The position in the UK is very different. As Finegold and Soskice comment 'England is the only one of the world's major industrial nations in which the majority of students leave full-time education or training at the age of sixteen' (1988, p. 23). Although participation rates in post-compulsory education have risen in recent years, they have still not reached 50 per cent of the age group. Moreover, despite the then Manpower Services Commission's original intentions, the work-based training offered by the Youth Training Scheme has never been extended to cover all young people, whether employed or unemployed, and in 1988 Training Commission officials estimated that as many as 100,000 young people each year entered jobs which offered little or no formal training (Goulbourn, 1988, p. 14). Evidence generated by the Training Agency's Youth Cohort Study survey project indicates that even this estimate may be over-optimistic. A report from the Youth Cohort Study covering the fortunes of 8000 1984 school-leavers (Training Agency, 1989) showed that 51 per cent of survey respondents in work claimed to have received no training or instruction as part of their job.

If the overall quality of the UK's workforce, in low pay and other sectors, is to be brought up to international standards, improving provision for the 16–18 age group is vital. A number of proposals for action in this area exist, coming from bodies such as the CBI (1989), and the National Association of Head Teachers (NAHT, 1982, 1987). While there are differences of emphasis and detail between these proposals, a number of common themes emerge. Firstly, the current tangle of competing education and training provision for the 14–18 age group needs to be made more coherent (Cantor, 1985; Bolton, 1985; Evans and Watts, 1985; NAHT, 1987), with greater parity of status between 'academic' and 'vocational' courses (Cantor, 1985, p. 23; NAHT, 1982, 1987); and the sixth form curriculum, despite the government's rejection of the Higginson Committee's proposals, needs to be broadened away from the traditional A level model.

Secondly, the balance of the alternatives facing school-leavers at 16 should be altered to increase the incentives to remain in full-time education (Finegold and Soskice, 1988, p. 39; Micklewright, Pearson, and Smith, 1989; CBI, 1989, pp. 19–25). One means of achieving this would be to improve the quality of careers guidance available to young people, and by providing young people with a pattern of education and training that, through the concept of 'careers for all', would offer 'clear and worthwhile goals which bring a return that is tradeable in the market place' (CBI, 1989, p. 19).

Another way forward would be to help balance the disparity in financial returns available from different choices at 16. At present, there is only very limited, discretionary support for students staying on in full-time education between the ages of 16 and 18. The vast majority receive nothing, and are entirely dependent upon their families for support. Those leaving the education system can expect either to go onto a Youth Training Scheme with a weekly allowance, or enter paid employment. As the youth labour market tightens under the force of demographic change, the likelihood of increasingly well-rewarded employment at 16 seems set to rise, thereby further adding to the disincentive to remaining in education. The most frequently suggested answer to this imbalance is the payment of Educational Maintenance Awards (EMAs) to those remaining in post-compulsory education. EMAs could be paid on a blanket basis, perhaps replacing child benefit payments for the age group (Micklewright, Pearson and Smith, 1989), or on a discretionary basis to those most in need (CBI, 1989, p. 36).

The extension of universal provision of education and training to this age group would have the benefit of helping to overcome the problem of disadvantage being passed from one generation to the next via negative class and cultural attitudes towards the value of education and training (Ashton, 1988, pp. 4–7; Willis, 1977; Brown, 1987; Cantor, 1985; Micklewright, 1989). It would also neutralize peer group pressure that helps perpetuate and reinforce this culture. Developments along the lines being proposed by the CBI would also help head off the threat posed to Youth Training Scheme-style training by tightening labour markets and the possibility of employers opting for higher youth pay, rather than training, as a means of attracting a dwindling pool of young people into their employment.

There can be little doubt that reform of education and training provision for this age group, and the removal of the option of employment without properly structured high-quality training, would help bring the quality of the UK workforce closer into line with those of its competitors. It would also offer all employers, whether in low-pay sectors or elsewhere, a more solid foundation upon which to build any subsequent training and re-training.

The problem that remains, however, is whether employers, the government, and other actors in the policy making community have the commitment to follow through on the policy options outlined above. In particular, if a voluntarist approach is pursued, the role of employers is crucial to the success of change in this area. The CBI Task Force makes the assumption that it will be possible to persuade all employers to abstain, on a voluntary basis, from offering young people paid employment with no training. As has been illustrated above, a significant number of employers currently choose to offer this option. It is open to question just how far the members of the CBI Task Force are representative of all sections of British employers, and to what degree their recommendations would command the practical support of employers who currently see no need for any training for their young employees. Will employers in the low-pay sectors be willing to fund the full wages costs of a two-year scheme that involved trainees spending substantial periods of time studying for nationally recognized vocational qualifications, as the CBI are suggesting. The experience of the Youth Training Scheme to date suggests that they might not.

Overall, the three areas for policy development outlined above offer a number of ways forward. Some of the changes being suggested are undoubtedly easier to institute quickly than others, but all require for their success, the involvement of a wide variety of actors, including government, employers, the trade unions, local authorities, and bodies such as the Training Agency and National Economic Development Office. In particular, there is a need for government and leading employers to make it clear to the business community as a whole that the UK can no longer afford to allow the waste in human potential that is represented by the current low levels of vocational education and training received by certain sections of the nation's workforce.

7 CONCLUSION – THE DANGERS OF STANDING STILL

The strategies that have been discussed above are all narrowly-focused, in that they directly address issues relating to vocational education and training. Either singly, or taken together, they could help produce change and improvement in both the volume and quality of the vocational education and training offered to workers in low-paid jobs. Nevertheless, these strategies, while necessary, are by no means, on their own, sufficient to solve the problems of the low-pay sectors. They can offer important help in improving skills supply, and in increasing the job mobility of some individuals, thereby enabling them to leave low-paid employment for better jobs, but without being part of some broader change they will not alter the basic pattern of skill utilization in the low pay sectors. Altering the skills, knowledge and competences of those who carry out low-paid jobs, in itself, will not automatically change the nature of the jobs they undertake.

As this chapter has stressed, issues such as companies' product market choice and the utilization of competitive strategies based on price rather than quality play a significant part in structuring managements' perceptions of the level of skills they require. External pressure aimed at providing skills in excess of those levels is likely to produce sub-optimal results unless and until the perceptions that underlie them are also changed. This in effect means altering the competitive strategies of significant sections of the British economy towards the provision of higher quality goods and services, while at the same time closing off the option of relying on low pay as a source of competitive advantage. Such a shift in competitive strategy would bring with it a requirement for new methods of work organisation and job design, and for human resource management-style personnel management strategies aimed at securing the active commitment of the workforce.

The example of the current uncertainties facing the Youth Training Scheme illustrate the scale and nature of the problem that has to be faced. The Youth Training Scheme represents the major achievement of the Manpower Services Commission and was hailed by its then-director as, 'the most significant development in education and training since the Education Act of 1944' (*Times Higher Education Supplement*, 24 January 1986). Yet, as has been outlined above, the scheme has never covered both the young employed and unemployed as was originally intended, and is now threatened by demographic change and tightening of the youth labour market. The reasons for these difficulties are fairly simple; the scheme has failed to change the underlying assumptions of the majority of British employers, not least in the low-pay sectors, towards the need to train the mass of young workers. The contrast between this situation and that in West Germany could not be more stark. Despite facing a far larger fall in the numbers of young people entering the labour market than in the UK, there is no sign of any threat to the 'dual system' of apprenticeships from West German employers seeking to bid up youth wages and offer little in the way of training. As a senior official concerned with marketing the Youth Training Scheme admitted, 'realistically, it must be recognised that within the UK we do not have an education and training culture to match that of our main international competitors. Many young people and their employers fail to see training as an investment for the future' (Goulbourn, 1988, p. 15). The Youth Training Scheme underlines the difficulties of attempting to increase the supply of skills while the underlying level of demand remains low.

As this chapter has sought to demonstrate, current policies are arguably failing to address this basic problem. Besides the risk that certain aspects of policy may encourage employers to rely still further on low pay as a competitive strategy, attempts to reform British vocational education and training appear to rely upon institutional innovations designed to increase the supply of training available, while leaving untouched the underlying structural forces and attitudes that limit the demand for better vocational education and training. Until the jump from vicious to virtuous circle of causation is made, sustainable improvements will continue to prove elusive.

Indeed, Fonda (1989) suggests that the current product market strategies of many UK firms mean that there is a strong likelihood that even if government is able to stimulate an increase in the volume of training, it will occur at the lower end of the skills spectrum. The result will be that British training will produce large numbers of people equipped to:

> perform today's low value-added tasks ... while the rest of the European Community focuses on training and education to pursue innovation and value-added business strategies (and the UK sinks to the bottom of the EC in terms of GDP per head of population) (Fonda, 1989, p. 7).

Jarvis and Prais (1989, p. 70) have also voiced concern that the low level and narrow focus of some vocational qualifications currently being specified by British employers through the National Council for Vocational Qualifications run the risk of producing, 'a certified semi-literate under-class – a section of the workforce inhibited in job-flexibility, and inhibited in the possibilities of progression'. The general drift of these comments has been echoed by the CBI Task Force report (1989, pp. 30–1), which is critical of the National Council for Vocational Qualifications' concentration on narrowly defined skills rather than promoting broader-based competences.

The two models of labour market development outlined in this chapter also raise the question of with whom exactly Britain intends to be competing in the 1990s. There is a risk that the 'low-skills equilibrium' that currently exists will, unless tackled swiftly, ensure that an increasing number of sectors (and not just those characterized by low pay) will have no option but to concentrate on production at the lower end of the quality spectrum. Fonda (1989, p. 6) claims that 'far too many' British companies 'are aiming to survive by ... focusing all their attention on being the lowest-cost supplier in their industry'. The logical consequence of this tendency, as Sharp, Shepherd and Marsden (1987, p. 37) underline is 'that the United Kingdom's specialisation in less sophisticated products will increasingly put it into competition with ... low wage, but increasingly productive countries', a point echoed by Greenhalgh and Gregory (1989). As John Banham, the Director-General of the CBI has emphasized, it is open to question how sustainable such a strategy is, given the increasing skill levels and very low wages found in the developing world (*Lifeskills News*, 6, June 1988). Various commentators (Streeck, 1989; Fonda, 1989; New and Myers, 1986) have all suggested that the high-skill, high-wage, high value-added route is 'almost certainly the only viable long term strategy for a highly developed economy' (New and Myers, 1986, p. 26).

The danger must be that the longer we delay action to improve our overall skills base, and to increase the length of education that the majority of our working population undergo, the more out of step with other developed and developing economies the UK becomes. Unless progress is made, many UK low-pay manufacturers will find themselves vulnerable to being squeezed between high-quality production from Europe, the USA, and Japan and low-cost production from developing countries which is supported by levels of low pay impossible to sustain in the UK (Greenhalgh and Gregory, 1989). In the private services sector, an increasing infiltration of foreign-owned companies with very different competitive strategies and management philosophies from their British-owned counterparts may take place. In the public services, foreign competition is not a threat, but demographic change and tighter labour markets are. Unless work organization, pay and conditions, and more flexible recruitment strategies are adopted to meet the needs and expectations of new sources of labour, many of the low-pay areas of the public services are likely to be struggling to fill vacancies and maintain services in the 1990s.

Ultimately, the issues outlined above pose two sets of questions for policy-makers, whether in government, the Training Agency, companies or trade unions. The first is: what type of competitive strategy they wish to see spearheading the British economy in the 1990s, and what measures are needed to secure its widespread achievement? If the answer is one based on the production of high-quality goods and services, as the quotes at the beginning of this chapter tend to suggest, then it follows that one part of the solution ought to be a major upgrading of the skills base in those areas where companies are locked into a low-skills/low-pay strategy. The second question is: what are the social and economic costs of not adopting this competitive strategy, and instead leaving large swathes of the economy reliant for their long-term survival on price cutting? The answers to these questions will determine the degree to which, and the effectiveness with which, the structural problems described in this chapter are tackled.

Note

1. The author would like to record his thanks to Peter Nolan, and Professor Keith Sisson, for their helpful comments and suggestions concerning this chapter. As ever, any errors, omissions, or weaknesses of argument remain the sole responsibility of the author.

References

Ashton, D. N. (1988) 'Sources of variation in labour market segmentation: a comparison of youth labour markets in Canada and Britain', *Work, Employment and Society* , 2 (1) (March: 1–24).

Bach, S. (1989) *Too High a Price to Pay? A Study of Competitive Tendering for Domestic Services in the NHS*, Warwick Papers in Industrial Relations 25 (Coventry: University of Warwick, IRRU).

Basnett, D. (1982) *The Future of Collective Bargaining* (London: Fabian Society).

Bolton, E. (1985) 'An HMI perspective', in Watts, A. G. (ed.), *Education and Training 14–18: Policy and Practice* (Cambridge: Careers Research and Advisory Service) 11–14.

Bosworth, D. (1989) 'Barriers to growth: the labour market', in Barber, J., Metcalf, J. S. and Porteous, M. (eds), *Barriers to Growth in Small Firms* (London: Routledge).

178   *Training for the Low-paid*

Brady, T. (1984) *New Technology and Skills in British Industry* (Brighton: University of Sussex, Science Policy Research Unit).

Brown, P. (1987) *Schooling Ordinary Kids: Class Culture and Unemployment* (London: Tavistock).

Cantor, L. (1985) 'A coherent approach to the education and training of the 16–19 age group', in Worswick, G. D. N. (ed.), *Education and Economic Performance* (London: Gower): 13–24.

Cockburn, C. (1987) *Two-Track Training, Sex Inequalities and the YTS* (London: Macmillan).

Confederation of British Industry (CBI) (1989) *Towards a Skills Revolution – a Youth Charter* (London: CBI).

Craig, C. *et al.* (1982) *Labour Market Structure, Industrial Organisation and Low Pay* (Cambridge: Cambridge University Press).

Darling, P. and Lockwood, P. (1988) *Planning for the Skills Crisis – a Chance to Score* (London: Institute of Personnel Management).

Davis, R. (1987) 'How Avis did it', *The Director* (November: 47–7).

Devine, M. (1989). 'The Shape of jobs to come?', *Focus on Training*, 22 July: 4–5.

Employment for the 1990s (1988) Cm 540 (London: HMSO).

Evans, K. and Watts, A. G. (1985) 'Introduction', in Watts, A. G. (ed.), *Education and Training 14–18: Policy and Practice* (Cambridge: Careers Research and Advisory Service): 3–10.

Fennell, E. (1989) 'Savouring success', *Focus on Training*, 21 May: 6–7.

Finegold, D. and Soskice, D. (1988) 'The Failure of training In Britain: analysis and prescription', *Oxford Review of Economic Policy*, 4 (3) (Autumn): 21–53.

Fonda, N. (1989) 'In search of a training strategy', *Personnel Management* (April): 6–7.

Further Education Unit (FEU) (1988) *The Leisure, Tourism and Crafts Industries* (leaflet) (London: FEU Information Centre).

Goulbourn, T. (1988) 'The way forward – NTI objective 2', *Youth Training News*, 49 (September–October): 14–15.

Greenhalgh, C. and Gregory M. (1989) 'Why manufacturing matters', *Employment Institute Economic Report*, 4 (8) (October).

Gurdon, M. (1989) 'A tough line on training', *Personnel Today* (27 June): 16–17.

Hayes, C. and Fonda, N. (1988) 'Education, training and business performance', *Oxford Review of Economic Policy*, 4 (3) (Autumn): 108–19.

Hillier, R. (1989) 'Making training a key factor in business performance', *Employment Gazette* (May): 219–24.

Jarvis, V. and Prais, S. J. (1989) 'Two nations of shopkeepers: training for retailing in France and Britain', *National Institute Economic Review* (May): 58–73.

Keep, E. and Mayhew, K. (1988) 'The assessment: education, training and economic performance', *Oxford Review of Economic Policy*, 4 (3) (Autumn): i–xv.

Kennedy, C. (1987) 'Can we catch up in the quality race?', *The Director* (November): 44–6.

Lane, C. (1988) 'Industrial change in Europe: the pursuit of flexible specialisation in Britain and West Germany', *Work, Employment and Society*, 2 (2) (June): 141–68.

Layard, R., Piachaud, D. and Stewart, M. (1978) *The Causes of Poverty*, background paper, 5, Royal Commission on the Distribution of Income and Wealth (London: HMSO).

Lunn, T. (1989) 'Age of the new-image employer', *Sunday Times* (2 July).

Manpower Services Commission (MSC) (1981) *A New Training Initiative: An Agenda for Action* (London: MSC).

Manpower Services Commission/National Economic Development Office (MSC/NEDO) (1984) *Competence and Competition* (London: NEDO).

Manpower Services Commission/National Economic Development Office/ British Institute of Management (MSC/NEDO/BIM) (1987) *The Making of Managers: A Report on Management Education, Training and Development in the USA, West Germany, France, Japan and the UK* (London: NEDO).

Metcalf, H. (1988) 'Careers and training in tourism and leisure', *Employment Gazette* (February): 84–93.

Micklewright, J. (1989) 'Choice at sixteen', *Economica* (February).

Micklewright, J., Pearson, M. and Smith, S. (1989) 'Has Britain an early school-leaving problem?', *Fiscal Studies*, 10 (1) (February): 1–16.

Nash, T. (1989) 'Short on skills', *The Director* (March): 50–3.

National Association of Head Teachers (NAHT) (1982) *16–19: A Future for All* (Haywards Heath: NAHT).

National Association of Head Teachers (NAHT) (1987) *NAHT Action Plan – A Policy 14–18* (Haywards Heath: NAHT).

National Economic Development Office/Training Commission (NEDO/TC) (1988) *Young People and the Labour Market – A Challenge for the 1990s* (London: NEDO).

National Economic Development Office/Training Agency (NEDO/TA) (1989) *Defusing the Demographic Time Bomb* (London: NEDO).

New, C. C. and Myers, A. (1986) *Managing Manufacturing Operations in the UK 1975–1985* (London: British Institute of Management).

Nolan, P. (1988) *Pay, Productivity and UK Industrial Performance: An Overview*, position paper for Warwick/IRS Conference 'Pay, Performance and Productivity' (February) (Coventry: University of Warwick, IRRU).

Nolan, P. (1989) 'Walking on water? performance and industrial relations under Thatcher', *Industrial Relations Journal*, 20 (2) (Summer): 81–92.

Nolan, P. (forthcoming) 'The Productivity Miracle?', in F. Green (ed.), *The Restructuring of the UK Economy* (Brighton: Wheatsheaf) (forthcoming).

OECD (1977) *Alternation Between Work and Education: A Study of Educational Leave of Absence at the Enterprise Level* (Paris: OECD).

Parsons, D. (1987) 'Tuning into trends – Tourism and related leisure jobs', *Employment Gazette* (July): 337–45.

Pell, C. (1989) 'Forward planning is a way through the funding jungle', *Transition* (January): 10–13.

Pettigrew, A., Sparrow, P. and Hendry, C. (1988) 'The forces that trigger training', *Personnel Management* (December): 28–32.

Pickard, J. (1989) 'Crawley: a town in search of a labour force', *Personnel Management* (May): 46–50.

Piore, M. J. (1971) 'The dual labour market: theory and implications', in D. M. Gordon (ed.), *Problems in Political Economy: An Urban Perspective* (Lexington: D.C. Heath): 93–7.

Platt, Baroness (1987) 'The short term solution', *Focus on Adult Training*, 14 (December): 6–7.

Pointing (1986) 'Retail training in West Germany', *MSC Youth Training News* (April): 2–3.

Pond, C. (1983) 'Wages Councils, the unorganised, and the low paid', in G. S. Bain (ed.), *Industrial Relations In Britain* (Oxford: Basil Blackwell): 179–208.

Rigg, M. (1989) 'What keeps adults interested in training?', *Transition* (July): 10–12.

Roberts, J. (1989) 'Training is the key – The 1988 National Training Awards', *Employment Gazette* (January): 7–13.

Sharp, M. and Shepherd, M. (1987) *Managing Change in British Industry* (Geneva: International Labour Office).

Smail, R. (1987) 'Low pay in Britain – the latest survey', *Low Pay Review*, 29 (Spring): 4–9.

Steedman, H. (1987) *Vocational Training In France and Britain: Office Work*, Discussion Paper, 14 (London: National Institute of Economic and Social Research).

Steedman, H. and Wagner, K. (1987) 'A second look at productivity, machinery and skills in Britain and Germany', *National Institute Economic Review* (November): 84–95.

Steedman, H. and Wagner, K. (1989) 'Productivity, machinery and skills: clothing manufacture in Britain and Germany', *National Institute Economic Review* (May): 40–57.

Storey, J. (ed.) (1989) *New Perspectives on Human Resource Management* (London: Routledge).

Streeck, W. (1985) *Industrial Relations and Industrial Change in the Motor Industry – An International View* (Coventry: University of Warwick, IRRU).

Streeck, W. (1989) ' Skills and the limits of Neo–Liberalism: The enterprise of the future as a place of learning', *Work, Employment and Society*, 3 (1) (March): 89–104.

Training Agency (1989) *England and Wales Youth Cohort Study, Cohort 1, Sweep 2* (Sheffield: Training Agency).

Training Commission (1988) *The Funding of Vocational Education and Training – Some Early Research Findings*, Background Note, 2 (Sheffield: Training Commission).

Training for Employment (1988) Cm 316 (London: HMSO).

Webb, T. (1988) 'Workplace agreements – a union approach to training', *Transition* (May): 23–4.

White, G. and Palmer, S. (1987) 'Contracting out and the cleaning-up question', *Personnel Management* (May): 44–7.

Willis, N. (1989) 'A worker's right to train', *National Westminster Bank Quarterly Review* (February): 13–21.

Willis, P. (1977). *Learning to Labour* (Farnborough: Saxon House).

Witherspoon, S. (1987) *YTS: A Second Survey of Providers* (London: Social and Community Planning Research).

6 Job Training, Individual Opportunity and Low Pay[1]

Paul Ryan

'Wanted ... supermarket assistants with imagination' (Job ad, *Cambridge Evening News*, September 1989)

'Two enthusiastic early morning cleaning staff required for offices' (Job ad, *Cambridge Weekly News*, October 1989)

The low-paid are arguably the most disadvantaged segment of the British labour force in terms of training and self-development. Amongst employees, they receive the least training and enjoy the least opportunity to use skill in their work. They are also worse placed than the long-term unemployed and the early school-leavers upon whom public training subsidies have increasingly become focussed.

The training problems of the low-paid are in many ways a microcosm of those of the wider workforce. Widespread individual interest in training combined with limited incentives and opportunities to train; skill shortages, in terms of both quantity and quality; low managerial interest in employee development; the tension in government policy between the needs of individuals and employers – these attributes of training in Britain are particularly striking for low-paid employment.

Against such a background, there are several reasons to improve training for the low paid. We may wish firstly to improve equity, in terms both of inequality of individual opportunity, notably to acquire skill and higher pay, and of inequality of outcomes, in the shape of lower pay dispersion. Secondly, efficiency should also be increased. The dearth of training opportunities for the low paid coexists with skill shortages in more rewarding work. The words of an earlier enquiry into low pay remain relevant today: it is 'possible that there is a shortage of training opportunities which could enable low paid workers to qualify for higher paid jobs for which there is a shortage of labour' (NBPI, 1971, p. 35). Upgrading the skills of the low paid may

181

then increase output, reduce unemployment and even weaken inflationary pressure in the labour market (Ashenfelter, 1978).

These goals are not however identical and may not be fostered simultaneously by improving the skills of the low-paid. In particular, if a segmented labour market recycles low-paid jobs within the labour force, improvements in pay will prove weaker for the low-paid as a whole than for the recipients of training themselves. The importance of such offsetting effects is particularly difficult to assess.

Partly as a result, this chapter concentrates upon the first objective: the enhancement of opportunity. That goal is also of interest in its own right. Individual opportunity has moved up the policy agenda lately, as White Papers call for its improvement and EC, employer and trade union documents propose rights to training. Yet opportunities for individuals continue to be one of the least impressive attributes of British training practice, not least amongst the low-paid.

The analysis of low pay and skills depends heavily upon the sources of low pay. This chapter therefore discusses first the definition and interpretation of low pay (section 1); the degree to which the low-paid stand to benefit from training is discussed in section 2, followed in section 3 by the incentives and opportunities for training which face the low-paid. Public policy is assessed in section 4, followed by conclusions in section 5.

1 DEFINITION, CHARACTERISTICS AND CAUSES OF LOW PAY

The low-paid are heterogeneous in composition and needs, particularly with respect to skills and training. The 16 year old engineering apprentice, the 36 year old married mother in a part-time job and the 56 year old unskilled male labourer are all likely to be low-paid but the reasons for their low pay, together with their interest in skill and access to it, are likely to differ considerably. This section deals with the problem of heterogeneity, seeking to exclude the subset of the low-paid for whom skill is either no problem or of no interest and to focus upon the skill problems of the remainder.

The detailed definition of low pay is not important here, as the composition of the low-paid is not highly sensitive to the bounding of low pay. Females account for 70–90 per cent of the category on conventional criteria of low pay (Table 6.1, cols 1–2). Part-time workers predominate amongst females. Other over-represented

Table 6.1 Composition of low-paid and low-income groups by definition of low pay (percentage shares of total low paid or low income employment)

| | Composition of | | |
| | Low-paid employment in New Earnings Survey as ratio of male pay: | | Low income[c] group in PSI survey |
Category	0.49[a] (%) (1)	0.67[a] (%) (2)	(%) (3)
Females, part-time[b]	58.3	42.3	54.2
full-time	29.2	31.0	29.8
all females	87.5	73.3	84.0
Males, part-time[b]	0	2.8	10.7
full-time	12.5	23.9	5.3
all males	12.5	26.7	16.0
All	100.0	100.0	100.0
Share of low paid in total employment	11.5	34.0	28.3

Source: Cols 1–2, Brosnan and Wilkinson (1988) Table 3.
Col 3, unpublished tabulations from Rigg (1988), restricted to employees aged 22–59.

Notes:
a. Hourly rates of £2.20 and £3.00 in April 1986.
b. Reduced by the exclusion of employees with earnings below National Insurance threshold (overwhelmingly part-timers).
c. Annual income of £4000 or less (see Table 6.5).

groups include young workers and unskilled adult men. The incidence of low pay is also high in less skilled occupations in agriculture, personal services and light manufacturing.[2]

The causes of low pay are however important. If low pay reflects participation in, lack of interest in, or inability to benefit from training, the policy implications are different than if it reflects exclusion from skill and good jobs. Competitive theory looks to the former; segmentation theory to the latter.

In a competitive market, pay moves to equate demand and supply and low pay results from either low productivity during training or low labour quality. Employees in training whose productivity is consequently low must pay for it by accepting low wages (Becker, 1975). Competitive wage structure produces low pay for employees not in training as the interactive effect of low levels of skill, ability, motivation, commitment to the labour force and willingness to perform unpleasant work. In this view, low wage employment is 'often badly paid, not because it gets less than it is worth, but because it is worth so appallingly little' (Hicks, 1963, p. 82).

Within the competitive paradigm, human capital theory has concentrated its attention upon low levels of schooling and training amongst the low-paid (Mincer, 1974). If the lot of the low-paid is to be improved, improvement of their labour quality is the recommended policy, with remedial schooling and vocational training as promising delivery vehicles. In any case, low pay is the best that can be expected during the training period itself.[3]

For segmentationists, low pay is generated by the characteristics of jobs more than by those of workers. In the large organizations which dominate modern employment, pay is an attribute of the job rather than the worker, depending upon a complex and interdependent set of attributes of the product market, the employer and the production technology which determine employer ability to pay and employee ability to extract high wages. Skilled workers will be found in low-paid jobs if they lack bargaining power or if their employers either lack economic rent in their product markets or are averse to sharing it with them.[4]

Segmentationists therefore seek to reduce low pay by concentrating in the first place upon jobs rather than upon workers, encouraging employers to improve job quality through a mix of minimum wages, industrial restructuring, social security, training subsidies and high employment levels (Doeringer and Piore, 1971, Chapter 8). While orthodoxy tends to see such policies as inefficient, in a segmented labour market they may raise efficiency.[5] Policies to improve the skills of the low-paid are then seen as secondary. They may help low paid individuals to move up the queue for more highly-paid vacancies but they make no direct contribution to reducing the stock of low-paid jobs.

Problems of measurement and interpretation make it difficult to assess the empirical claims of the two theories of low pay. Those who favour a competitive interpretation point to the above average incidence of disability, health problems and low qualifications amongst men and lower attachment to paid employment and careers amongst women (NBPI, 1969). Most females who work part-time choose to do so despite the close association between part-time work, occupational segregation and low hourly pay. Similarly, one-half to two-thirds of females working in low-paid occupations express no interest in promotion or training, often in association with substantial household responsibilities.[6] Finally, a large minority of both the long-term unemployed and participants in public training schemes, who when in work gravitate towards low-paid jobs, show low levels of numeracy and literacy (DE, 1988c; TA/DES/ALBSU, 1989).

At the same time, low pay may be associated with low labour quality without being caused by it, whilst pay differentials between employers and industries have increasingly been treated as non-compensating and explained in terms of employer ability to pay, etc.[7]

This chapter seeks therefore to concentrate upon the 'involuntary' component of low pay by excluding those actually receiving training, particularly amongst young workers; those least likely to learn much from training because of disability, attitudes, etc. particularly amongst unskilled adult males; and those who would not be interested in more skilled, responsible and better-paid work if it were made available to them, particularly amongst married females – even if their choices may be heavily contingent upon occupational segregation and the low availability of subsidized childcare (OECD, 1988; Humphries and Rubery, 1984).

Although it is impossible to quantify the importance of such exclusions, the segmentationist interpretation of low pay is taken as the more appropriate for most of the unmarried females and the unskilled adult males who receive low pay, together with a large minority of the married females, in the sense of having little choice about low pay and securing little or no training in return for it.

One exclusion is however possible as well as desirable: low-paid young workers. As the pay and training of young workers have been the subject of much economic analysis and policy action, this chapter will concentrate where possible upon the adult low-paid. The corollary is an orientation towards continuing (adult) training rather than initial (youth) training.

2 DO THE LOW PAID NEED MORE SKILL?

A case for improving the training opportunities facing the adult low-paid has to answer three questions: do they have less skill than other employees; can they benefit from more skill; and do they themselves want more skill? Positive answers to all three create a strong case, whereas negative ones on any count weaken it.

Comparative Skill Levels

The low-paid are in key respects the least skilled of employees. The picture is clearest for formal qualifications, where the share without qualifications is the highest and the share with higher qualifications is the lowest amongst the low paid (Table 6.2).[8]

At the same time, the association between pay and qualification is less than overwhelming. The proportion of employees possessing intermediate qualifications is only slightly lower for the low paid when allowance is made for higher ones (Table 6.2).[9] A substantial minority of higher-paid workers, particularly males, has no qualifications at all.[10] Similarly, more than a third of skilled manual males and more than a half of craft, professional and managerial females are low-paid (Atkinson *et al.*, 1982). Many females with vocational qualifications work part-time in low-paid personal service occupations (Elias, 1988, Table 4.1).

The issue is complicated further by the heterogeneity of skill. Qualifications represent the formal end of the skill spectrum. Differences appear smaller, and may even be reversed, for skills which are

Table 6.2   Highest qualification level attained by pay category and sex (Great Britain 1986; full-time employees aged 20–69[a]; row percentages)

| | | | | | Highest Qualification[c] | | | |
| | | | | | CSE/ | | | |
Sex	Pay category[b]	Sample size	Any higher	A/O level	commercial/ apprenticeship	Foreign/ other	None	All
Females	Low	696	3.9	37.3	16.4	4.1	38.3	100.0
	Other	1350	27.9	36.6	12.2	2.0	21.4	100.0
	All	2046	19.7	36.9	13.6	2.7	27.1	100.0
Males	Low	418	9.5	34.8	15.5	0.7	39.5	100.0
	Other	4223	25.8	29.7	12.4	3.5	28.7	100.0
	All	4641	25.3	30.1	12.7	3.3	29.6	100.0
Both	Low	1114	5.9	36.4	16.1	2.8	38.7	100.0
	Other	5573	26.3	31.4	12.3	3.1	26.9	100.0
	All	6687	22.9	32.1	13.0	3.1	28.9	100.0

Source: OPCS, *General Household Survey 1986*, Table 9.18.

Notes:
a.   Employed for at least 31 hours in the reference week, including paid overtime, excluding full-time students.
b.   Low: usual weekly gross earnings less than or equal to £100.
     Other: usual weekly gross earnings greater than £100.
c.   Qualification categories detailed in *General Household Survey 1986*, pp. 250–1; CSE grade 1 included in A/O category.

uncertified (and usually informally developed). Case studies suggest that requirements for dexterity, judgement and concentration are often higher for the low-paid, reflecting greater demands from less automated work; and that the feminization of much low-wage work is closely associated with low formalization and recognition of what can be substantial skill requirements (Craig *et al.*, 1982, pp. 80–2).[11]

The result is some uncertainty concerning the relative skill level of the low-paid. What is clear is that the skills of the low-paid fall short in the most transferable dimensions of skill, those certified by a formal qualification; and that any superiority which the low-paid may possess in uncertified and informal skills is of little help to them, given that such skills tend to be specific to low-paying firms, occupations or sectors.

The Benefits of Training

Training may help the low-paid, whether or not they possess less skill than the average, by leading to improved pay and employment stability. The benefits of training to the low-paid have been a topic of controversy. Orthodox economics expects a competitive labour market readily to translate increased skill into higher productivity and pay. By contrast, dual labour market theory, the more restrictive variant of segmentationism, depicts the low-paid as trapped in dead-end jobs within a secondary labour market from which most are unable to escape because of discrimination, location, etc. while rigid job requirements prevent increased skill from raising worker productivity within secondary jobs. Evidence on the dispute can be sought from both the US and the UK.[12]

US Manpower Programmes

The federal government has since the early 1960s sponsored and financed a series of programmes of vocational preparation and training (Bassi and Ashenfelter, 1986). Membership of their fluctuating client group has been dominated by disadvantaged workers, mostly unemployed before entry but, when employed, heavily concentrated in low-paid jobs.

It was the proclaimed failure of such programmes to improve the employment and earnings of the disadvantaged which fostered an institutionalist revival in the late 1960s in the form of dual labour market theory.[13] However, as dualist criticism proved increasingly non-statistical, its conclusions have appeared impressionistic.[14] A battery of subsequent econometric studies has been widely interpreted as disproving the dualist conclusion by showing that training programmes do indeed increase the earnings of the disadvantaged, particularly amongst females.

The issue is actually far from settled. The benefits of manpower programmes to low-wage workers have been judged by one survey to be 'modest, in part because it is not easy to solve the employment difficulties of the hard-to-employ and in part because the resources devoted to any one individual are fairly modest' (Bassi and Ashenfelter, 1986, p. 149). Benefits are also rendered uncertain by selection bias. As participation in training is likely to be associated with unmeasured personal attributes such as ability and motivation, statistical associations between training and earnings are readily distorted if training picks up the influence of ability and motivation. To the extent that participants are more (or less) able or motivated than non-participants – which depends on selection criteria – the higher (or lower) post-training earnings gains of participants may then reflect the difference in their ability or motivation rather than the effects of the training itself.

The only guarantee against selection bias is the clinical trial, in which applicants are allocated randomly to participant and control groups. In its absence, the best that can be done to gauge training benefits is to construct a comparison group of composition as similar as possible to the participant group. But second best proves poor, as the estimated size of participants' benefits is highly sensitive to the choice of comparison group. A wide range of estimated training benefits, including zero and negative values, is generated by plausible alterations in the comparison groups chosen for the research (Lalonde, 1986).

More soundly-based evidence of individual benefits is however available from the single programme to adopt an experimental design, the National Supported Work Demonstration of the mid-1970s, which assigned applicants randomly either to that programme or to an 'untreated' control group. Gains in annual earnings proved substantial for participants, with increased hours of work dominating female benefits, and increased hourly pay, male benefits (Lalonde, 1986, Tables 1, 4, 5).

However, individual benefits from National Supported Work Demonstration have a bearing upon skills only in the most general sense, as that programme lacked any technical training, its content being limited to work experience and group counselling.

One small programme devoted to work experience and attitudes cannot establish the conclusion that training helps low-paid individuals, let alone the low-paid as a whole. Dualist scepticism about the benefits of training the low-paid has yet to be rebutted by US evidence.

British Work Histories: the National Training Survey

Although the UK has also developed major public training schemes, evaluation of the benefits of programmes such as the Youth Training Scheme and Employment Training remains rudimentary, relying heavily upon limited outcome measures (e.g. hiring rates) and lacking the benefit of even comparison groups.[15] More useful evidence is available instead from the individual work histories recorded retrospectively by the National Training Survey of 1975–6 (Claydon, 1980) and analyzed in respect of training primarily by Greenhalgh and Stewart (1987).

Undertaking training is associated with upward occupational mobility in the *National Training Survey*, in that receipt of any full-time vocational training between 1965 and 1975 was associated with a benefit of 3–8 per cent in expected hourly earnings in 1975, reflecting the greater advancement along the occupational pay hierarchy of those who received training than of those who did not. (The higher estimates refer to females.) More extended training proved particularly valuable if it led to a qualification. Acquisition of a qualification below first degree level was associated with a further earnings benefit of between 2 and 10 per cent.[16] The benefits of training to individuals are likely to be even higher in practice, as *National Training Survey*-based research does not capture any intra-occupational pay increases.[17]

These results refer to the average employee. Concentrating on the low-paid, many, particularly young males, moved up the occupational hierarchy between 1965 and 1975 (Metcalf and Nickell, 1982, section 6).

Greenhalgh and Stewart conclude that the association of training with upward mobility is particularly marked amongst the low-paid. We now examine their results in detail in order to elaborate the links between low pay, training and mobility. The first step is to examine the incidence of mobility amongst those who receive training; the second the reverse – viz. the incidence of training amongst those who are upwardly mobile. In each context we seek differences between the strength of these links for the low-paid relative to that for the more highly paid.

Starting with those who have received training, we find that the low-paid are the most likely to show upward mobility, particularly if they are female. While 65 per cent of the initially low-paid females who received any full-time training between 1965 and 1975 had moved upwards by up to two occupational categories by 1975, only 28 per cent of the equivalent group on the next rung up the occupational ladder in 1965 had done so by 1975. The equivalent rates for males are 57 and 46 per cent, indicating a lower differential in favour of the low-paid (Table 6.3, cols 3 and 6 combined).[18] Comparing males and females directly, low-paid females with training were the more likely to move up two occupational classes (33.5 as against 24.2 per cent; Table 6.3, col 6).[19]

Thus upward mobility is indeed most commonly associated with training amongst the low-paid, particularly females.

However, training does not appear tied particularly closely to mobility amongst the low-paid in other respects. In the first place, the closer association of training with mobility amongst the low-paid is to some extent spurious, as regression towards the mean raises absolute mobility rates for the low-paid as a whole, with and without training (Table 6.3, cols. 3–4, 6–7).

This difficulty may be countered by comparing the mobility experiences of those who did and did not receive training within pay categories. The extent to which training leads to upward mobility is then not generally greatest amongst the low-paid. Ratios of upward mobility rates amongst those with training relative to those of their occupational peers without training prove higher for the low-paid only when attention is restricted to longer distances of travel (two categories; Table 6.3, cols 5, 8).

The fact that such ratios are uniformly higher for females than for males reflects the low mobility rates attained by females who received no training. For women, lack of training is particularly damaging for upward mobility.

The association of the training–mobility link with low pay is further qualified by the fact that training is by no means necessary for upward mobility. ('Training' is limited here to the full-time variant for which data are readily available.) Only a minority of employees who moved up one occupational category between 1965 and 1975 received any full-time training during that decade (45 per cent; Table 6.4, col. 6). Moreover, the incidence of training amongst upwardly mobile males is, at 38 per cent, least for the low-paid.

Table 6.3   Training and upward mobility by occupational level and sex, British employees, 1965–75[a] (percentages)

Sex (1)	1965 Occupational[b] pay category (2)	Incidence of upward mobility within category					
		Move of one category – Training 1965–74[c]			Move of two categories – Training 1965–74[c]		
		Any (3)	None (4)	Ratio (5)	Any (6)	None (7)	Ratio (8)
Females[e]	38–70	31.0	12.4	2.5	33.5	8.4	4.0
	71–90	22.7	7.6	3.0	5.5	2.3	2.4
	91–130	13.3	6.8	2.0	NA	NA	NA
	131+	NA	NA	NA	NA	NA	NA
	All[d]	20.9	8.6	2.4	16.8	5.1	3.3
Males	38–70	33.1	16.2	2.0	24.2	7.9	3.1
	71–90	30.8	12.2	2.5	14.7	8.7	1.7
	91–130	25.8	18.2	1.4	NA	NA	NA
	131+	NA	NA	NA	NA	NA	NA
	All[d]	28.5	15.1	1.9	16.3	8.5	1.9
Both	38–70	32.5	14.5	2.2	27.0	8.1	3.3
	71–90	29.9	11.1	2.7	13.6	7.2	1.9
	91–130	24.4	14.7	1.7	NA	NA	NA
	131+	NA	NA	NA	NA	NA	NA
	All[d]	27.5	13.1	2.1	16.3	7.5	2.2

Source: derived from Greenhalgh and Stewart (1987) Tables 1, 2.

Notes:

NA   not applicable

a. Includes all members of NTS sample who were employed in both years and who reported their earnings at the time of interview (13,621 males and 8350 females). Base: employees in the relevant occupational category who did (or did not) receive training during 1965–75, percentage shares of mobility patterns 1965–75 (immobile and downwardly mobile shares not shown).

b. Occupations grouped (for both 1965 and 1975) by average hourly earnings of male employees in 1975.

c. Receipt of any full-time training directly related to subsequent employment.

d. Weighted mean (excluding NA categories).

e. Excludes single females (presumably those who were single in both years as they accounted for only 2.7 per cent of the sample; Greenhalgh and Stewart, 1987, Table 1).

It is even lower for upwardly mobile low-paid females (27 per cent). But the key factor for low-paid women is gender rather than pay, as receipt of full-time training is less common amongst upwardly mobile females at all occupational levels than it is amongst even low-paid males (Table 6.4, col. 6).[20] While the role of gender is exaggerated by the limitation of scope to full-time training, its importance cannot be doubted.[21]

A third area of difficulty involves causality. To be able to infer that receipt of training actually causes occupational mobility we would

Table 6.4   Upward mobility and training by occupational level and sex,
British employees, 1965–75 (percentages)

Sex (1)	Occupational pay category (2)	Employment share 1965 (3)	Incidence of training[a] in group, 1965–74 (4)	Incidence of upward move of one group 1965–75 (5)	Share of (5) with training[a] 1965–74 (6)
Females	38–70	22.8	13.1	14.9	27.4
	71–90	28.7	16.1	10.0	36.6
	91–130	39.5	14.2	7.7	24.6
	131+	8.9	13.4	NA	NA
	All[b]	100.0	15.4	10.4	29.5
Males	38–70	9.4	22.8	20.0	37.7
	71–90	35.2	30.2	17.9	52.3
	91–130	32.7	38.7	21.2	47.1
	131+	22.6	29.8	NA	NA
	All[b]	100.0	31.2	19.5	48.1
Both	38–70	13.2	18.7	17.8	34.0
	71–90	33.5	27.5	16.3	50.4
	91–130	34.6	32.7	17.9	44.7
	131+	18.7	28.2	NA	NA
	All[b]	100.0	25.2	17.2	45.2

Source: derived from Greenhalgh and Stewart (1987) Tables 1, 2.

Notes: as for Table 6.3.
a.   Full-time training (of any duration) only; evening and part-time training excluded.
b.   Weighted mean (NA categories excluded).

want to know two things: first, the possibility of controlling for the selection bias which so drastically limited the conclusions to be drawn from US manpower programmes; secondly, the nature of the links between training and mobility.

Selection bias is to be expected for NTS training histories, given that private agents, be they individuals or employers, are expected to select positively around ability and motivation in the allocation of training. Analysts of the *National Training Survey* have sought to remove such bias with fixed effects models, which in effect rely upon the individual's work history to generate comparison groups for the trained and the untrained alike, thereby avoiding any assumption of direct comparability between the two groups. As the returns to training remain significant in such models, causality appears highly likely. Unfortunately, however, the extent to which the returns achieved by low-paid and other employees differ remains to be investigated with fixed effects models (Nickell, 1982; Greenhalgh and Stewart, 1987). [22]

Finally, if training and mobility are indeed causally associated, little is known about the mechanisms involved. Does training precede, accompany or follow mobility? Does it require a change of occupation or employer? A change of employer may be particularly important if the low-paid are to benefit from training. Their work least commonly offers the prospect of promotion related to training along the job ladders of internal labour markets. It is not surprising therefore that only amongst the low-paid is earnings growth positively related to turnover. [23]

Information about mechanisms is needed also to establish the degree to which benefits to low-paid individuals are benefits to the low-paid as a whole. If a change of employer or occupation is typically required for individuals to realize the benefits of training, then collective benefits to the low-paid are likely to be less than if the gains can be realized within a given job, as employers are likely to seek in the former instance to fill the vacancy with another low-paid worker.

The upshot is that, although training is neither necessary nor sufficient for upward mobility, it benefits most of the low-paid who undertake it. The benefits are not in fact unusually high for the low-paid but it does appear likely that the low-paid are distinctive in having to change employers in order to realize them.

Interest in Training

The final aspect of need for skill is desire itself. If the low-paid do not perceive a need and wish to act on it, no amount of demonstration of objective needs will result in appropriate action.

The attitudes of the low-paid are frequently ambivalent. They tend to take the narrowest and most instrumental view of training, seeing it heavily in terms of access to jobs and, as they already have a job, showing least interest in it on that account. They are also the least prone to envisaging training in the future.

Gender again differentiates strongly amongst the low-paid. Females are the more prone to express lack of interest in promotion and in changing the type of work they do, as well as to indicate that they are not considering training as a future option (Table 6.5). [24]

To some extent the attitudes of the low-paid reflect low incomes; to

Table 6.5   Interest in training and promotion by sex and income, GB
1987 (percentages in income group giving indicated response)

Statement	Sex	1987 Income Group[a] (£000 pa)			
		<4	4–8	>8	All
I am interested in promotion	F	51	35	28	42
or furthering myself in my	M	28	27	20	24
present kind of work (Disagree)[b]					
I am interested in changing the	F	34	41	43	37
type of work I do	M	17	31	40	33
(Disagree)[b]					
Education and training is not	F	22	12	8	18
important to me	M	19	20	10	16
(Agree)[b]					
I am not considering training	F	57	39	41	49
in the future	M	45	47	38	43
(Agree)					
Base[c]	F	518	295	125	1082
	M	213	403	517	1295
	All	731	698	642	2377

Source: Rigg (1988) unpublished results; sample limited to employees aged
22 years or more (plus females about to reenter the labour market).

Notes:
a.   'Personal total take-home income from all sources' at time of survey
     (June–August 1987).
b.   Includes agree (or disagree) 'strongly' as well.
c.   Totals include 'income not specified' (145 female, 163 male).

some extent more limited experience and horizons, interacting to
reduce awareness, interest and confidence (Rigg, 1988 pp. 40–9, 106);
to some extent, for married females in particular, a competing
commitment to domestic responsibilities.

Nevertheless, three-quarters of the same low-income workers
express confidence in their ability to learn new skills; two-thirds,
interest in changing the kind of work they do; and only one-third,
satisfaction with the opportunity to use skills on their current job
(Rigg, 1988, p. 42, Tables 4a, 7.2b). Not surprisingly, low-paid
individuals are especially likely to express interest in training if it is
expected to lead to better pay (FE UK, 1989).

The issue of desire is therefore complex. However, where the
link between training and improved pay and occupational status is

perceived by the low-paid, the desire for training is widespread, particularly amongst males and single females. For them the question then becomes one of access and cost.

3 THE DETERMINANTS OF TRAINING AND THE LOW-PAID

Interest in training is only one condition for the improvement of the skills of the low-paid. Training must also be available, and then at a price which individuals are willing and able to pay. The low-paid tend to be worst placed on both counts. This section first considers evidence on the training received by the low-paid and then analyses its source.

Extent of Training Amongst the Low-paid

The training experiences of the low-paid are impoverished, in ways which differ by sex. Taking males first, the proportion of employees who received any full-time training during 1965–74 was least for the lowest-paid occupations (Table 6.4, col. 4). The inverse link between pay and training amongst males remains intact after the imposition of controls for age, race, qualifications and family type. Indeed, the closest correlate of training activity amongst males, after age, is occupational status (and, therefore, pay; Greenhalgh and Stewart, 1987, Tables 4, 5).

The link between pay and access to training is less important for females, not least because the primary correlate of training activity is gender. Females of all occupational levels receive less full-time training than do even low-paid males (Table 6.4). Moreover, the direction of the link between pay and training is mixed amongst females. Low-paid married females show somewhat higher receipt of full-time training than do their more highly-paid counterparts once controls are imposed for other personal characteristics.[25] However, low pay is not without disadvantage for females. Evening training for married females and both types of training for single females are each much less prevalent amongst the low-paid (Greenhalgh and Stewart, 1987, section 3).[26]

The Economics of Training

In the absence of public intervention, there would be two key influences upon the level of training activity amongst the low-paid: the individual and the employer. Competitive theory emphasizes the role of the individual; institutional theory, that of the employer.

The availability of training to the low-paid is not a problem in competitive theory. Employers are willing to offer as much training as employees demand given that, in the case of general (transferable) skills, they need not finance the training which they provide. Trainees pay for it instead by accepting a wage equal to their net value product in training. If, in the extreme, trainees produce nothing and use up scarce resources, as in full-time instruction off the job, then they must pay for that by foregoing all pay and parting with a fee to cover direct training costs (Becker, 1975). The key agent is then seen as the trainee. The employer provides training when it is the most efficient provider, but it is the trainee who has to pay in any case. Questions about the access of the low-paid to training are then treated as questions about trainee willingness and ability to pay for training and not about the availability of training opportunities.

In practice, however, employers finance most or all of whatever training they provide, while employees receiving such training sacrifice little or nothing (Deloitte, Haskins and Sells, 1988; Jones, 1986). The distribution of training costs is heavily skewed towards employers because of limited and rigid differentials in pay (and labour costs) between trainees, untrained workers and trained workers.[27] Employers react by substituting recruitment of the skilled for training the unskilled, leading to undersupply of training places and skill shortages; by slanting the content of training towards skills specific to their own needs; and by rationing access to training according to the ability and retainability of prospective trainees, particularly in association with length of service in internal labour markets (Ryan, 1984a, 1987; Marsden and Ryan, 1990b).[28]

Access to training provided by employers is likely to be particularly scarce for the low-paid, who are poorly placed to compete for a limited supply of opportunities. They have already been passed over for vacancies in more highly-paid jobs. They have to take what is left: jobs with low pay and low training content. The individual attributes emphasized by orthodox theory are secondary when it comes to getting training from employers: even those low-paid workers who are able and willing to finance their own training will have trouble finding employers willing to provide it.

Evidence: The Two Routes to Skill

The low level of training activity amongst the low-paid is generated in the first instance by the difficulty of getting training from employers.

Table 6.6   Attributes of recent training by income category, sponsorship and sex, all adult employees, 1987 (percentage of all employees aged 22–59 in category who had received training during previous three years)

Sex	Sponsor and Duration of training		Income category (£000 pa)[a]			
			<4	4–10	10+	All
Both	Employer	all	14	28	42	29
		3+ days	8	22	36	23
	Self	all	5	7	6	6
	Either[b]		18	32	46	33
Female	Employer	all	14	33	44	25
		3+ days	8	24	35	17
	Self	all	4	6	9	5
	Either[b]		18	37	50	29
Male	Employer	all	13	24	42	32
		3+ days	10	21	37	28
	Self	all	8	5	6	6
	Either[b]		17	28	45	36

Source: Rigg (1988) unpublished tabulations.

Notes:
a.   Definition in Table 6.5.
b.   Excludes training courses lasting less than 3 days in the case of employer-sponsored training only.

The incidence of employer-provided training is almost negligible in subcraft manual occupations (Rigg, 1988, Table 2c). It falls off with income at a rapid rate. As few as one in twelve of the low-paid report having received from an employer during the previous three years any training (broadly defined) lasting three days or more (Table 6.6).

Moreover, training provided by employers to the low-paid is more often delivered informally and on the job, as well as being part-time and short duration, than is the case for other employees (Table 6.7). However, it is no less commonly associated with gaining a qualification, which is least frequent amongst higher-income groups.

The frequency of training amongst the low-paid is underestimated in the PSI data as a result of subsequent earnings mobility amongst those who receive training, which results in upward truncation bias in estimates of the effects of low pay on training.[29] At the same time, other information also suggests that the low-paid gain little training from their employers.[30]

Low access to employer-based training need not be the end of the

Table 6.7   Attributes of recent training provided by employers by income category, adult employees, 1987 (percentage of employees aged 22–59 in income category with 3 or more days of employer-provided training whose training exhibited the particular attribute)

	Income category (£000 pa)			
Attribute of training	*<4*	*4–10*	*10+*	*All*
Location				
a on the job	35	22	6	16
b off job, on premises	6	10	8	8
c off the premises	60	68	86	75
Full-time share	62	77	87	79
Duration less than 3 weeks	60	69	79	72
Qualification obtained	32	42	27	33
Base	75	181	223	479

Source: Rigg (1988) unpublished tabulations.

story for the low-paid. Self-sponsorship may provide an alternative route to skill. The low-paid may be able to turn to the courses provided by technical colleges, proprietary schools and correspondence schools in order to sponsor their own training.

Self-sponsorship is so different a route from employer sponsorship that Malcolm Rigg (1988) talks in terms of two distinct training markets. It is less oriented towards induction and the needs of current jobs and more towards changes of occupation and employer; more towards longer courses leading to qualifications; it is much less commonly subsidized by employers through pay and course fees and it may even earn employer hostility; and it is associated with lower perceived benefits in terms of pay and promotion, in the short term at least.[31] In short, self-sponsorship is both more costly and more risky for the trainee than is employer sponsorship.

The PSI findings can be used with more confidence as a guide to the relative level of training activity along the two routes to skill and its relationship to low pay, given that truncation bias appears broadly similar for absolute levels of activity on each route.[32]

In practice, self-sponsorship is more common amongst the unemployed than amongst employees and it accounts for only 17 per cent of recent training events reported by adult employees.[33] Instead of acting as a widespread alternative to employer sponsorship, it involves even fewer low-paid workers than does employer training. Although the differential importance of employer sponsorship is least for low earners, that reflects the paucity of low-paid travellers, particularly females, along either route and the rapid growth of traffic along the employer route as income rises, not any substantial amount of self-sponsorship amongst the low-paid (Table 6.6).[34]

The three factors which help explain low levels of self-sponsorship are access, finance and motivation (Finegold and Soskice, 1988, p. 36). Although small cell sizes make it difficult to use the PSI results to disentangle their contribution to training sponsorship amongst the low-paid, some general indication can be provided nevertheless of their nature and significance.

Taking access to training first, although it is likely to be less of a problem than for employer-sponsorship, suitable courses may not be available, whether locally from technical colleges and Skillcentres or nationally from correspondence and Open College courses. But the more fundamental obstacles involve people's ability and willingness to pay for training, given the limited extent of the assistance available to employees who seek to sponsor their own training (Rigg, 1988, p. 77; FE UK, 1989).

Individual ability to pay is curbed by the nature of human capital as an asset – notably the difficulty of using it as collateral against which to borrow to cover training costs. The result is severe rationing of finance amongst individuals who lack assets (Becker, 1967). Difficulty on this score appears widespread in practice. Individuals who sponsor their own training have to finance much or all of it themselves, relying as a result upon a variety of sources, including personal earnings, family income and assets, local authority and MSC grants and public benefits (Table 6.8). By contrast, recipients of employer-sponsored training are usually fully financed by the employer, through full coverage of course fees and provision of normal earnings.[35]

Ability to pay for training is likely to be particularly limited amongst the low-paid. Although the overlap between low pay and low household income is only partial and suitable data on household assets are scarce, most of the low-paid live in households with low resources taking the life-cycle as a whole (Layard *et al.*, 1978; Atkinson *et al.*, 1982; Bazen, 1988). Such people face the greatest difficulty of financing training, both internally, out of either existing assets or current savings, and externally, from potential lenders to whom they can offer little or no collateral.

The PSI study suggests that financial difficulty is particularly intense amongst the low-paid, although larger sample sizes would be needed to provide clearer answers. Lower-income groups appear to

Table 6.8   Sources of funding for recent self-sponsored training by level of
income, adults, 1987 (percentage of persons[a] in income category with such
training who received any funding from particular source)

Cost category	Funding source	Income category (£000 pa)		
		<6	6+	All
Course	Self	33	65	50
Fees	Family/relatives	8	0	6
	Employer	0	2	2
	Public	49	33	51
Maintenance	Own pay	37	73	47
	Family/relatives	8	13	11
	Grant/allowance	33	17	28
	Public benefits	27	8	19
	Loan (ex-family)	2	2	1
Base		63	48	111

Source: Rigg (1988) unpublished tabulations.

Notes:
a.   Members of labour force aged 22–59 (plus intending female re-entrants).

rely on the widest variety of funding sources, in contrast to the
dominance of the individual's own earnings and assets in the more
affluent categories. There is also tentative evidence that wider family
resources play little role in cushioning the adverse effects of low pay
when it comes to the finance of training (Table 6.8).

Similarly, the share who report that at some earlier time they
would have liked to have undertaken training but had been unable to
do so is higher than average for the low-paid, the unqualified and
part-time workers. Amongst such respondents, financial difficulties
and family commitments were mentioned by 47 per cent of the low
paid, as against 38 per cent of all respondents.[36] Similarly, amongst
those who could envisage taking training in the future, the low-paid
were particularly likely to mention difficulty in finding the finance (41
per cent), while the high-paid emphasized lack of time (43 per cent).
Finally, while local authorities are particularly likely to help low
earners to pay course fees, only 29 per cent of low-paid individuals
who sponsor their own training receive such help.[37]

Inability to finance training is not universal amongst the low-paid.
One in twenty of the low-paid in the PSI survey had sponsored some
training for themselves during the previous three years. They had
funded it with a mix of personal, family and public resources,

amongst which public funds (low or free course fees plus training grants and allowances) appear to have been much more important than family resources (Table 6.8; Rigg, 1988, pp. 77–8).

The other individual attribute relevant to self-sponsorship of training is willingness to invest in it (amongst individuals who are interested in it and have access to finance in the first place). The ambivalence already noted in the desires of the low-paid for training (section 3) may turn into widespread reluctance when the issue of paying for it is raised. The returns to investment in skill will be low, and with them the willingness to finance training, under several circumstances particularly likely to characterize the low-paid: expectation of leaving the labour force soon, as for older workers and many young females; low ability to learn and low scholastic achievement; membership of groups which face discrimination, notably females and minorities; lack of information about training and employment options; lack of employer interest in skills learned and qualifications gained; and low skill differentials within low-wage sectors. These varied influences may reduce the willingness of many low-paid workers to sponsor their own training.

Little evidence is available on the willingness of the low-paid to finance training. The reliability of attitude surveys is suspect. More useful information is potentially available from takeup of the Career Development Loans scheme, which offers subsidized loans (ranging between £300 and £5000) to pay for up to 80 per cent of the fees and (for full-time courses) some or all of the living expenses associated with vocational courses of up to one year's duration (DE, 1988d).

Not enough information has yet become available about Career Development Loan take-up to permit a clear inference about willingness to sponsor one's own training in general, let alone that of the low-paid in particular. Demand for the finance has thus far remained modest. After fourteen months of national Career Development Loan availability, only one in every 20,000 economically active individuals (5400 persons) had applied for a loan. A modest budgetary allocation (roughly £1 million per annum) has thus sufficed to cater for the 76 per cent of applicants judged creditworthy by the commercial banks which administer the scheme.

Low levels of demand for Career Development Loans are at least partly the result of poor information and ungenerous assistance. The scheme is still in its early days; it has received little publicity. Its subsidy component is limited to an 'interest holiday' which lasts until three months after completion of the course and which amounts to only £350 for the average course.[38] Its reach is limited by government encouragement to participating banks to follow normal commercial criteria in vetting applications.

However, the occupational status of employed applicants (2955 loans approved) suggests that both the low-paid and the high-paid are over-represented within a low overall level of Career Development Loan activity. Roughly 55 per cent of such loans have gone to the three lowest paid occupational categories. Sales, service and less skilled manual occupations appear to show the highest levels of Career Development Loan takeup (Table 6.9, cols 4, 5).[39]

In conclusion, the low-paid face particular difficulty along both of the routes to skill. Employer provision involves little cost or risk to the individual but few low-paid adults can gain access to it. Sponsoring one's own training is costly and risky and the low-paid are generally the worst off when it comes to assessing the investment, finding the finance for it and bearing the risks involved.

There is therefore a problem of incentives for the low-paid, but its domain is confined to the subsidiary, precarious route of self-sponsorship; and to the minority of low-paid individuals who possess adequate finance and information about vacancies. The more fundamental problem is that of opportunity, notably in the labour market, in terms of low access to the employers' training resources. Lack of opportunity in the capital market, in terms of access to finance, is irrelevant to that problem, given the low costs and risk involved. But it is a major constraint upon the alternative – viz. sponsoring training oneself, where willingness to pay has yet to be tested seriously.

4   TRAINING POLICY AND THE LOW-PAID

British politics have in the 1980s seen a resurgence of the liberal, enabling ideal of improving incentives and opportunities for individuals to better their economic lot. Rights to training have even been proposed in recent years by sources as diverse as the European Commission, trade unions and even employers associations (CEC, 1984; Willis, 1989; CBI, 1989). These ideals have much to offer the low paid, given the impoverishment of their opportunities to acquire skills. This section considers the degree to which such goals in practice affect training policy for the low-paid.

Table 6.9 Career Development Loans approved by current and intended occupation of employed applicants, Great Britain, 1989

CODOT occupational category (1)	CODOT group (2)	Index of weekly pay[a] full-time adults (3)	Employment share[b] (%) (4)	Share of CDLs approved[d] by occupation			CDL occupational categories (8)
				Current or last (%) (5)	Intended (%) (6)	(6)–(5) (7)	
Professional and Technical	II, III IV, V	129.1	24.3	25.5	46.3	20.8	Professional, Commercial, Computer, Health, Flying (0.5)
Managerial[c]	VI	125.1	5.8	3.4	11.3	7.9	Management
Make, Repair Process	XII, XIII XIV	93.9	19.4	7.6	1.7	–5.9	Making and Processing Automotive, Engineering (general)
Construction	XVI	91.9	2.6	3.9	3.2	–0.7	Construction
Transportation	XVII	88.9	7.4	5.4	17.0	11.6	Driving
Sales and Service	VIII IX, X	79.6	12.8	19.7	10.1	–9.6	Hotel and Catering Service/Selling
Farm, Paint Other	XI, XV XVIII	76.9	7.4	22.9	3.0	–19.9	Other, Flying
Clerical	VII	74.9	20.3	11.6	7.4	–4.2	Clerical, Commercial Shorthand, Typing, Office Mach
All	I–XVIII	100.0	100.0	100.0	100.0	0	All
Base			133 178	2 955	4 716		

Source: Department of Employment, Cols 1–4: New Earnings Survey (1988), Tables 86, 87; Cols 5–8: unpublished data.

Notes:
a. Gross weekly earnings of full-time employees on adult rates whose pay was unaffected by absence; by CODOT category.
b. Shares of full-time employees in NES sample; by CODOT category.
c. Except general management.
d. Includes loans made to unemployed and self-employed applicants; by CDL category.

Contemporary Policy

Public training policy certainly promises much for individual opportunities. According to a 1988 White Paper,

> the government's objective, and the country's need, are both clear: to open up many more opportunities for adults to train, retrain, acquire additional skills or upgrade those they already have, throughout their working lives (DE, 1988a, p. 40).

Incentives to individuals are also considered, but in a detached, optimistic mood. 'Everybody can benefit from training. Nobody is too old, too junior or too senior or in too specialised a job' (DE, 1988, p. 49).[40]

Things change quickly when it comes to the choice of methods. Training opportunities for individuals are to depend almost wholly upon employer provision. The government promotes a dichotomy between responsibility for training the employed, which is to fall to employers, and that for the unemployed, which falls to itself. No particular role is allocated to individuals beyond the generality that 'individuals must also take much greater responsibility for their own development' (DE, 1988a, p. 40). There is no mention of individual rights to training.[41]

An employer-led strategy for improving individual opportunity could make sense were employers to provide opportunities suitable in quantity and quality. In fact, both the utilization of skill and the provision of training by British employers leave much to be desired (Campbell and Warner, 1990). The White Paper concedes the latter difficulty in passing but then, in the upbeat mood which increasingly characterizes such documents, goes on to argue that 'what is needed is whole-hearted employer commitment . . . an increasing number of highly successful companies are now beginning to show the way . . . the rest of the country must follow'. Completion of the argument is tastefully left to the reader. What must happen will happen, so presumably individuals will obtain adequate training opportunities from employers.

That logic is unlikely to impress the low-paid. Of all employees they report receiving from their employers not only the least training and opportunity to use skills, but even opposition to sponsoring their own training. To present their employers to them as the source of enhanced opportunity is to invite ridicule. With some honourable exceptions, employers of the low-paid will be the last to be converted to the importance of human resource development, if they ever get there at all.

While reliance upon employers to provide training opportunities is by no means new,[42] it has in key respects intensified in the 1980s. Training opportunities for low paid adults have been curtailed by the elimination of Training Opportunities Scheme (TOPS) courses, the reorientation of a cutback, commercialized and finally privatized Skillcentre system towards the needs of employers and by the concentration of public training funds upon youth unemployment (Ryan, 1984b; Keep, 1987).

The augmentation of training opportunities for employees is not however to be left wholly to employers. Two initiatives are geared primarily to individuals. Firstly, Career Development Loans were made available nationally in 1988 to individuals prepared to finance their own training. As noted above, the Career Development Loan scheme remains small scale, little publicized and stands symbolically last on the policy agenda (DE, 1988b, p. 52).[43] But it is the only programme, excepting the funding of higher education, to give financial assistance directly to individuals for training.

Secondly, individual access to training has been promoted through subsidies to distance and open learning technologies. Public seed money has been provided through the Open Tech and Open Learning programmes and the Open College. Computer terminals have been installed in Jobcentres, workplaces and union offices, *inter alia*, to provide individuals with information about training opportunities.

The resources available to the latter set of programmes are however minute compared to those involved in employer training. Moreover, they involve no long-term implicit subsidy to individuals, as they are required to attain commercial independence within short periods (Manpower Services Commission, 1987, Table 1.1; TC, 1988, pp. 45–7; Deloitte, Haskins & Sells, 1987). Not surprisingly, the dominant category of Open College customer has been the employer rather than the individual acting on his or her own behalf.

Policy Alternatives

The weakness of current policies means that it should not be too difficult to improve policies towards low pay and skills. The key questions are how to do it, and how much of it to do. The discussion is limited at this stage to policies which address directly the skills of the low-paid.

Either employers or individuals can be encouraged to sponsor more training. It is helpful to distinguish here between occupational, internal and secondary labour markets. Occupational markets depend upon processes of training and certification which give individuals portable qualifications which are therefore not specific to particular employers. Internal markets develop skills which are employer-specific, avoid certification and replace the qualification by the company as the focus of individuals, employment security. Secondary markets are largely unstructured and casual and offer employees little prospect of either skill acquisition or promotion (Marsden, 1986; Marsden and Ryan, 1989, 1990). Most low-paid workers function in secondary markets.

Individual opportunities to train can be enhanced under any of these three structures, but policy content should suit the institutional context (Raffe 1988; Marsden and Ryan 1988, 1990b). Reliance on employer sponsorship appears more appropriate where internal labour markets predominate; reliance upon individual sponsorship, where occupational and secondary markets are present.

As British labour markets have moved unevenly from occupational towards both internal and (in the 1980s) secondary structures, the implicit orientation of the 1988 White Papers to internal and secondary markets, in which training is dominated by employer perceptions of their own needs and employees are left to get what they can out of employers, does at least correspond to the institutional realities of contemporary Britain. From this standpoint, encouraging increased employer provision does indeed look the more promising route.

There is little doubt that low-paid workers would welcome increased employer training provision, given its low cost/low risk attributes. The problem is one of feasibility. By all means encourage employers to do more training. But long experience indicates that it takes more than exhortation to elicit from employers a significant increase in training opportunities for the low-paid. It is difficult for public policy to influence training within internal markets, where employers prefer specificity and heterogeneity rather than standardization and certification of skills. It is even more difficult to improve employer training in secondary markets, particularly in the small plants and firms in which many of the low-paid work. Finally, an attempt to do either by statutory means is almost inconceivable at present, given the acceptance of employer perceptions of skill needs implicit in an 'employer-led' training strategy (Keep, 1990).

Favouring individual sponsorship provides at the minimum a

valuable complement to exhortation under all types of labour market structure. Where internal markets predominate, the deficiencies of employer training provision, in terms of quantity, quality and equity, can be reduced by increased public provision of subsidized vocational education and training – as has been the case in France and Sweden. The case for such action is even stronger for secondary markets, where employer provision is least impressive of all.

Individual sponsorship is particularly congruent with occupational markets, which emphasize individual ownership of qualifications. Occupational structures live on in the UK, particularly in professional, craft and secretarial work. Occupational principles remain at least nominally present in the Youth Training Scheme, Employment Training and National Vocational Qualifications, to the extent that such schemes have been geared towards skill families and the certification of trainees under a revamped national set of vocational qualifications. The advantages of occupational structures for training, skills usage and individual liberty are not widely appreciated (Marsden and Ryan, 1989a).

Training for occupational markets may be provided in an educational institution, as by technical colleges or Skillcentres, and/or at the workplace, under a suitably regulated apprenticeship system, as in West Germany and in some Industrial Training Board sectors in Britain. A key difficulty is that the apprenticeship route remains largely closed to adults. The former routes, all of which involve self-sponsorship, could readily be fostered by public policy.

A variety of considerations point therefore towards encouraging individual sponsorship of training. As individual sponsorship is more costly and risky to individuals than is employer sponsorship, such a policy must seek to reduce both the cost and the risk, both of which are particularly powerful deterrents to the low-paid.

The Career Development Loan scheme could provide a useful vehicle, given that 84 per cent of early participants gained a qualification, mostly relevant to a new occupation. The occupational pattern of Career Development Loan activity suggests that takeup is geared towards upward mobility, in that the more highly paid occupational categories show a greater surplus of aspiration over origin in take-up patterns (Table 6.9, cols 5, 6).

The fillip provided by Career Development Loans to self-sponsored training can be increased by boosting the implicit subsidy from its present low level. Raising the coverage of course fees to 100 per cent in the case of low-paid participants would be a step in that direction, albeit a modest one (FE UK, 1989). An explicit grant element could be introduced, for example by public payment of one-half of course fees. If the low-paid are to be targeted, any grant component could well be means-tested. However it is done, the subsidy content of Career Development Loans could be increased greatly before it would amount to a substantial use of public funds or jeopardize the principle that trainees should make a contribution of their own.

Costs to individuals could also be reduced by increasing public subsidy of fees in vocational courses, whether provided by Local Authority further education or by private training bodies. Income taxation could also be brought into line with European practice by making personal outlays for training a deductible expense (Finegold and Soskice, 1988, p. 36).

A further selective contribution, addressed primarily to numerous low-paid mothers and lone parents, would be to expand public subsidy of childcare. The least that could be done would be to move from tax liability to tax deductibility in the treatment of outlays on childcare outside the home; the most, generous direct subsidy to parents. The long-term unemployed currently have access to what is effectively a full-cost subsidy: childcare expenses of up to £50 per week are paid to lone parents participating in Employment Training. There is thus no objection of principle to the extension of childcare subsidy to training sponsored by the low-paid, which would allow many part-timers to consider full-time training and work for the first time.

The risks associated with self-sponsorship of training arise primarily from uncertainty about job prospects with both current and alternative employers. Two aspects are particularly important. First, assuming that a certified skill is acquired, there is the risk that employers who prefer to train informally for their own needs in internal labour markets may not value the qualification, in which case employees will in turn have less incentive to invest in acquiring it. A vicious circle of this kind has been observed in the Youth Training Scheme (Raffe, 1988). Even in occupational markets, adult entry may be impeded by the absence of training and certification opportunities apart from those provided by employers and by the restriction to teenagers of access to the latter, as is still usually the case under apprenticeship.

Individuals can reduce this risk by considering vacancy patterns before choosing a training course. Such planning is expected of applicants for a Career Development Loan. Career Development

Loan take-up patterns suggest its presence, in that individuals who take out loans show an orientation not only towards upward mobility but also towards jobs where occupational structures are well developed, in that adults can acquire qualifications which are recognised by employers. Thus in Table 6.9 aspiration to a particular occupational category is greater than might be expected from prevailing pay levels in the clerical and driving categories, where such structures are well established (e.g. typing courses, HGV licences). Similarly, aspiration is less than expected in the construction, making and repairing categories, where qualifications, though widespread, are obtained mostly through employer-based initial training and lie therefore outside the reach of adults (Table 6.9).[44]

Public policy can seek to reduce the risk that suitable jobs may not be available to individuals sponsoring their own training by fostering both occupational structures and their accessibility to adults, particularly in craft and technical fields. The current National Vocational Qualifications effort would promise more in this respect were it constructed less around employer-perceived needs and work-based assessment and more around transferable skills and broader forms of assessment.

Secondly, as training may not lead to a qualification or a new job, the individual faces the risk of being even worse off than before, in that the previous job is unlikely to be available. While low-paid jobs may not be generally scarce, their incumbents often fear the loss of whatever job rewards they currently enjoy. Such risks could be reduced by statutory rights to training leave, as provided by law to adult employees in both France and Sweden, but they would still remain substantial. Take-up of leave entitlements has remained low in France as a result of not only of low prior educational attainments and loss of pay, but also of weakened job security, given widespread employer disfavour (OECD, 1976; Jallade, 1982). Low-wage employers tend to be especially hostile to self-sponsored training and, as it is not easy to enforce job rights upon reluctant employers, the risk of not getting one's old job back would remain substantial. Nevertheless, establishing such a right would demonstrate that the state is backing the individual and at least guarantee compensation if the employer chose to abrogate it.

A policy which reduces the cost and risk of sponsoring one's own training would undoubtedly increase the extent to which individuals do so. Such a policy could be expected to elicit a strong response from the low-paid. It will be unpopular with low-wage employers, who usually prefer to limit their employees' horizons to their current job tasks. But such a policy offers various advantages. It develops a stunted part of training provision and bolsters occupational structures in the labour market. By reducing the dependence of the low-paid on their employers, it puts pressure on those employers to pay attention to employee development and even to raise pay. It avoids the resistance provoked by policies which require employers to do particular things about training (Keep, 1990). Finally, it aligns well with the dominant ideology and it can contribute to its stated desire to encourage individual initiative.

How far policies favouring self-sponsorship should be carried is less readily determined. From the standpoint of efficiency, the resulting cuts in both skill shortages and the wastage of human abilities in low productivity employment may justify substantial intervention, although the balance of costs and benefits remains to be determined. From the standpoint of equity, such policies offer a clear opportunity to a group who have in the past decade received little more than advice both to feel grateful to have a job and to accept lower pay in order to keep it. Other social groups do much better. Mandatory grants cover the tuition costs of most undergraduates to the tune of £15,000 or more per capita. Managerial and professional employees benefit from the lion's share of employer training at little cost or risk to themselves. To offer the low-paid only a short-lived interest holiday on a bank loan hardly constitutes a fair deal.

5   CONCLUSIONS

This chapter has drawn together several aspects of skills and low pay amongst adult workers. First, the skills of the low-paid are deficient, particularly those which are certified and transferable. Secondly low-paid individuals usually benefit significantly from training, though the mechanisms remain obscure. The link between these two phenomena is the difficulty experienced by the low-paid in acquiring training. Their ability to gain access to the more desirable route to skill, the low-cost/low-risk one provided by employers, is the lowest of all. The low-paid are also amongst the worst placed to sponsor and finance their own training, with its high costs and risks. Although substantial numbers, particularly females, are resigned to and even tolerant of their situation, many of the low-paid describe themselves as trapped.

The training needs of the low-paid constitute the intersection of two wider sets: the training problems of the British economy and the needs of the low-paid. Consideration of their intersection leads to consideration of the two sets in their own right.

Taking training problems first, the decay of occupational structures in labour markets, inadequate employer appreciation of skill and provision of training, the imbalance between the financial character-istics of training sponsored by employers and individuals – these attributes all apply to the wider economy as well. Individual opportu-nities require improvement across the board. Such a broad focus would help the low-paid in turn by avoiding the stigmatisation of participants as low-quality workers, a factor which has damaged the Youth Opportunities Programme, Youth Training Scheme and Em-ployment Training in turn.

It is also likely that the low-paid would benefit indirectly from increased training for others. More skilled supervisors and managers would be able to make better use of the existing abilities of the low-paid. Alternatively, if better-paid workers were trained to fill skill shortages, job vacancies and training opportunities would open at an intermediate level at which the low-paid could in turn aim.

Secondly, there are the needs of the low-paid. What the low paid need to break out of the circle of low resources and low achievement is by no means limited to training. Those amongst the low-paid whose literacy and numeracy are deficient require remedial education before training proper can be of much use to them. If that task is not addressed, then the educational standards achieved by today's children will have to be raised if their low achievers are to prove more suitable recipients of training when their turn comes.

Moreover, in a segmented labour market, the aggregate benefits derived by the low-paid from training are undoubtedly less than the sum of individual gains. Indeed, the presence of significant aggregate benefits may depend upon the pressure exerted upon low-wage employers by reduced availability of low-wage labour.

More generally, for the low-paid as a whole the need is not primarily one of training and possibly not one of training at all. Females with household responsibilities dominate the low-paid. Those with young families are likely to rank affordable childcare above training in any hierarchy of needs, as well as to describe it as a precondition for training.

For the low-paid in general, a national minimum wage is arguably a more important need than training, particularly to those who will keep their jobs and, for the low-paid as a whole, particularly if few will lose them. The latter requirement points towards an intermediate role for training, as one of several ingredients in the policy mix advocated by the 'Swedish model' of bargained wage floors, expansionary demand management, industrial restructuring and worker re-training. Such policies seek to avoid creating unemployment as a result of minimum wages by redeploying resources from low to high value-added sectors to an extent and with a speed which the labour market alone cannot achieve. In doing so, they offer training to those who wish to leave their current line of work or whose current jobs are lost as a result of minimum wage policy (Calmfors, 1986; Fraser, 1987).

The Swedish model has done well in practice, and not only in Sweden. Sustained by broadly consensus politics and centralized bargaining institutions, the four Nordic economies have attained low inequality of pay along with high employment. The reduction of economically dysfunctional pay differentials has in turn given an incentive to low-wage employers to mechanize, improve their products and develop their labour forces in order to survive (Field, 1984; Rowthorn, 1989).

Such policies are a long way from home in Britain at present. Here prevailing policy espouses market forces without considering when and why they may fail. It advocates enhanced opportunities for individuals but in practice offers little. Training opportunities for the low-paid require improvement with or without the other ingredients in the Swedish model. As employers have little to offer the low-paid, government should be encouraged to put its money where its mouth is. Individuals in general and the low-paid in particular should be given a quantum improvement in opportunities to arrange their own training.

The Career Development Loans scheme offers a promising start. A major increase in the subsidy offered to individuals sponsoring their own training would both increase opportunities and foster occupational structures in the wider labour market. It would also help to reduce the enormous, inefficient and unfair disparity which prevails at present between the economics of employer-sponsored and self-sponsored training.

Notes

1. I would like to thank Ken Mayhew for encouraging me to produce the paper on which this chapter is based. The assistance of the Policy Studies Institute (in the persons of Malcolm Rigg and Karen MacKinnon), OPCS and the Department of Employment in providing access to unpublished data is gratefully acknowledged. I also thank Sir John Cassels both for an invitation to give a talk to the PSI seminar on 'The real skills shortage' which stimulated the development of much of this analysis and, along with Christine Greenhalgh, Ewart Keep, S. J. Prais, David Raffe, W. S. Siebert, David Stanton, Hilary Steedman, Frank Wilkinson and participants at the Oxford seminar, for helpful comments and suggestions. Finally, thanks are also due to David Marsden for his help in the area of our common research interests and to Gale Smith for making me awareness of the training-related obstacles facing low paid women.

2. The proportions of full time males who were either aged less than 21 or who were employed in subcraft manual occupations and who were low-paid both exceeded 40 per cent in the 1977 Family Expenditure Survey (Atkinson *et al.*, 1982, Tables 7, 8).

3. Recent developments in efficiency wage theory have revised the competitive prediction of the equalization of wages per efficiency unit across all employers, thereby permitting a different interpretation of low pay, as the result, e.g., of costless monitoring of employee effort in a world where most monitoring is not costless (Shapiro and Stiglitz, 1984).

4. Similarly, low productivity during training is not necessarily associated with low pay. Norms of fair pay combined with bargaining power commonly require employers to pay standard rates to trainees, particularly adult ones (Ryan, 1984, 1987). A review of segmentationism is provided by McNabb and Ryan (1989).

5. Second-best complications notwithstanding, allocative efficiency should generally improve alongside a reduction in the dispersion in the prices at which labour power of given quality is traded – and a significant dispersion in that price is a central attribute of a segmented labour market (Ryan, 1981). Orthodox critics of a statutory minimum wage commonly neglect this general equilibrium case for it in favour of the partial equilibrium one against it (Forrest, 1984). Economic efficiency should gain more generally from linking the elimination of low productivity jobs to economic expansion and retraining for employment in expanding sectors marked by high value product and pay (see section 5 of the text, below).

6. Martin and Roberts, 1984, Tables 4.16, 5.22, 5.26; Hunt, 1988, pp. 168–70.

7. The low-paid can be the less skilled in a segmentationist as well as a competitive theory of the labour market, as high-wage employers are in a position to select the most skilled workers and have a clear interest in doing so (Marsden and Ryan, 1989b). However, segmentation may be so intense that the lower-paid could be the more skilled, as in a

'dualist' rather than a 'queue' formulation of segmentation (Doeringer and Piore, 1971, Chapter 8). Perhaps the most persuasive evidence of segmentation is provided by labour mobility, in the form of low quit rates in high-wage sectors and determination of the pay of mobile workers by employer rather than personal characteristics (Ryan, 1980; Krueger and Summers, 1987). Gross (1990) provides the first detailed empirical study of the links between product markets, technology and pay in Britain.

8. As part-time workers are likely to be less qualified and lower paid than are full-timers, the discrepancy in qualifications by pay would be even greater were they included.

9. When the highly qualified are excluded from each pay category, the share of employees with intermediate qualifications remains lower amongst the low-paid, at 38.7 per cent as opposed to 42.6 per cent, but the difference is clearly much smaller.

10. The other sides of the coin are more familiar: (i) the limited role of schooling and qualifications in explaining the variance in pay across individuals (Layard *et al.*, 1978, Chapter 4; Marsden, 1983, Table 11.3); and (ii) the low level of qualification amongst British managers (Sadler, 1989).

11. An outstanding example is clothing, where employment is dominated by female sewing machinists, most of whom are low-paid according to standard criteria, but whose skills, for the most part uncertified, remain substantial despite the subdivision of labour and the rationalization of training (Thomas, Moxham and Jones, 1969; NBPI, 1969; Davenport, Totterdill and Zeitlin, 1986; James, 1987; Steedman and Wagner, 1989; see also note 31, below).

12. The 'strict' formulation of dual labour market theory (Piore, 1970, Doeringer and Piore, 1971, Chapter 8) has largely failed to win support from patterns of mobility in the wider labour market, as opposed to the inner city urban labour markets for which it was originally formulated. Although some writers argue that segmentationism must be rejected if the working poor are not in fact trapped in a clearly defined secondary market (Mayhew and Rosewell, 1979; Metcalf and Nickell, 1982), the key issue lies elsewhere, in the existence of a significant dispersion in job rewards for comparable workers (McNabb and Ryan, 1989).

13. 'The central task of manpower policy is to move secondary workers into primary jobs. My own assessment of the "new manpower" programmes is that in this regard (moving secondary workers into primary jobs) they have been for the most part unsuccessful' (Piore, 1970, p. 63). Subsequent dualist assessment proved more qualified: 'The overall results of the decade of manpower policy are still a matter of dispute. What I think is not disputable is that the attempt to cull improvements out of the theory of human capital have proved disappointing' (Piore, 1973, p. 253). Bluestone (1970) cites Secretary of Labour (and labour economist) George Schultz's 1969 statement to Congress that the 'realities of the jobs available,' i.e. the rigidity of low wage employment with respect to a more highly trained labour supply, have constrained the 'full achievement of our expectations' (p. 18).

14. Although a detailed statistical assessment had been undertaken in an earlier report (Doeringer, 1969), the leading dualist assessment of manpower programmes largely excluded statistical evidence, limiting itself to average durations of employment in secondary jobs as evidence of confinement of the working poor to the secondary segment (Doeringer and Piore, 1971, pp. 168–9).

15. Exceptions include Deakin and Pratten (1987), who concentrate upon outcomes for employers under YTS.

16. Nickell, 1982, Table 1; Greenhalgh and Stewart, 1987, Table 6. The detailed effects of qualifications on pay are reported only by Nickell and then for males only.

17. The weakness of the earnings data provided by the NTS has led, in all the research cited here, to the measurement of job rewards by the average pay of male members of an individual's detailed occupational category, derived separately from the 1975 General Household Survey. The low-paid in NTS research are therefore those working in occupations for which average male earnings in 1975 were low. See also Metcalf and Nickell (1982), Stewart and Greenhalgh (1984), Greenhalgh and Stewart (1985).

18. It is tempting to attribute at least part of any close relationship between training and mobility to an association between low pay and training for young male workers (who are included in these NTS samples). However, absolute rates of upward mobility of those with training amongst low-paid males are similar for a low-paid category dominated by adults: married females (Table 6.3, cols 3, 6).

19. As some of the training recorded must have been unassociated with upward mobility, truly associated training must have applied to a smaller minority of individuals.

20. The frequency with which the upwardly mobile low-paid received training becomes higher when the distance travelled is raised from one occupational category to two, at 38 and 48 per cent for females and males respectively (unreported tabulations).

21. The training categories which could not be included (evening, part-time and non-vocational) are more commonly undertaken by females. Thus part-time and evening training amount to roughly 43 per cent of vocational training events reported by females, as against only 19 per cent for males (estimated from Greenhalgh and Stewart, 1982, Table 1; 1987, Table 1). Although the difference between the sexes in the contribution of training to mobility is therefore overestimated by the data in Table 6.4, the bias appears small, as only evening training shows much association with mobility (Greenhalgh and Stewart, 1987, pp. 187–8).

22. Not even the fixed effect models used on the NTS will eliminate selection bias from the training effect if individual effects such as ability or motivation interact with training participation in determining earnings. The likelihood of difficulty can be illustrated from one of the more sophisticated evaluations in the US manpower literature. Ashenfelter (1978) used both a fixed effects model and a matched comparison group but still estimated returns to training which remained

sensitive to assumptions about prior earnings variation and which now appear dubious in the light of estimates based upon strictly experimental evaluation (Lallonde, 1984).

23. Low-paid full-time manual male employees in 1971 who changed employers during the ensuing twelve months registered a much larger increase in earnings during that period than those who remained with the same employer. However, amongst those who were not low-paid, the reverse was observed (DE Gazette, 1977, Table 2). Although no information is available on the role of training in such moves, the difference suggests that a change of employer may well be required if the low-paid are to capture the benefits of training. Similarly, only the low-paid express more interest in changing employer than in seeking promotion within their current employment (Rigg, 1988, Table 4a).

24. The data in Tables 6.5–6.8 derive from a recent survey conducted by the Policy Studies Institute, which drew upon a national sample of 2581 economically active individuals (Rigg, 1988). Special tabulations provided by PSI for this analysis refer in all cases to adults (aged at least 22 years) and in most cases to employees only. The survey sample was drawn from postal addresses and is thus strictly representative neither of employees nor of the labour force. Various design and response attributes mean that secondary earners without training (a category which includes many low paid female part-timers) may be underrepresented (Rigg, 1988, Chapter 10), although breakdowns of the lowest-income group between males and females, as well as between part-time and full-time females, are comparable to those in studies of low pay (Table 6.1).

25. Although low-paid married females also receive less full-time training than do more highly-paid ones, regression analysis attributes this entirely to other personal characteristics such as age and family size and suggests a positive *ceteris paribus* effect for low pay on training activity (Greenhalgh and Stewart, 1987, Tables 3, 4). It is not clear why low pay should lead more married females, but not males or single females, to undertake more full-time training than their more highly-paid counterparts – nor indeed, given that, why the same difference does not appear for evening training.

26. The PSI results show a similar pattern, with a 'steep rise in the incidence of reported training at incomes of £6000 a year or more for people in employment,' controlling for personal characteristics (Rigg, 1988, p. 19). However, as the PSI pay variable is measured *after* training, this positive relationship captures the effects of training on pay as well as those of pay on training (see note 29).

27. The unimportance of costs to trainees for employer-provided adult training is indicated also by the finding that only 3 per cent of recipients receive less than their normal pay (Rigg, 1988, p. 81).

28. Such phenomena may be interpreted also as optimal contracts when skills are for technological reasons wholly employer-specific (Carmichael, 1983), although a more general analysis must recognize the dependence of skill specificity upon wage structure as well.

29. The size of the truncation bias in the PSI's estimates of the effects of

low pay upon training (note 26) is unknown, even if it is unlikely to account for most, let alone all, of the association between low pay and low training. It does however prevent any inference from the greater strength of the relationship between income and training in the PSI survey than in the NTS (where measurement of occupational level prior to training by Greenhalgh and Stewart avoids such bias) that the training-related disadvantages of the low paid have increased over time.

30. Case studies document the low interest of low-wage employers in employee development. British clothing employers have attracted particular attention for their continuing pursuit of a deskilled section-alized organization of work, linked to standardization of products in retail markets dominated by chain stores. In contrast to West Germany, and in contradiction to predictions that computerization of production combined with increased consumer interest in variety will force a reversal of strategy in favour of skill-intensive 'flexible specialization,' British employers, their ITB and skill certification bodies (NCVQ) have remained wedded to narrow job categories and skill requirements, whether training is intensive or casual (see note 11; Zeitlin, 1988).

31. Rigg (1988), Tables 5.12a, 2a, 2c, 5.8a, 5.9a, 3a; p. 82.

32. As training is associated with greater short-term perceived benefits, in terms of pay and (particularly) promotion, when it is employer-sponsored than when self-sponsored (Rigg, 1988, Table 3a), truncation bias is likely to be stronger for the former category. The implication is that the incidence of employer-sponsored relative to self-sponsored training amongst the low paid is also underestimated by the PSI data. This bias is however small, as the difference in the short-term perceived gains in pay which resulted from training is itself small (Rigg, 1988).

33. Only a minority (43 per cent) of recent individually sponsored training, representing less than 4 per cent of all individuals, was initiated by employees, mostly those who wanted more than their employers could or would provide (Rigg, 1988, p. 15).

34. Surprisingly, the increase of training activity with income indicated in Table 6.6 is little different for females than for males.

35. Similarly, workers who can envisage training in the future commonly anticipate various financial obstacles to sponsoring their own training (Rigg, 1988, Tables 5.8a,b, 5.9a,b, 7.6a).

36. Based on unpublished results from Rigg (1988).

37. Rigg (1988), pp. 129–30, 131, 56, 77.

38. An average CDL value of £2280 for an average of 10 months' suspended interest payments (given a 7-month average course dura-tion) amounts to an average government interest payment of £349 at an assumed CDL interest rate of 18.3 per cent (APR). The accom-panying loan guarantee provided to participating banks involves a further public subsidy, depending upon the unknown prevailing default rate. The value of the loan to the low-paid individual may of course be considerably greater than the sum of these two elements, as finance would otherwise usually be more expensive or unavailable.

39. As banks are encouraged to follow conventional criteria in assessing applications, the low-paid are likely to be more strongly represented in CDL applications than acceptances, though data on this are as yet unavailable. The data in Table 6.9 are at best suggestive as they involve two different occupational classifications (CODOT and a CDL-specific one) which have been matched only from brief labels and are therefore subject to error. The content of the 'Other' category is particularly likely to differ between the two sources.

40. The lack of attention to incentive problems related to training contrasts with that related to job search by the unemployed, where a serious problem is inferred and policy response is to be emphatic (DE, 1988b, p. 49).

41. Employer provision was emphasized even more strongly in the second of the 1988 White Papers: 'The prime responsibility for this investment (in the skills and knowledge of our people) lies with employers'. A modern training system 'must be planned and led by employers, because it is they who are best placed to judge skill needs' (DE 1988b, pp. 4, 38).

42. In the policy debate of the early 1960s, 'the provision of more and better opportunities for individuals was largely a by-product of pursuing a strategy geared to the needs of employers', reflecting a 'very strong tendency to associate policies which affect employers with economic objectives and those which directly affect individuals with social objectives' (Lindley, 1983, pp. 347–8).

43. Despite its intention to outline 'the strategy towards unemployment and training which the Government intend to pursue over the lifetime of this Parliament and the steps which they intend to take to implement it,' the first of the 1988 White Papers did not even mention CDLs, which had been available in pilot schemes since 1986 and were about to go national (DE, 1988a, p. 4). Low publicity for CDLs contributes to the finding that none of a sample of 48 low paid workers had heard of the scheme nine months after its national launch (FE UK, 1989).

44. Such an inference is suggested by discrepancies in the broad tendency for the difference between actual and aspired occupational categories to increase with prevailing pay levels in Table 6.9 (columns 7, 3).

The number of categories available is not large enough to permit the use of multivariate analysis to separate the effects of pay levels and qualification structures in promoting interest amongst CDL recipients. Nor are there suitable measures of the qualifications held by members of different occupations: existing measures concentrate upon academic rather than vocational qualifications (IER, 1989). A further factor which may dampen interest in courses oriented towards manual skills is the inadequacy of a one-year loan to finance training durations of up to three years. However, as such training is generally unavailable to adults, training duration is unlikely to matter in practice at present.

References

Ashenfelter, O. (1978) 'Estimating the effects of training programmes on earnings', *Review of Economics and Statistics*, 60 (February).

Atkinson, A. B., Mickelwright, J. and Sutherland, H. (1982) *Low Pay: a Preliminary Look at Evidence from the FES* (London: Low Pay Unit).

Bassi, L. J. and Ashenfelter, O. (1986) 'The effect of direct job creation and training programmes on low skilled workers', in Danziger, S. H. and Weinberg, D. H. (eds), *Fighting Poverty: What Works and What Does Not* (Cambridge, Mass: Harvard).

Bazen, S. (1988) 'On the overlap between low pay and poverty', ICERD discussion paper, 120 (London School of Economics).

Becker, G. S. (1967) 'Human capital and the personal distribution of income: an analytical approach', Woytinsky Lecture, University of Michigan; reprinted in Becker (1975).

Becker, G. S. (1975) *Human Capital* (Chicago: University of Chicago) 2nd edn.

Bluestone, B. (1970) 'The tripartite economy: labour markets and the working poor', *Poverty and Human Resources Abstracts*, 5.

Brosnan, P. and Wilkinson, F. (1988) 'A national minimum wage and economic efficiency', *Contributions to Political Economy*, 7 (March).

Calmfors, L. (1986) 'Comment', in Bosworth, B. P. and Rivlin, A. M. (eds), *The Swedish Economy* (Washington, D.C.: Brookings).

Campbell, A. and Warner, M. (1990) 'Training strategies and micro-electronics in the engineering industries in the UK and West Germany', forthcoming in Ryan, P. (ed.), *International Comparisons of Vocational Education and Training* (Lewes: Falmer).

Carmichael, L. (1983) 'Firm-specific human capital and promotion ladders', *Bell Journal of Economics*, 14 (Spring).

Confederation of British Industry (CBI) (1989) 'Towards a skills revolution – a youth charter', interim report of the Vocational Education and Training Task Force (London) (mimeo).

Commission of the European Communities (CEC) (1984) *Social Europe* (December).

Claydon, S. (1980) 'Counting our skills: the National Training Survey', *Employment Gazette*, 88 (November).

Craig, C., Rubery, J., Tarling, R., and Wilkinson, F. (1982) *Labour Market Structure, Industrial Organisation and Low Pay* (Cambridge: Cambridge University Press).

Davenport, E., Totterdill, P., and Zeitlin, J. (1986) 'Training for the clothing industry: a strategy for local government intervention', unpublished report to the Greater London Council.

Deakin, B. M. and Pratten, C. (1987) 'Economic effects of YTS', *Employment Gazette*, 95 (October).

Deloitte, Haskins and Sells (DHS) (1988) 'Study of Employers' Training Activities', Report to Manpower Services Commission (Sheffield).

Department of Employment (DE) (1988a) *Training for Employment*, Cm 316 (London: HMSO).

Department of Employment (DE) (1988b) *Employment for the 1990s*,
   Cm 540 (London: HMSO).
Department of Employment (DE) (1988c) *The London Labour Market*
   (London: HMSO).
Department of Employment (DE) (1988d) *Career Development Loans*,
   information booklet (London: Department of Employment).
Department of Employment (DE) Gazette (1977) 'How individual people's
   earnings change', *Department of Employment Gazette*, 85 (January).
Doeringer, P. B. (1969) 'Low income labor markets and urban manpower
   programs: a critical assessment', Manpower Administration, US Depart-
   ment of Labor (Washington, D.C.: GPO).
Doeringer, P. B. and Piore, M. J. (1971) *Internal Labor Markets and
   Manpower Analysis* (Lexington: D.C. Heath).
Elias, P. (1988) 'Family formation, occupational mobility and part-time
   work', in Hunt (1988).
FE UK (1989) 'The next rung up: training, enterprise and unskilled
   workers' (London: Full Employment UK).
Field, F. (1984) 'Policies against low pay: an international perspective',
   research paper, 84/4 (London: Policy Studies Institute).
Finegold, D. and Soskice, D. (1988) 'The failure of training in Britain:
   analysis and prescription', *Oxford Review of Economic Policy*, 4 (3)
   (Autumn).
Fraser, N. (1987) 'Economic policy in Sweden: are there lessons from the
   Swedish model?', *International Review of Applied Economics*, 1 (June).
Forrest, D. (1984) *Low Pay or No Pay?*, Hobart paper, 101 (London:
   Institute for Economic Affairs).
Greenhalgh, C. and Stewart, M. B. (1982) 'The effects and determinants of
   training', Warwick Economic Research Paper 213, Department of Eco-
   nomics (University of Warwick).
Greenhalgh, C. and Stewart, M. B. (1985) 'The occupational status and
   mobility of British men and women', *Oxford Economic Papers*, 37
   (March).
Greenhalgh, C. and Stewart, M. B. (1987) 'The effects and determinants of
   training', *Oxford Bulletin of Economics and Statistics*, 49 (May).
Gross, M. (1990) 'Labour market segmentation: the role of product market
   and industry structure in determining labour market outcomes. A test for
   the United Kingdom', unpublished Ph.D. dissertation (University of
   Cambridge).
Hicks, J. R. (1963) *The Theory of Wages* (London: Macmillan) 2nd edn.
Humphries, J. and Rubery, J. (1984) 'The reconstitution of the supply side
   of the labour market', *Cambridge Journal of Economics*, 8 (December).
Hunt, A. (ed.) (1988) *Women and Paid Work* (London: Macmillan).
Institute for Employment Research (IER) (1989) *Review of the Economy
   and Employment*, vol. 2, Occupational Studies (Coventry: University of
   Warwick).
Jalladde, J.-P. (1982) *Alternate Training for Young People: Guidelines for
   Action* (Berlin: CEDEFOP).
James, R. (1987) 'The excess cost of training', *Clothing World* (January).
Jones, I. S. (1986) 'Apprentice training costs in British manufacturing

establishments: some new evidence', *British Journal of Industrial Relations*, 24 (November).

Keep, E. (1987) 'Britain's attempts to create a national vocational education and training system: a review of progress', Warwick papers in Industrial Relations 16 (University of Warwick, IRRU).

Keep, E. (1990) 'Training for the Low-paid' (Chapter 5 in this volume).

Krueger, A. B. and Summers, L. H. (1987) 'Reflections on the inter-industry wage structure', in Lang, K. and Leonard, J. S. (eds), *Unemployment and the Structure of Labour Markets* (Oxford: Basil Blackwell).

Lalonde, R. (1986) 'Evaluating the econometric evaluations of training programmes with experimental data', *American Economic Review*, 76 (September): 604–20.

Layard, R., Piachaud, D., and Stewart, M. B. (1978) *The Causes of Poverty*, Background Paper, 5, Royal Commission on the Distribution of Income and Wealth (London: HMSO).

Lindley, R. M. (1983) 'Active manpower policy', in Bain, G. S. (ed.), *Industrial Relations in Great Britain* (Oxford: Basil Blackwell).

McNabb, R. and Ryan, P. (1989) 'Segmented labour markets', in Sapsford, D. and Tsannatos, Z. (eds), *Current Issues in Labour Economics* (London: Macmillan).

Manpower Services Commission (MSC) (1987) *Annual Report 1986/87* (Sheffield: MSC).

Marsden, D. W. (1983) 'Wage structure', in Bain, G. S. (ed.), *Industrial Relations in Great Britain* (Oxford: Basil Blackwell).

Marsden, D. W. (1986) *The End of Economic Man? Competition and Custom in the Labour Market* (Brighton: Wheatsheaf).

Marsden, D. W. and Ryan, P. (1988) 'Apprenticeship and labour market structure: UK youth employment and training in comparative context', paper presented to International Symposium on Innovations in Apprenticeship and Training (November) (Paris: OECD).

Marsden, D. W. and Ryan, P. (1989a) 'Employment and training of young people: have the government misunderstood the labour market?', in *Education and Training UK 1989* (Newbury: Policy Journals).

Marsden, D. W. and Ryan, P. (1989b) 'Statistical tests for the universality of youth employment mechanisms in segmented labour markets', *International Review of Applied Economics*, 3 (June).

Marsden, D. W. and Ryan, P. (1990a) 'The structuring of youth pay and employment in six European economies', in Ryan, P., Garonna, D., and Edwards, R. C. (eds), *The Problem of Youth: the Regulation of Youth Employment and Training in Advanced Economies* (London: Macmillan) (forthcoming).

Marsden, D. W. and Ryan, P. (1990b), 'Initial training, labour market structure and public policy in Britain and the FRG', in Ryan, P. (ed.), *International Comparisons of Vocational Education and Training* (Lewes: Falmer) (forthcoming).

Martin, J. and Roberts, C. (1984) *Women and Employment: a Lifetime Perspective*, Social Survey Report, SS 1143 (London: HMSO).

Mayhew, K. and Rosewell, B. (1979) 'Labour market segmentation in Britain', *Oxford Bulletin of Economics and Statistics*, 41 (May).

Metcalf, D. and Nickell, S. (1982) 'Occupational mobility in Great Britain', in Ehrenberg, R. (ed.), *Research in Labour Economics*, 5.

Mincer, J. (1974) *Schooling, Experience and Earnings* (New York: Columbia University Press).

National Board for Prices and Incomes (NPBI) (1969) *Pay and Conditions in the Clothing Industry*, Report 110, Cmnd 4002 (London: HMSO).

National Board for Prices and Incomes (NBPI) (1971) *General Problems of Low Pay*, Report 169, Cmnd 4648 (London: HMSO).

Nickell, S. (1982) 'The determinants of occupational success in Britain', *Review of Economic Studies*, 49 (January).

Organisation for Economic Cooperation and Development (OECD) (1976) *Developments in Educational Leave of Absence* (Paris: OECD).

Organisation for Economic Cooperation and Development (OECD) (1988) 'Women's activity, employment and earnings: a review of recent developments', *OECD Employment Outlook 1988* (Paris: OECD).

Piore, M. J. (1970) 'Jobs and training', in Beer, S. and Barringer, R. E. (eds), *The State and the Poor* (Cambridge, Mass: Winthrop).

Piore, M. J. (1973) 'The importance of human capital theory to labour economics: a dissenting view', *Proceedings of 26th Annual Meeting of the Industrial Relations Research Association*.

Raffe, D. (1988) 'Going with the grain: youth training in transition', in Brown, S. (ed.), *Education in Transition* (Edinburgh: Scottish Council for Research in Education).

Raffe, D. (1989) 'The transition from YTS to work: content, context and the external labour market', paper presented to Annual Conference of British Sociological Association (March).

Rigg, M. (1988) 'The impact of vocational education and training on individual adults', final report to Training Agency VET Funding Study (London: Policy Studies Institute).

Rosenberg, S. (1980) 'Male occupational standing and the dual labour market', *Industrial Relations*, 19 (Winter).

Rowthorn, R. (1989) 'Wage dispersion and employment: theories and evidence', paper presented to 9th World Congress of the International Economics Association (Athens) (August).

Ryan, P. (1980) 'The empirical analysis of labour market segmentation', paper presented to Conference on Low Pay and Labour Market Segmentation in Advanced Economies (Berlin) (July).

Ryan, P. (1981) 'Segmentation, duality and the internal labour market', in Wilkinson, F. (ed.), *The Dynamics of Labour Market Segmentation* (London: Academic Press).

Ryan, P. (1984a) 'Job training, employment practices and the large enterprise: the case of costly transferable skills', in Osterman, P. (ed.), *Internal Labour Markets* (Cambridge, Mass: MIT Press).

Ryan, P. (1984b) 'The New Training Initiative after two years', *Lloyds Bank Review* (April).

Ryan, P. (1987) 'Trade unionism and the pay of young workers', in Junankar, P. N. (ed.), *From School to Unemployment? The Labour Market for Young People* (London: Macmillan).

Sadler, P. (1989) 'Management Development', in Sisson, K. (ed.), *Personnel Management in Britain* (Oxford: Basil Blackwell).

Shapiro, C. and Stiglitz, J. (1984) 'Equilibrium unemployment as a worker discipline device', *American Economic Review*, 73 (June).

Steedman, H. and Wagner, K. (1989) 'Productivity, machinery, and skills: clothing manufacture in Britain and Germany', *National Institute Economic Review*, 109 (May).

Stewart, M. B. and Greenhalgh, C. A. (1984) 'Work history patterns and the occupational attainment of women', *Economic Journal*, 94 (September).

Thomas, B., Moxham, J., and Jones, J. A. G. (1969) 'A cost–benefit analysis of industrial training', *British Journal of Industrial Relations*, 7 (July).

Training Agency/Department of Education and Science/Adult Literacy and Basic Skills Unit TA/DES/ALBSU (1989) 'Literacy and numeracy in YTS: a report' (Sheffield: Training Agency).

Training Commission TC (1988) *Annual Report 1987/88* (Sheffield: Training Commission).

Willis, N. (1989) 'A worker's right to train', *National Westminster Bank Quarterly Review* (February).

Zeitlin, J. (1988) 'The clothing industry in transition: international trends and British response', *Textile History*, 19.

7 Lower Incomes and Employment: A CBI Analysis[1]

CBI

British business has as its objective the achievement of a high-productivity, high-pay, high-employment economy. While there is widespread support from many quarters for that objective, there is far less consensus on the best methods of achieving that end and on the steps which should be taken in the shorter term to tackle such issues as low incomes, low pay and employment incentives. The purpose of this chapter is to provide an analysis of these issues from a business perspective, and to set out the CBI's views on the way forward.

The employer's perspective is based on two fundamental considerations. First, the continued expansion of the wealth creating sector demands an unequal distribution of income in order to offer a meaningful system of incentives and, therefore, there will necessarily always be a 'lower-income' group of some sort. Secondly, CBI members are concerned that effective policies should be developed which assist those members of society whose incomes are insufficient to meet their needs and who would otherwise experience poverty, although such policies should so far as possible not damage work incentives.

That low pay is the major cause of poverty seems to have come to be accepted by many as almost a truism. However, there is little consensus on what constitutes poverty or, indeed, on what level of pay can be held to fall within the pejorative category 'low pay'. More importantly, not everyone on low earnings is automatically subject to poverty, as our analysis will indicate.

The structure of this chapter is as follows:
- in section 1, we briefly examine the concept of 'poverty' and the variety of definitions which have been put forward over the years;
- in section 2, we similarly review the various definitions of 'low pay' which have been used over recent years;

- in section 3, the demand side of the picture is examined, for example whether low-paid jobs are offered by particular sectors of the economy or by certain types of companies;
- In section 4, the chapter seeks to provide an analysis of the main characteristics of those groups of individuals who fall into the lowest-paid categories of employees. We look at such issues as whether individuals are in low-paid jobs because of their personal characteristics, for example their lack of educational attainments or skills – the supply side of low pay;
- in section 5, the link between low pay and poverty is explored in order to assess the extent to which low pay is likely to lead to individuals or families experiencing poverty;
- finally, in section 6 the chapter explores the various approaches which have been adopted in the past to tackle the problems associated with lower incomes and some possibilities for the future.

1 DEFINITIONS OF POVERTY

Definitions of poverty fall into two main categories, either absolute or relative definitions, although there is in practice a degree of overlap between them.

The first serious attempts to define and measure poverty were undertaken in the late nineteenth and early twentieth century by Charles Booth and Seebohm Rowntree. In his studies conducted in the 1880s, Booth did not lay down a specific level of income below which a family could be defined as in poverty; within rough guidelines, interviewers were left to decide for themselves who was poor. However, in 1899 Rowntree sought to arrive at a more scientific evaluation of poverty.[2] He calculated the level of income necessary 'for the maintenance of merely physical health'. Food, rent and household sundries were deemed to be the three essentials for physical health. Relying heavily on an early American survey, Rowntree calculated the dietary requirements of people of various ages and sexes. These in turn were used to draw up actual food requirements and, consequently, food costs. Minimum rent was calculated at that level actually paid, while clothing was calculated as the minimum essential (adequate to keep a man in health and not so shabby as to injure his chances of obtaining respectable employment). In addition, families were given extra amounts to cover fuel and other household sundries. Thus, Rowntree calculated income levels for various family groups which could be accepted as the absolute minimum necessary. This formed the poverty line.

In a second study, Rowntree developed a 'human needs scale' which tried to take into account changing perceptions of need by adding extra allowances for personal sundries such as a daily newspaper, trade union subscription and tobacco, etc.[3] He also made allowances for 'inefficiencies' of expenditure and diet. Although Rowntree sought to calculate the level of 'absolute' or subsistence poverty, his calculations were not as scientific as superficially they appeared. For example, the minimum nutritional needs were based on a study of the dietary requirements of American prisoners – not a group necessarily representative of the population as a whole! Or again, in the case of clothing and rent, minimum requirements were based on actual expenditure, not an objective assessment of absolute necessities.

It might be expected that state levels of support might reflect some objective and scientific estimate of income sufficient for subsistence. In fact, the Beveridge Report[4] relied heavily on Rowntree's work. Beveridge acknowledged that 'the determination of what is required for reasonable human existence is to some extent a matter of judgement, estimates of this point change with time and, generally, in a progressive community upwards'. The scale rates recommended were based on Rowntree's human needs scales, but in most cases below those calculated by Rowntree. They were not a scientific assessment of minimum requirements, but a measure of what could be afforded by the post-war government and a political decision as to what should be paid. In setting National Assistance benefit levels, the precursor of Supplementary Benefit and Income Support, Beveridge's recommended levels were followed, increased to take some, but not full, account of inflation between the time the Report was published and their introduction in 1948. Since the initial creation of the safety net, ideas of 'absolute necessities' have become more subjective and little attempt has been made to revive this approach.

The second definition of poverty commonly used is that of relative poverty. For example, Peter Townsend defines poverty in terms of 'relative deprivation' – the position of those who 'lack the resources to obtain the types of diet, participate in the activities and amenities which are commanded by the average individual or family, [those who] are, in effect, excluded from ordinary living patterns, customs or activity'.[5] In order to produce a deprivation standard – or poverty line – Townsend drew up a deprivation index of 60 items, including dietary, household, family, recreational and social deprivations. Such measures of poverty also aim to be scientific and objective like those based on 'absolute necessities', but again the choice of factors by which deprivation or poverty is to be measured introduces a substantial measure of subjectivity and, therefore, controversy.

Attempts to measure poverty scientifically whether in absolute or in relative terms are therefore full of pitfalls, as even this brief review has indicated. As a result, the level of the safety net provided by the state – currently Income Support – is often accepted as the 'poverty line'. While inevitably standards and views will vary amongst individuals, it is probably fair to say that in practice most people would accept that to live on an income below that provided by Income Support is to experience poverty.

2 DEFINITIONS OF LOW PAY

Just as definitions and measures of poverty vary, so do views as to what constitutes low pay. The conclusion reached when the possibilty of a statutory national minimum wage was examined by a government-appointed Inter-Departmental Working Party of officials in the late 1960s was that what constitutes low pay is essentially a matter of subjective judgement.[6] Since then, no universally, or even widely accepted, definition of low pay in the UK has emerged.

Definitions of low pay can be split into two broad classifications: poverty-based definitions and relative definitions. Poverty-based definitions seek to define a 'living wage', that is the level of pay which is necessary to support individuals and their dependants on income levels at least equal to those provided by state benefit arrangements. In determining the living wage for a given family, and therefore the low pay benchmark, one approach is to calculate the gross earnings before tax and national insurance necessary to generate a net income equivalent to Income Support levels. However, in making such a calculation, various assumptions have to be made about the numbers and ages of wage earners and dependants, about housing costs (which vary significantly across regions) and work expenses. Depending on the assumptions made, so the gross earnings needed in order to generate take home pay equivalent to Income Support will vary. A rather similar approach is to use Family Credit as a measure of low pay. Once again, however, Family Credit will vary with the assumptions made about the numbers and ages of the children in the family.

The strength of poverty-based definitions of this type is that they relate earnings to the level of income which the state regards as a minimum or poverty threshold; family units whose earnings fall below these levels could be regarded as in poverty. However, in order to arrive at a benchmark figure for low pay a whole series of assumptions must be made about the family unit and it⌣ circumstances. As a result, the benchmark level arrived at by such means loses its validity because it must be based on the circumstances of a minority. As the assumptions are varied, so the earnings target will vary.

The second approach to defining low pay is based on relative definitions. This has the major advantage of not requiring arbitrary assumptions as to family size, composition, etc. A worker is considered to be low paid simply if his or her earnings are low relative to other workers. There are four relative definitions that have been put forward over the years to which reference is frequently made in pay bargaining and debate over public policy. These are earnings below:

- the gross earnings of the lowest decile of male manual workers (used by the Royal Commission on the Distribution of Income and Wealth in its 1978 Report);
- two-thirds of average male manual workers' gross earnings (the TUC's traditional definition);
- two-thirds of median gross earnings of all male employees (the Low Pay Unit definition);
- 68 per cent of national gross earnings for both men and women (this level was adopted by the Committee of Independent Experts which monitors implementation of the European Social Charter established by the Council of Europe and is known as the 'decency threshold').

Applying these four definitions to the average earnings figures contained in the 1988 New Earnings Survey produces the various measures of low pay recorded in Table 7.1.

Perhaps the first and most obvious point to be made about these various relative definitions is the sheer scale of the spread of low pay thresholds they produce and, as a result, the enormous differences in the number of people who are held to be low-paid. Secondly, all are based on gross average earnings figures of various types. The figures

Table 7.1   Low pay definitions, April 1988

	Weekly earnings £	No. of employees* (million)
lowest decile of male manual workers	119.40	1.9
2/3 average male manual gross earnings	133.73	2.8
2/3 median gross earnings of all males	143.67	3.6
68% national gross earnings for both male and female	148.50	3.8

Source: CBI calculations from 1988 New Earnings Survey.

Note:
* Number of employees with earnings falling below these levels are those for full-time employees on adult rates in April 1988.

used therefore include such items as shift and overtime premium payments and a wide range of allowances, bonuses and other payments as well as basic pay. All four approaches involve taking some proportion of such gross average earnings for all hours worked and setting that as the target for basic pay for a standard week or even converting it to an hourly rate by dividing total earnings for all hours worked by some assumed number of normal weekly hours (normally 39). Such an approach produces targets for basic weekly and hourly rates which bear no relation to reality. Moreover, any widespread attempt to implement such targets, apart from the potentially serious impact on the costs, competitiveness and employment levels in British firms, would simply result in moving the goal posts, by raising the level of average earnings in subsequent years. This is particularly true of the definition of low pay adopted by the Royal Commission on the Distribution of Income and Wealth, which takes the lowest decile of male manual workers as its measure.

3   WHERE ARE THE LOWER-PAID JOBS?

While it may be impossible to produce a satisfactory definition of low pay, quite obviously this is not to deny that there are people who fall at the lower end of the earnings scale. In order to simplify our analysis of where the lower-paid are and who they are, we have taken as our measure those adults in full-time jobs with gross earnings of less than £125 a week in April 1988. It must be stressed that there is no special significance attached to this figure. It has been adopted purely for analytic convenience. In all, about 2.2 million adults in full-time employment had gross weekly earnings below £125 in April 1988.

This section examines the distribution of lower-paying jobs among industries, region and occupations. As Bazen has pointed out in studying the distribution of low pay,[7] it is necessary to differentiate between *concentration* (which may be defined as the proportion of all low-paying jobs found in a particular industry, occupation, age group or region) and *incidence* (which is defined as the proportion of workers in a particular industry, occupation, age group or region who are in lower-paying jobs). The importance of those two concepts becomes clear in our analysis.

Industrial Distribution

Low pay is commonly associated with particular industries. However, we need to differentiate between concentration and incidence. In Table 7.2 we have taken 11 sectors and show the extent of lower pay within them.

Table 7.2 highlights the fact that all industries contain some lower-paid workers. However, there is considerable variation across industries. The concentration of male lower-paid workers (i.e. the proportion of all those we have classified as lower-paid) is particularly high in the distribution trades and, perhaps surprisingly, in the banking and financial services sector. These two sectors account for nearly 40 per cent of all lower-paid men. For female employees, lower pay is concentrated in these two industries as well as pro-fessional and scientific services and footwear and clothing. In all, over 70 per cent of all lower-paid female employees are to be found in these four sectors of the economy alone.

A rather different pattern emerges when we look at the incidence of lower pay, i.e. the proportion of the workforce within a sector who may be regarded as lower-paid. For example, although a significant proportion of all low-paid workers are employed in the finance sector, the *incidence* of low pay for men is relatively low. However, in certain industries, the opposite case of low concentration combined with high incidence is found. The most obvious cases are in the textiles industry and the clothing and footwear industries where only 2.7 and 1.9 per cent of low-paid males and 5.2 and 1.4 per cent

Table 7.2   Lower pay in selected industries, April 1988

SIC (1980)	Industry	Males Inc* (%)	Males Conc* (%)	Females Inc (%)	Females Conc (%)
0	Agriculture[1]	31.6	6.1	–	–
1	Energy & Water Supply Industries[2]	0.9	0.5	9.0	0.6
25	Chemical Industry	3.6	0.9	28.5	1.4
32	Mechanical Engineering	4.9	2.7	43.2	1.9
33–34	Electrical Engineering	5.2	2.2	37.7	4.4
43	Textiles[1,3]	19.4	2.7	63.9	5.2
45	Footwear & Clothing[1,3]	25.7	1.9	74.4	14.0
64–65	Retail Distribution	23.8	19.6	61.4	20.6
66	Hotel and Catering[1]	48.0	8.0	67.5	8.4
8	Banking & Finance, etc.[1]	8.3	19.3	25.0	18.6
93–95	Professional & Scientific Services	8.5	8.0	24.8	18.8
	All Industries	9.3	100	34.8	100

Source: CBI estimates based on 1988 New Earnings Survey, Part C, Tables 66–69, those earning adult rates only.

Note:
*   Incidence and concentration respectively.
1.   Manual males only.
2.   Non-manual females only.
3.   Manual females only.

respectively of all low-paid females are found. Yet for each industry the incidence of lower pay is significantly above the average at 19.4 and 25.7 per cent respectively for men and 63.9 and 74.4 per cent respectively for women.

Occupational Classification

Table 7.3 looks at the occupational distribution of the lower-paid, taking a selection of 11 occupational groups from the New Earnings Survey to provide a broad indication of the pattern. For male workers, lower pay tends to be concentrated in those occupations which employ lower skilled employees. So a high proportion of all lower-paid men are found, for example, in transport, materials handling, catering, cleaning and clerical work. For low-paid women,

Table 7.3   Lower pay by selected occupations, April 1988

Occupation	Males		Females	
	Inc* (%)	Conc* (%)	Inc (%)	Conc (%)
Professional & Related Supporting Management & Administration	1.2	1.1	3.9	0.5
Professional & Related in Science, Engineering, etc.	2.1	1.9	10.4	0.4
Managerial (excluding general management)	3.4	2.7	17.7	1.6
Clerical & Related	12.8	12.8	33.6	41.0
Selling	17.0	8.5	64.0	10.5
Catering, Cleaning, Hairdressing, etc.	31.8	13.7	66.2	16.0
Farming, Fishing etc.	31.8	6.7	–	–
Processing, Making, Repairing & Related (metal & electrical)	4.7	8.0	43.7	1.6
Construction, Mining & Related	11.7	4.5	–	–
Transport, Operating, Materials & Related	13.3	14.2	52.2	1.1
General Labourers	26.6	4.1	–	–
Total for all occupations	9.3	100.0	34.8	100.0

Source: CBI estimates based on 1988 New Earnings Survey, Part D, Tables 92–93, those earning adult rates only.

Note:
* Incidence and concentration respectively.

the highest concentration is found among clerical workers (41 per cent); followed by catering, cleaning and other services and selling. However, the incidence figures reinforce the view of the importance of the link between lower skill levels and lower pay. So, the incidence of low pay climbs above 25 per cent for men in general labouring, catering and cleaning and farming. For women, it reaches more than 60 per cent in selling and catering and cleaning services.

Regional Distribution

Table 7.4 shows the regional distribution of lower pay. As with the industrial distribution, lower-paid employment is to be found in all regions. The concentration figures indicate that the regional variation in low pay is not so wide as the industrial distribution. Three regions have markedly low concentrations of low pay for both men and

Table 7.4 Lower pay by region, April 1988

Region	Males		Females	
	Inc* (%)	Conc* (%)	Inc (%)	Conc (%)
Greater London	4.6	8.3	13.5	6.1
South East	7.7	15.1	31.0	17.6
East Anglia	8.7	3.9	42.5	4.3
South West	11.2	9.0	40.9	8.7
West Midlands	10.4	11.3	44.1	11.8
East Midlands	10.3	8.2	45.5	9.2
Yorks & Humber	11.0	10.1	42.1	10.1
North West	10.9	12.0	39.1	12.2
North	9.8	5.5	42.4	6.1
Wales	13.6	6.0	42.2	4.8
Scotland	11.6	10.7	38.8	9.0
UK all regions	9.3	100.0	34.8	100.0

Source: CBI estimates based on 1988 New Earnings Survey, Part E, Table 114, those earning adult rates only.

Note:
* Incidence and concentration respectively.

women: East Anglia, Northern England and Wales. A high concentration of low pay is found for both sexes in the South East, West Midlands, Yorkshire and Humberside and North West England.

To some extent, of course, such figures simply reflect the differential distribution of employment between regions, but this is by no means the whole story, as the incidence figures reveal. A good example is the South East. Although the region contains more than 15 per cent of all lower-paid men and 17.6 per cent of lower-paid women, the proportion of workers of both sexes within the region who are lower-paid is below the national average. Conversely, Wales contains only 6 per cent of all lower-paid men and 4.8 per cent of all lower-paid women, but 13.6 per cent of men and 42.2 per cent of women working in that region are lower-paid.

4 CHARACTERISTICS OF LOWER-PAYING INDUSTRIES

Types of Firms

It is often asserted that small firms pay lower wages than larger firms. Whilst of course such generalizations need to be treated with caution,

Table 7.5 Percentage of total employees in selected manufacturing industries employed in small firms

SIC 1980	Industry	% of employees in small firms
25	Chemical Industry	28.2
32	Mechanical Engineering	45.4
33–34	Electrical Engineering	28.1
43	Textiles	57.3
45	Footwear & Clothing	53.5
	Total Manufacturing	40.4

Source: CBI estimates based on Business Monitor PA 1003, DTI (HMSO, 1988) Table 8.

Note:
Figures refer to total employees in industry (manual, non-manual, full-time, part-time, adults, juveniles, men, women).

empirical evidence has tended to support this view, showing earnings differentials between firms of differing sizes to be considerable on average. The Bolton Report, for example, noted that the difference in earnings between employees in small and large firms was in the order of 20 per cent on average.[8]

Table 7.5 details the proportion of the total workforce of five manufacturing industries working in small manufacturing firms, defined in the Bolton Report as a firm employing between 10 and 200 employees.

Table 7.5 does illustrate that those manufacturing industries which had the highest incidence of lower pay, as illustrated in Table 7.2, are among those with the highest proportion of employees in small firms. The Bolton Committee also examined the service industries and although the data was relatively dated (even in 1971), it did suggest that small firms in the service sector were likely to have a higher incidence of low-paid workers. It must be emphasized, however, that there are such enormous differences between small firms – between for example a high tech consultancy and a seaside cafe – that company size is one of the less useful perspectives on lower pay.

What is perhaps considerably more important is the productivity and efficiency of individual organizations. Throughout the 1960s the National Board for Prices and Incomes (NBPI) issued numerous reports in which a recurring theme was the link between lower pay and industrial inefficiency. The theme was clearly stated in the *Fourth General Report* in 1969, which said 'In ... as improving the position of the low paid ... the main remedy is to be found in the improvement of efficiency'.[9]

Attempts to assess whether lower-paid employees tend to be concentrated in particular sectors because, on average, efficiency levels are lower in those sectors face major difficulties. No one measure of efficiency produces valid comparisons as industries differ so greatly with respect to activities performed, markets or productive processes. Nevertheless, previous studies have tended to rely on one of two measures: a comparison of average rates of return on capital employed by industry or a comparison of average net output per employee by industry. Perhaps as a result of such limitations, the results of such studies have been far from conclusive.

Comparing the average rates of return on capital employed appears to be the most common definition when comparing broadly classified industries, despite the fact that any data are usually from listed companies and therefore largely exclude the small firm sector. Duncan concluded that there is no obvious relationship between inefficiency, as indicated by a low return on capital, and low pay.[10] Indeed, he suggested that the reverse is true. The Bolton Committee concluded from the results of its sample inquiry that the rate of return on capital tends to decrease as company size increases although the difference is not very great. In terms of comparisons of average net output per employee Duncan indicated that productivity tended to be below average in low-paying industries.

The fact that attempts to measure the average efficiency of an entire industry in order to examine the underlying reasons for lower pay lead to inconclusive results is perhaps hardly surprising. One major disadvantage of such studies would appear to be their inability to isolate the contribution of labour as opposed to that of capital. The relative efficiency with which sectors utilize these resources is therefore difficult to explore. In any case, such macro approaches involve averaging together results from such very different organizations as to call the entire concept into question. What should not be in doubt from practical experience is that high pay goes hand in hand with high productivity and high performance at the level of the individual business.

Low growth Sectors

Lower-paying industries are often said to be characterized by slow or negative rates of economic growth. In attempts to measure industrial growth, previous studies have often used comparisons of rates of growth in employment. The assumption is that industries where there are lower-paid workers are mostly industries where employment is contracting. However, while the concentration of lower pay is high in those manufacturing industries with declining or static employment levels, there have been large increases in employment in service sectors with similar concentrations of lower pay.

Other indicators of industrial growth include estimates of changes in output and productivity. However, as has been noted many lower-paying industries are labour intensive and traditional methods of measurement of productivity such as output per head do not distinguish between the contribution of labour and/or capital. It is therefore not possible to suggest that there is a simple relationship existing between lower pay and industrial growth.

Sex Composition

In many of those sectors where large numbers of lower-paid employees are to be found, women make up an above average proportion of the workforce. Table 7.6 illustrates this, using the same eleven sectors as we have used in earlier tables.

Skills Composition

It is often assumed that the only characteristic shared by lower-paying industries is a relatively low level of skill on average across the workforce. Yet again, however, the picture is far from simple. Previous surveys of manufacturing industries have indicated no tendency for lower-paying industries to employ relatively high proportions of unskilled labour. Indeed there is slight tendency for industries with a high proportion of unskilled men to have slightly higher earnings relative to other industries.

5   WHO ARE THE LOWER-PAID?

To what extent is it possible to define the lower-paid in terms of their 'personal characteristics'? It is, for example, commonly argued that lower pay reflects low individual productivity because of lower skill levels or inexperience. In this section the various individual factors to which lower pay might be attributed are explored. It should be

Table 7.6   Employment of women as a proportion of total employment and proportion of women part-timers in selected industries

SIC 1980	Industry	No. of women in industry (000)	Women as % of industry workforce	% of women part-timers*
0	Agriculture	69.8	24.6	37.4
1	Energy & water Supply Industries	72.5	16.3	18.9
25	Chemical Industry	107.0	30.4	12.0
32	Mechanical Engineering	121.5	16.5	20.7
33–34	Electrical Engineering	205.6	32.0	10.6
43	Textiles	101.0	48.4	11.6
45	Footwear & Clothing	212.6	73.4	10.8
64–65	Retail Distribution	1368.6	63.2	58.8
665	Hotel Trade	175.0	64.4	47.3
8	Banking & Finance etc.	1323.1	50.3	26.2
93–95	Professional/Scientific Services	2277.9	72.4	51.3
	All industries and services	10,251.1	46.1	42.8

Source: CBI estimates based on Department of Employment *Gazette* (August 1989).

Note:
* Percentage of women in the sector who work part-time.

emphasized that this section is concerned with trying to identify explanatory factors – not with trying to 'blame' the plight of the lower-paid on their individual shortcomings!

It is important to recognize that lower-paid workers do not form a constant group somehow separate from the rest of the employed population. Individuals tend to experience lower pay at particular times of their working lives. Many move in and out of lower pay at intervals. Evidence of the transitional nature of the lower-paid for many falling into that category at any one time is provided by the Department of Employment's study of a matched sample of individuals over the period of 1970 to 1974.[11] In the five consecutive surveys those full-time manual men who were in the lowest decile of the distribution of earnings were a continually changing group. As Table 7.7 shows, only 2.9 per cent of all male manual workers were in the bottom decile of the earnings distribution in all five surveys. By contrast, over one in five of all male adult manual employees fell into that category for at least one of the five years. Thus, for a very high

Table 7.7   Full-time manual men (aged 21 and over) working in each April from 1970 to 1974: numbers in relation to the lowest-paid tenth

In lower-paid tenth	Sample numbers	% of total
In all five surveys	419	2.9
In all four surveys	314	2.2
In all three surveys	406	2.8
In two surveys	561	3.9
In one survey	1369	9.6
In none of the surveys	11,266	78.6
Totals	14,335	100.0

Source: Department of Employment *Gazette* (January 1977) Table 3 (summary).

proportion of the lower-paid at any given time, the prospects are that they will move out of the lower-paid category fairly rapidly as they acquire skills, experience or simply better paying jobs elsewhere. Nonetheless, there does remain a residual group falling consistently in the lower-paid category year after year.

Age

One of the most striking characteristics of the lower-paid is their very different distribution between age groups. Lower pay is prevalent at both ends of the age spectrum but particularly among young employees. As Table 7.8 shows, 36 per cent of those male under 21 are lower-paid and just under 16 per cent of those males over 50 are lower-paid. As a general pattern, earnings rise rapidly with age on average through the late teens and early twenties. More people then tend to fall back into lower pay as they start to approach retirement age.

The explanation for young people being so prone to low pay is likely to lie in the fact that they lack the skills, experience, expertise and on-the-job training which they need to be able to fill the higher-paying jobs. Naturally over time these attributes tend to be acquired, and upward occupational mobility therefore becomes possible. Evidence of this was found by Metcalf and Nickell[12] who examined occupational mobility among male workers between 1965 and 1975. They discovered that half the 15–19 age group had moved up the occupational ladder between 1965 and 1975 and such movement was found to be associated with vocational training, stable

Table 7.8   Lower pay by age

	Males		Females	
	Inc* (%)	Conc* (%)	Inc (%)	Conc (%)
Under 18	87.6	11.2	88.6	5.8
18–20	53.2	24.8	73.6	21.1
21–24	20.1	17.6	40.9	19.1
25–29	8.9	10.6	23.7	10.0
30–39	5.1	11.2	24.5	13.1
40–49	4.3	8.8	30.5	17.1
50–59	6.9	10.7	34.6	12.7
60–64	12.0	5.1	39.3	1.2
All ages	11.3	100.0	36.6	100.0

Source: CBI estimates based on 1988 New Earnings Survey, Part E, Table 124.

Note:
Incidence and concentration respectively.

employment histories and good health. Although this study was conducted some years ago it is likely that such patterns have not significantly changed.

Low pay among older workers may be accounted for by a number of factors. While there is no evidence that they are less productive than younger workers, older workers are more likely to suffer long-term health problems and this may mean that they are moved to lighter duties with lower pay rates and less likelihood of earning bonuses. More serious health problems may lead to long periods of absence from the workplace and consequent job changes. This in turn can lead to loss of earning potential, with the loss of payments reflecting increased responsiblity or incremental rises.

Skills and Educational Background

On average, the lower an employee's qualifications on leaving school and the lower his skill level, the lower his hourly earnings level is likely to be. However, it is open to argument whether it is length of education that causes higher earnings or some other factors which underlie both of these, for example pre-school influences, personal drive and determination or family background, which may facilitate access to certain jobs. Furthermore, only a proportion of any variation in earnings can be accounted for by educational achievement alone. Layard found that the spread of earnings within any educational group after a given number of years' work experience is only 7 per cent less than the spread of earnings in the whole population with the same number of years of work experience.[13] Even for people who enter the labour market with almost identical length of education and qualifications, and roughly similar personal characteristics, there are after a number of years in the labour market very large differences in earnings. None of this, however, is to deny the importance of education and skill acquisition in opening up higher earnings opportunities for individuals.

Broken Employment Histories

Periods of unemployment are closely linked with lower pay. Those who have experienced periods of unemployment tend to have lower than average weekly earnings. Data from the 1978 Cohort study of the unemployed men conducted by the then DHSS gives details of their employment status in the year prior to registration.[14] The study confirmed that a high proportion of unemployed men are more likely to have held semi-skilled or unskilled manual jobs and therefore received lower wages. Furthermore, those who remained unemployed for three months generally had low incomes when they were in work. Many males move regularly between unemployment and low-paid jobs; going back over a period of five years it appears that 78 per cent of the sample had at least one spell of registered unemployment; more than two in five had had at least two spells and a quarter had had three or more.

Interrupted work histories mean that employees are unable to move up in service-linked pay arrangements. Although incremental scales are more common in non-manual jobs, a broken employment record means that individuals' ability to increase their earnings through moving to different types of work or by taking on more responsibility, etc. are curtailed. Furthermore, many fringe benefits, such as eligibility for occupational sick pay, which help to boost the income of the lower-paid have length of service conditions attached.

Women are particularly likely to have interrupted work histories because so many leave work to have children. Interruptions associated with childbearing are often followed by part-time work and, compared with uninterrupted careers, lower hourly pay and lower occupational status.[15]

6 LOWER PAY AND POVERTY

In the public debate about low pay and poverty, there is on occasion a tendency to equate the two. This is wholly inappropriate. In general, the single most important means for individuals or households to avoid poverty is to have access to paid employment. As Table 7.9 indicates, the key determinant of where households are ranked in

Table 7.9   Household income and economic activity, 1986

	Households ranked by original income				
	Bottom fifth	Next fifth	Middle fifth	Next fifth	Top fifth
Economically active people per household	–	0.6	1.2	1.8	2.2

Source: *Social Trends*, 19, Central Statistical Office (HMSO, 1989).

terms of income is the number of economically active people per household. Those households in the lowest bands of income typically have no economically active members. The same is true of other countries. In the USA, for example, in 1984 a majority of adults heading poor families did no paid work at all and only 17 per cent worked full-time.[16]

The importance of participation in the labour market as a means of avoiding poverty lies not only in the immediate income which paid employment generates. Employment also provides an opportunity for individuals to acquire rights to a higher income in old age, through the accumulation of pension rights via SERPS, an occupational pension scheme or a personal pension. In brief, the most effective means for a household to avoid poverty or dependence on state benefits is, as a general principle, to have one or more of its members in economic activity.

The emphasis on the position of households in terms of income leads on to a second important point in the debate about the relationship between low pay and poverty. It should not be assumed that all those who receive lower pay live in lower-income households. The two cannot be equated in that simple manner. We have already seen for example that many young employees have relatively low earnings. This tells us nothing, however, about their household

Table 7.10   Families where both husband and wife work[a]

	Proportion of two-earner families	Proportion of low-paid wives[b]
In poverty (less than Supplementary Benefit)	0.6[c]	0.2
On the margins of poverty (at or above but less than 140% Supplementary Benefit)	4.1	1.2
Not poor	95.3	98.6
Total	100.0	100.0

Note:
[a]   Full-time workers only.
[b]   On the weekly definition.
[c]   Subject to statistical error.

circumstances, which will vary radically between those living at home with parents also in full-time employment and those heading up households in their own right. In practice, most young people with lower pay are unlikely to be in households experiencing or close to poverty. Table 7.9 has already illustrated the key importance of the number of economically active people per household, with the top fifth of households in terms of income containing on average more than two economically active people. Another illustration of the importance of the number of earners is provided by Bazen's analysis, showing only 0.6 per cent of two-earner families to be classified as in poverty, as Table 7.10 illustrates. Layard's study indicated that only one in five of those employees in the bottom 10 per cent of wage earners was also in the 10 per cent of households with the lowest incomes. All of this serves to emphasize that in judging incomes – and designing suitable measures to assist lower income groups – attention has to be focused on the household unit.

Although, as we have shown, the most important factor in moving households out of the low-income category is for them to have access to paid employment, there are nonetheless a large number of families where their income from paid employment is insufficient to achieve this. Table 7.11 illustrates the point.

Table 7.11 shows the number of families not on supplementary benefit, living both in and on the margins of poverty. The DSS include information on those living on 140 per cent of Supplementary Benefit. This reflects suggestions that, because families on supplementary

Table 7.11   Estimated numbers of families and persons with incomes close to Supplementary Benefit level, 1985

Employment status	Income below Supplementary Benefit level[2]		Income below 140% of Supplementary Benefit level*	
	Families (000)	Persons including children (000)	Families (000)	Persons including children (000)
1 Over pensionable age (60 for woman, 65 for man)	770	960	2720	3690
2 Under pensionable age: Family head or single person:				
a. Normally in full-time work or self-employed	240	560	980	2900
b. Sick or disabled for more than 3 months	50	60	210	330
c. Unemployed for more than 3 months	320	510	490	730
d. Others	230	340	510	810
Total under pensionable age:	830	1460	2190	4780
Of which large families (3 children or more)	50	250	220	1190
Total of 1 and 2	1600	2420	4910	8460

Source: DSS, analysis of Family Expenditure Survey and analysis of Annual Statistical Enquiry of Supplementary Benefit Claimants.

Notes:
*   Excluding Supplementary Benefits recipients.
1. The estimates of those not in receipt of supplementary benefit are based on DSS analysis of income and other information recorded by respondents to the 1985 Family Expenditure Survey (FES). The estimates of those in receipt of Supplementary Benefit are derived from the Annual Statistical Enquiries of Supplementary Benefit Claimants at December 1984 and February 1986. The estimates relate only to people living in private households; families and persons in institutions are not sampled in the FES.
2. The Supplementary Benefit level is taken as being the scale rate(s) appropriate to the family, using the long-term rates for pensioners only, but with heating additions for people of 70 years and over and children under five, included as part of the scale rate where the head is a householder. Income refers to net income *less* net housing costs *less* travel to work expenses where appropriate.
3. The comparison is based on the family's income in the normal employment situation of the family head. Therefore, where the head of the family has been off work due to sickness or unemployment for less than thirteen weeks at the time of the survey, the family's normal income when the head was in work was used in determining the level of income.

benefit received additional special needs payments, the basic rate of Supplementary Benefit is not an accurate measure of what the State regards as a minimum income. In addition, some claimants received the long-term rate of Supplementary Benefit which was specifically paid to reflect the fact that the basic rate of Supplementary Benefit cannot meet long-term needs adequately. Those where the head of the family was in full-time employment or self-employed form roughly 15 per cent of families in poverty, around 240,000 families.

One of the reasons that so many families with access to paid employment are nonetheless in poverty is their failure to take up the benefits to which they are entitled. Various benefits are available to families where the head of the household is in paid work, the most important being Family Credit and Housing Benefit. The take-up of Family Income Supplement (the forerunner of Family Credit) was traditionally low, at around 50 per cent; estimates in 1983-4 for example indicated that 150,000 of those entitled to claim did not do so.[17] On average, it was estimated that non-claimants were losing £7.10 per week. In its original predictions, government estimated that around 750,000 families would be eligible for Family Credit, but this figure was revised down to 500,000 in March 1989.[18] Government has indicated that only around 30–40 per cent of those eligible are claiming Family Credit, leaving around 350,000 in poverty if the level of Family Credit is taken as the poverty line. Of course, a proportion of these are likely to be above the level of Income Support and thus not in poverty according to that measure.

The take-up of Housing Benefit is also low. Around 60 per cent of those eligible do not claim. On average £2.30 per week at 1984 estimates was unclaimed. With the introduction of the Community Charge all social security benefit recipients will have to pay a proportion of their Community Charge and of their incomes or benefit payments. This could lead to a drop in income and an increase in those below the poverty line, judged by Income Support levels. In addition, Housing Benefit may not meet a family or an individual's full housing costs where these costs are deemed to be more than is judged reasonable.

One-parent families are particularly likely to experience poverty. This is partly because in employment women, who form the major breadwinner in most one-parent families, are more likely to be in occupations and sectors where lower pay levels predominate. In addition, those unemployed single parents dependent on social security benefits are likely to find that moving into paid work is not financially attractive, particularly after taking account of childcare costs, because total net family income is less in employment than in unemployment.

7 MEASURES TO AID THE LOWER-PAID

In this section, we look briefly at the main existing mechanisms for providing assistance for those in lower paid employment. We then go on to assess one particular proposal which has been put forward periodically over the years, namely the concept of a Statutory National Minimum Wage. We conclude by outlining the CBI's favoured strategies for safeguarding the incomes of lower earners and enhancing the employment and earnings opportunities of those who might otherwise find themselves permanently outside employment or confined to lower paid jobs.

Existing State Assistance

Over the years, many different types of regulation for the lower paid have been debated and a variety of measures put into effect. A concise chronology of these is attached in Appendix 1. At present the two principal mechanisms through which the government seeks to safeguard or assist the lower-paid are:

- the Wages Council system; and
- Family Credit, which provides state benefits for those in work.

The operation of the 24 Wages Councils (plus two which have ceased to function in practice) is now regulated by the Wages Act 1986. This gives them powers to set minimum adult basic rates and overtime rates for some 2.75 million workers, primarily in such sectors as retailing, hotels and catering and clothing manufacture. A further 400,000 or so workers in agriculture in England and Wales and in Scotland have statutory minimum rates and other conditions set by Wages Boards under the Agricultural Wages Acts. The Wages Councils and Boards have, of course, a lengthy history, dating back to the Trade Boards established in 1909. Over the years, the various Boards and Councils and the legislation governing them have been revised to reflect changing needs and circumstances, most recently by a significant reduction in the scope of Wages Council Orders under the terms of the 1986 Act. Details of the minimum weekly rates set by the 24 Wages Councils are shown in Appendix 2.

While Wages Council legislation has involved the setting of blanket minimum pay levels with no regard to personal circumstances, Family Credit (previously Family Income Supplement) is specifically designed to assist those heads of families with children (whether male or female or single parent) whose wages are deemed to be insufficient to meet their needs. Effectively the scheme is designed to ensure that families are able to attain a minimum standard of living.

Family Credit is payable where the net weekly income of the family is below the so called 'applicable amount' (in August 1989, £54.80); in such cases the maximum credit is payable. Where earnings are above the applicable amount family credit is reduced by 70 per cent of the person's earnings where these exceed the applicable amount. The maximum Family Credit was based on the following rates in August 1989:

	£
Adult credit	33.60
Child – under 11	37.30
11–15	12.90
16–17	16.35
18	23.30

Family Credit replaced Family Income Supplement (FIS) in April 1988. The two schemes operated on similar lines but Family Income Supplement was calculated on gross earnings. This led to the creation of a very high marginal rate of taxation, over 100 per cent in some instances, causing some families to experience a drop in net income when their earnings rose. Furthermore, under the Family Income Supplement scheme benefit rates for dependants were lower for Family Income Supplement recipients than for unemployed claimants and therefore some families, particularly those with large numbers of children, could find themselves better off out of work.

The introduction of Family Credit has not been an immediate success in terms of its take up. Family Income Supplement was subject to very low take-up rates. In 1987 some 220,000 families were in receipt of Family Income Supplement. However DSS estimates indicated that only around 50 per cent of those people entitled to claim actually did so.[19] Early indications were that take-up rates for Family Credit were lower than for Family Income Supplement, perhaps around 30 to 40 per cent, as we noted earlier, and the government has recently relaunched the scheme. The low take-up of the scheme effectively means that a significant number of families are living on an income which the government has defined as insufficient to meet their basic needs, and they therefore could be considered as living in poverty. The reasons for low take-up are complex but a proportion are likely to be unaware of the scheme or if they are aware of it, wrongly believe that they are not entitled to claim. Some reports have suggested that because the benefit is now called 'Credit' potential recipients believe they will have to repay it at some future date – as with Social Fund Payments. In addition, some of those eligible may not claim because they feel stigmatized by receiving 'state handouts', or because they wish to remain independent or they may be discouraged by what they may perceive as complex and intrusive claim procedures.

A number of other measures have been adopted or considered over the years by governments to assist the lower-paid. Significant among these have been the Fair Wages Resolution, abolished in 1983, which required government contractors to observe the terms of relevant industry agreements or, in their absence, the general level of terms and conditions in the industry. Schedule 11 of the Employment Protection Act, repealed in 1980, applied broadly similar provisions to all employers. It should be emphasized that in both instances these measures were primarily used by relatively well paid groups of employees as means of side-stepping the rigours of pay policy in the 1970s, and not to improve the position of the lower paid.

The Concept of a Statutory National Minimum Wage

Since early in this century, the concept of a Statutory National Minimum Wage has been put forward from time to time. The most recent government inquiry into the possibility of a National Minimum Wage was conducted by an interdepartmental committee of officials in the 1960s. The inquiry working party published a report for discussion in 1969, looking at the arguments for and against a National Minimum Wage, possible forms it might take and the costs and other consequences.[20] The conclusions of that report were very far from endorsing the concept of a National Minimum Wage as an effective means of aiding those on low incomes, and no further action was taken.

Apart from government measures and initiatives, the issue of minimum pay targets has arisen regularly in negotiations in individual organizations and industries. In many instances trade unions have submitted claims based on the low-pay bargaining targets, which have been set by the TUC since the start of the 1970s. In some instances, employers have been prepared to set defined minimum pay levels for employees, through such mechanisms as minimum earnings levels (MELS) or minimum salary levels for particular age groups, which reflect and suit their organizations' particular circumstances. Such minima are, of course, not related to the domestic circumstances of individual employees. In a break with their past approaches, both the TUC and Labour Party approved a statement on 'Low Pay: Policies and Priorities' in 1986, which has as its central feature the introduction of a national minimum wage with statutory backing.

The CBI has repeatedly stated the desire of its members to see further progress towards a high-pay, high-performance economy. The key national goal of improving productivity at least to the levels achieved by other industrialized countries, and so enabling rewards to be improved significantly, has widespread backing and acceptance among employers. The CBI does not, however, believe that the adoption of minimum wage legislation is an appropriate or realistic means of raising the real pay levels of the lower-paid or that it represents an effective means of tackling poverty.

In the short term, the introduction of national minimum wage legislation could result in an immediate reduction in jobs for the lower-paid. Certain 'marginal' jobs would be lost since the revenue they generate would be insufficient to meet the additional costs of a minimum wage. Such reduction in employment would particularly affect the unskilled, inexperienced, younger adults and those approaching retirement age, the groups already most severely affected by unemployment. It is of course impossible to calculate the likely extent of such job losses, and the scale of them would vary depending on the level at which any minimum wage were pitched.

At least as significant as the impact on those jobs with pay levels falling below the minimum wage would be the impact at higher levels of the pay structure. There would be pressure from those employees just above the minimum wage threshold for pay rises to maintain their differentials over those being raised to the minimum wage, with knock-on effects throughout the pay structure of companies. The resulting addition to total employment costs could have serious adverse consequences on the UK's competitive position. Such effects would, moreover, not be a one-off occurrence. Every time the minimum wage was increased, there would be further losses of 'marginal' jobs and further ripples through the pay structure. If any attempts were made to set the minimum wage as a percentage of average earnings, every increase in it would produce an increase in the average, triggering a further rise in the minimum wage and so setting in motion an ever-rising spiral in labour costs. Employers would inevitably respond to such increases by further shedding of labour in an attempt to contain pay costs.

The CBI is wholly opposed to the idea that employers should be required to establish minimum pay levels which take no account of the circumstances of individual employers, of the nature of the work being undertaken, of the varying skills, abilities and responsibilities of individual employees and of variations in work patterns and in productivity between units. The emphasis on weekly cash earnings, moreover, fails to take account of the fact that employees benefit from remuneration packages made up of a variety of different elements. Employees may have relatively low weekly earnings, but have proportionately higher benefits in terms of pension, sick pay and holiday provisions.

The concept of a minimum wage has been put forward as a means of alleviating poverty. In practice, it would not be an effective method of doing so. The majority of those who stand to benefit from the introduction of a statutory minimum wage, always assuming that they were still in employment, would be likely to be younger single people or second earners in households with more than one source of income from employment. As we have already seen, the reality is that the great majority of those households with the lowest incomes do not contain any wage earner at all. They would, therefore, not benefit from the introduction of a minimum wage. Indeed, to the extent that such a policy initiative would result in higher prices and reduce their prospects of employment, they could actually be made worse off.

Alternative Strategies to Assist Low-income Families in Work

What, then, should be done to assist those employees in lower income households and to help those from households not currently represented in the labour market into paid employment? In this section, we outline some of the approaches favoured by the CBI. Given the scale of the issues, this is necessarily not a comprehensive or detailed programme for action. Rather, we have endeavoured to identify a limited number of areas and options for consideration where action might be taken which would have the effect of raising incomes or enhancing earnings opportunities without reducing work incentives or imposing prohibitive costs on the state.

Social Security-based Approaches

In its submission on lower incomes to the Royal Commission on the Distribution of Income and Wealth in 1977, the CBI stated that any general evaluations of sufficiency must compare the total income of a 'living unit' or household with its needs. The CBI continues to believe that if the government wishes to provide assistance to defined categories of households with incomes falling below a specified threshold, whether or not the head of household is in employment, such assistance is best provided directly by the state. Moreover, in view of the limited resources available, and the importance of maximizing assistance for those in need, the most appropriate approach is a careful targeting of state benefits.

One of the most obvious ways of taking working families out of poverty is to increase the take-up of social security benefits such as Family Credit and Housing Benefit. However, whilst this is easy to propose, it is apparently very difficult to achieve. The reasons why eligible families do not claim are varied but some of the money spent on advertising Family Credit could perhaps usefully be spent on ascertaining, in a more specific fashion than hitherto, the reasons for such poor take-up.

If the take-up of Family Credit cannot be improved, there would appear merit in pursuing the idea of building upon the Child Benefit system. Child Benefit has a take up level of almost 100 per cent and One Parent Benefit a take up of 93 per cent. Child Benefit is not taken into account when assessing income for Family Credit purposes and therefore an increase would directly raise family income. A rise would not adversely affect incentives to work because Child Benefit is regarded as income for Income Support purposes, and therefore any rise in Child Benefit would be offset by a decrease in Income Support.

The advantages of such an approach would be that it would directly raise the incomes of those families most likely to experience poverty – those with many children where the head of the household is in paid work – without damaging work incentives. However, in order to contain costs some way of clawing back benefit from those on higher incomes would need to be found. With the computerization of Inland

Revenue records not far away, this would presumably be feasible in due course.

Reducing the earnings threshold for Family Credit could also help those families where the breadwinner is able to obtain or take up only part-time work. This would be the case for many single-parent families, for example. At present the earning threshold is 24 hours or more per week and this might be reduced, in the first instance perhaps for one-parent families only.

In terms of extending assistance to low-earning households without children, one possibility is that the Family Credit scheme could be extended to help the other group for whom low wages are most likely to lead to poverty – older workers. The French example might well provide some lessons. The French government has recently finalized details of the 'minimum integration income' (RMI) which is designed to help those in poverty.[21] The amount payable under the RMI Scheme is calculated by taking into account the household income and topping it up to a level laid down by law. This level has been set on the principle that it should not be so near the statutory minimum wage as to discourage people from taking up employment. However those with part-time jobs or on training courses will be eligible, and in order that they are encouraged to take work or undergo training they will be able to earn up to a certain amount before the RMI is reduced. The scale rates of RMI vary according to whether the household consists of a single person, a single parent, a childless couple and according to the number of children. The scheme also has the benefit of ensuring that recipients obtain all the benefits to which they are entitled.

Labour Market Approaches

Major changes are currently taking place in the labour market and many of these will have a beneficial impact on those who experience poverty through low wages or inability to find paid work. The demographic changes in the composition of the labour force, with fewer younger people entering the labour force is predicted to give rise to a substantial increase in the number of women entering work. Of the new jobs which will be created up to the year 2000, some 80 per cent are expected to be taken by women.[22] Thus it is likely that many more families will be two-earner households taking many more households out of the lower-income category. Furthermore the introduction of career break schemes, avoiding the penalties of broken employment histories, and rising skill levels of women generally should lead to a consequent rise in women's pay rates.

Probably the single biggest barrier faced by the growing number of women with children wishing to return to paid employment is that of finding reliable, affordable childcare. In order to facilitate the return of women to work, the government should promote increased childcare provision. Many employers are looking at ways of helping with provision of childcare, and the removal or reduction of the tax liability on employees who use employer sponsored childcare arrangements would certainly help. More general tax relief on childcare costs would also be of value, although employers recognize that the issues here are far from simple. Local government schemes, adequately supported by central government, for out-of-school childcare should also be developed and many companies would be willing to help sponsor such schemes. The CBI believes there is an urgent need for the government to give serious consideration to all these possibilities.

The demographic trends towards an older workforce should assist in the breakdown of the dominant youth culture and lead to a greater appreciation of the role of older employees in the workplace and, through re-training where necessary, to increased wage levels. Among young people, the CBI's 'careership' proposals, by enhancing training opportunities for young people and therefore their skill levels, should help to deal with the problem of life-cycle poverty in the longer term. Projections of future skill needs show a continuing fall in the numbers of unskilled jobs. It has been argued that the most effective way of generating more youth training is to reduce trainee wages. High trainee wages erode the differential between an unskilled and a skilled job and act as a disincentive for both individuals and employers to train. However the CBI does not believe it is practical to hold down youth wages, as the market trend is in the alternative direction.

Consequently the CBI's Careership proposals[23] seek to provide all 16-year-olds entering the labour market with an education and training credit from the Exchequer and an employment contract from the employer. This would ensure that the choice between a job *or* training was replaced by a job *and* training. All young people would have the means of continuing in some form of education and training post-16, and youth wages would find their own market level. This would have the advantage that more young people would reach higher skill levels during foundation training which would enhance their job prospects in the short term. In addition, the broader base of training for this age group would make for easier career changes and updating of skills in later life.

We should not overlook possible scope for enhancing skill levels, and therefore earnings opportunities, for those lower-skilled, lower-paid employees currently in the workforce. Many unskilled workers are unaware how to go about enhancing their existing skills or finding out about suitable training courses. Full-Employment UK has identified a number of short-term options which could enable lower-paid workers to raise their skill levels. These ideas seem worthy of consideration by government. They include providing unskilled workers with access to Job Centres (outside normal working hours); in-depth interviews with employment advisers to draw up 'Job Plans'; career development loans; and low-interest enterprise loans for those wanting to become self-employed.[24]

Incentives for Employment

Despite all the reforms of recent years, the benefit and tax regimes still impose disincentives for certain groups to take up paid employment, unless they make an improbable immediate move into highly-paid work.[25] No one would argue that tackling these is a simple matter. What is important is that constant efforts should be made to identify and analyze them and to find mechanisms for minimising their impact.

One particular area of concern to the CBI is the present low levels of earnings disregards for many of the unemployed. While allowing the unemployed to earn certain amounts without loss of benefits has its critics,[26] the CBI believe that such measures are of value as they encourage people to maintain contact with the labour market, its disciplines and potential job openings. Given that part-time jobs represent the fastest growing type of employment, measures which enable at least certain groups of unemployed people to take such jobs without experiencing a crippling withdrawal of benefit have come in for well-merited consideration.[27] Measures of this type could play an important role in helping individuals back into the workforce and hence opening up opportunities for them to raise their, and their households', incomes.

Another area which has long been of concern to the CBI is that of National Insurance. The Government has over recent years introduced various changes to the operation of the National Insurance system, these have been designed to increase the take-home pay of lower-paid groups and encourage employers to offer more jobs by reducing employment costs. The changes in 1985 introduced lower National Insurance bands for those on low earnings and removed the very high marginal tax rates which occurred when employees crossed the lower earnings limit (LEL). However while the introduction of the various bands ameliorates the problem for those crossing the LEL it introduces similar disincentives to those on higher wages as employees were reluctant to raise their earnings by, for example, working extra hours where this could take them into a higher National Insurance bracket.

In the Chancellor's 1989 spring Budget changes, which came into operation in October 1989, were announced. Under the new arrangements, welcomed by the CBI as a first step, all employees were to pay contributions of 2 per cent of £43 once their earnings exceeded this level, and 9 per cent of the excess of their earnings over £43 until earnings reached £325. For employees the changes meant that the National Insurance system more nearly follow the tax system with an effective single rate of tax of 9 per cent with an allowance of £43, plus a charge of 82p (2 per cent of £43) for entering the system.

For those families with children the rise in net wages resulting from reduced National Insurance liability will be offset by the similar reductions in Family Credit and Housing Benefit. However, the change will benefit lower-paid women (in two-income households with no Family Credit entitlement) and young people. The changes will remove any disincentive upon employees to work extra hours or increase piecework productivity, or indeed to take on extra responsibility or training whereby small increases in earnings were initially on offer.

However, the varying National Insurance bands will still lead to anomalies from the employers' point of view. He or she will still experience the situation where a relatively small increase in gross pay can lead to a significant leap in National Insurance liability. This is bound to distort internal labour markets and affect employers' willingness to offer extra hours or wage increases. In the light of this and in the interests of simplicity, the CBI has called on the Chancellor to introduce the same changes to employers' National Insurance liability as he has for employees. In the longer term it would seem sensible to remove what is effectively a charge on entering the National Insurance system for both employees and employer.

8   CONCLUSION

In section 7 we focused on existing measures to assist the lower-paid and promote paid employment to counter poverty and possible new or alternative strategies for the future. Throughout, the emphasis has been on measures geared to help individuals or particular households. It would be wholly wrong, however, to ignore the wider perspective. For all of those on lower incomes, by far the most effective means of improving their position is to create a more wealthy total economy, founded on an internationally competitive and profitable business sector. If measures are adopted supposedly to assist lower income groups which have the effect of undermining competitiveness and investment, then in the not too long run they will be clearly self-defeating. What are needed are measures that so far as possible work with the drive towards a more successful economy, encouraging those who can to enter employment, enhancing their skill levels and hence their earning power. Only through such a strategy will we achieve the high-productivity, high-pay, high-employment economy, able to provide high standards of provision for those not able to participate actively in the labour market, that we all want to see.

Appendix 1: Minimum Wage Regulation in the UK: A Short Chronology

1888	Select Committee on the 'Sweating' System appointed; 1890 Report opposed legal regulation of wages in 'sweated' industries but proposed Fair Wages Resolutions for public contracts
1891	First Fair Wages Resolution adopted by Government
1906	Inquiry by Earnings and Hours Committee made authoritative wages data available for the first time
1908	Select Committee on Homework report showed 'sweating' prevailed amongst homeworkers and factory workers Recommended establishment of trade boards
1909	Trade Boards Act established Boards to set rates for 200,000 workers in four trades where wages were 'exceptionally low as compared with that in other employments' Fair Wages Resolution revised
1913	Trade Boards Act extended to five more trades
First World War	Minimum wages guaranteed to munitions workers (1916) and agricultural workers (1917)
1918	Wages (Temporary Regulation) Act extending protection of a minimum wage; Labour Party demand national minimum wage; Trade Boards (Amendment) Act, on advice of Whitley Committee, empowered Minister of Labour to create additional Boards easily; intended to encourage free collective bargaining where labour unorganized; Boards able to fix piece-rates, overtime rates and point at which payable
1919	Tripartite National Industrial Conference endorsed concept of statutory national minimum wage but no legislation resulted
1921	63 Boards covering 3 million workers
1922	Cave Committee recommended repeal of 1918 Amending Act
1924	Agricultural Wages Act set up Agricultural Wages Boards
1938	Holidays with Pay Act enabled Boards to require up to 1 week's holiday with pay
1924–39	Advent of seven more Boards plus Road Haulage Wages Board, covering a further 1.5 million workers
1939	Northern Irish Agricultural Wages Board inaugurated
Second World War	Compulsory arbitration, lessening Boards' significance

1944	Catering Wages Act
1945	Wages Councils Act converted Trades Boards into Wages Councils, extending their powers to deal with all aspects of pay and holidays; similar Act in Northern Ireland.
1946	Revised Fair Wages Resolution
1948	Agricultural Wages Act
1949	Agricultural Wages (Scotland) Act; in England, Scotland and Wales 400,000 workers covered
1953	Peak of 66 Wages Councils embracing 3.5 million workers
1959	Wages Councils Act, a consolidation measure
1968	Donovan Report reflected belief that Councils inhibited free collective bargaining and had not improved the relative position of the low-paid
1969	Government appointed Interdepartmental Working Party of officials to examine idea of statutory minimum wage
1970	TUC recommended voluntary national minimum wage
1971	Commission on Industrial Relations recommended elimination of five councils
1974–9	Labour government merged some Councils and abolished others
1975	Employment Protection Act enabled councils to fix, in addition to minimum pay and holidays, 'any other terms and conditions (of employment)'; also gave Secretary of State power to convert councils into Statutory Joint Industry Councils (SJICs); Schedule 11 requires employers to observe industry-wide agreements or, if none, to operate pay and conditions in line with others in same sector and locality
1979	Wages Councils Act, consolidating Employment Protection Act amendments
1980	Repeal of Employment Protection Act Schedule 11
1983	Abolition of the Fair Wages Resolution
1985	Government consultative paper set out options for Councils' reform or abolition
1986	Having given notice of intention to deratify ILO Convention No. 26 requiring signatories to maintain minimum wage fixing machinery, government enacted Wages Act 1986; it: – excluded workers under 21 years old from Wages Orders – restricted Councils to setting single minimum hourly rate, single overtime rate, plus ceiling on deductions for meals and accommodation – simplified procedures for abolition of individual Councils – abolished concept of SJICs
1986	TUC and Labour party adopt statutory minimum wage as policy. Reformed system of 26 councils fully operational, covering 2.25 million workers; in addition, Agricultural Boards, unaffected by 1986 Act, continue to set range of rates, overtime, piece-rates, holidays, holiday pay and sick pay
1988	Government consultation paper proposed abolition of Wages Council system

Appendix 2: Wages Council Rates, August 1989[28]

	Nos of workers aged 21 and over covered	Min. weekly rate (£)
Aerated water	5500	90.42
Boot & shoe repairing	5000	90.87
Button manufacturing	1000	82.89
Clothing manufacturing	147,000	82.19
Coffin furniture & cerement making	200	92.82
Cotton waste reclamation	300	82.48
Fur	1500	86.97
General waste materials reclamation	13,000	83.85
Hairdressing undertakings	64,000	85.80
Hat, cap & millinery	4000	82.19
Laundry	26,000	91.65
Licensed non-residential establishments	492,000	89.70
Licensed residential establishments	379,000	82.68
Linen & cotton handkerchief & household goods & linen piece goods	2500	85.80
Made-up textiles	3000	78.00
Ostrich & fancy feather & artificial flower	500	83.07
Perambulator & invalid carriage	2000	97.11
Retail bespoke tailoring	4000	97.50
Retail food & allied trades	465,000	96.72
Retail trades (non-food)	745,000	97.11
Rope, twine & net	2500	84.63
Sack & bag	1000	83.46
Toy manufacturing	11,000	84.43
Unlicensed places of refreshment	96,000	92.82

Notes

1. Produced by the Employment Affairs Directorate (September 1989).
2. Rowntree, B. S. (1902) *Poverty: A Study of Town Life* (London: Macmillan).
3. Rowntree, B. S. (1941) *Poverty and Progress* (London: Longmans Green).
4. Cmd 6404 (1942) *Social Insurance and Allied Services* (London: HMSO).
5. Townsend, P. (1979) *Poverty In The United Kingdom* (Harmondsworth: Penguin).
6. HMSO (1969) *A National Minimum Wage*.
7. Bazen, S. (1985) *Low Wages, Family Circumstances and Minimum Wage Legislation*, Family Income Support, part 10, no. 643 (May) (London: Policy Studies Institute).
8. Cmnd 4811 (1971) *Report of the Committee of Inquiry on Small Firms* (Bolton Report) (London: HMSO).
9. Cmnd 4093 (1969) *Fourth General Report, National Board for Prices and Incomes* (London: HMSO).
10. Duncan, C. (1981) *Low Pay – Its Causes and The Post-War Trade Union Response* (London: John Wiley).
11. *Department of Employment Gazette* (January 1977).
12. Metcalf, D. and Nickell, S. (1979 *Occupational Mobility In Britain*, Centre for Labour Economics, discussion paper, 60.
13. Layard, R. *et al.* (1978) *The Causes of Poverty*, Background Paper, Royal Commission on the Distribution of Income and Wealth (London: HMSO).
14. *For Richer, For Poorer?* (1984) DHSS Cohort Study of Unemployed Men, Research Report, 11 (London: HMSO).
15. Joshi, H. (1984) *Women's Participation In Paid Work: Further Analysis of the Women and Employment Survey* (London: Department of Employment).
16. Mead, L. (March 1988) 'The New Welfare Debate', *Commentary*.
17. *Social Security Statistics*.
18. *DSS Press Release* (19 March 1989).
19. *Social Security Statistics*.
20. HMSO (1969).
21. 'Minimum Integration Income In Force', *European Industrial Relations Review* (April 1989).
22. Labour Force Outlook to the Year 2000, *Employment Gazette* (April 1989).
23. *Towards A Skills Revolution – A Youth Charter*, CBI, 1989.
24. *The Next Rung Up*, Full Employment UK, (May/June 1989).
25. For a recent short analysis see Brandon Rhys Williams and Hermione Parker, *Stepping Stones to Independence* (Aberdeen University Press, 1989).
26. For example the critique of US disregards in Charles Murray, *Losing Ground* (Basic Books, 1984).

27. *The Employment Patterns of the Over-50s*, Report by the House of
     Commons Employment Committee.
28. *Industrial Relations Review & Report* (August 1989).

8 Low Pay – A Trade Union Perspective[1]

TUC

1 INTRODUCTION

The issue of low pay is one of traditional and legitimate trade union concern. Whilst the TUC would not accept that there is anything self-evident or self-perpetuating about the poor always being with us, the existence of underpaid, underprivileged and undervalued workers poses considerable economic and social problems and costs. Substantial evidence continues to emerge about the existence of an underclass of marginal workers who are effectively entrapped in those areas of employment which attract the lowest wage rates, the worst working conditions and, perhaps most worrying, the least chance of upward mobility within the job market. However, the profile of this worker has changed since the Beveridge prototype. It is no longer the case that the marginal worker is male and working in a sweatshop in a declining region of the UK. It is increasingly the case that such workers are female and frequently employed part-time in the public sector.

The issue is not simply one of social justice or political embarrassment. The macro-economic implications of low pay – so often ignored in the search for 'flexible labour markets' – entail not only wasted resources in terms of ill-trained, low-skilled, low-productivity workers (this in a time of a sharp fall in young entrants to the labour market, NEDO, 1988) but also a cost in terms of lost investment opportunities, and therefore reduced competitiveness.

Trade union organization, representation and participation in collective bargaining improve the wages of the low-paid, but by itself collective bargaining is not enough. Although European evidence suggests that strong and effective collective bargaining structures may go a long way to improve the position of the low-paid, it is increasingly questionable that in the UK such systems can adequately protect the low-paid worker. That is why the TUC is committed to the introduction of a statutory National Minimum Wage. This too, however, may not be sufficient. Those in poverty are not simply the

263

victims of poor employment prospects. Any comprehensive set of measures designed to improve their lot must also include reform of the tax–benefit structure to provide realistic incentives to those on the margins of the job market. They must also include a well thought out and consistent set of measures designed to improve access to the labour market, and especially for lone parents, to make it possible for many marginal workers actually to take up the opportunities available to them.

The Low-pay Problem

The problem of low pay has long been recognized in industrial societies. In the early part of this century, for example, legislation was introduced to establish minimum wages in 'sweated' trades, and regulation of minimum wage levels was widely carried out by Wages Councils. By 1987 about 2½ million workers were still covered by some sort of statutory provision which set minimum wages.

Low pay is heavily concentrated among certain groups in the labour force, notably women, young workers and workers from ethnic minority groups. Evidence from the New Earnings Survey (NES) shows that the problem is not confined to the traditional sweated industries in the private sector, but it is also common in the public sector, notably in the NHS and some local government services. However, low pay is concentrated in certain industries – notably clothing and hotel and catering – and in certain occupations, such as clerical workers and labourers. Low pay is found in all regions of the country although the South East has a lower share of low-paid workers in the regional workforce. Finally low pay is concentrated among the lower age groups up to the mid-20s and the older age groups from the mid-40s onwards.

On the TUC definition of low pay (two-thirds gross weekly male manual earnings) there are over 3 million full-time adult low-paid workers in Britain, about a fifth of the workforce. And there are probably even more low-paid part-time workers (measured in terms of the hourly equivalent to two-thirds of weekly earnings) raising the overall total to well over 6 million. Excluding overtime would raise the number of full-time adult low-paid workers on the TUC definition by about 1 million. The great majority of these low-paid workers – some two-thirds of the full-time workers and almost all the part-time workers – are women. There are about equal numbers of low-paid manual and non-manual full-time workers, but this is due to the very large numbers of low-paid non-manual women in the clerical and shopworking occupations.

Trends in Low Pay

Over the past ten years there have been conflicting influences on the number of low-paid jobs. Many low-paid full-time jobs were lost as a result of increasing unemployment which particularly affected lower grades, and structural change away from traditional manual to higher grade white collar jobs. According to the 1988 Labour Force Survey, most of the new jobs in the 1980s have been in the professional, managerial and associated jobs, and although not all are well paid, the overall effect is to reduce the proportion of low-paid jobs. This trend is set to continue into the 1990s. The number of low-paid full-time jobs on the TUC's definition has hardly changed since 1979.

The number of part-time jobs has dramatically increased, and there is a clear association between the growth of part-time work and low pay, because much of the increase is taking place in traditional low-pay industries. Part-time workers have experienced relatively low real increases in their pay. New Earnings Survey figures for part-time women indicate an annual real increase of about 1½ per cent over the last ten years. This compares with 2½ per cent for male average earnings. However, as these figures exclude about a third of the lowest-paid workers (who may be expected to have fared worse) the underlying average real increase for part-time workers will be significantly less.

Over the past ten years, however, the structure of earnings has spread outwards as those in higher-paid jobs have secured progressively higher increases. In the groups surveyed by the New Earnings Survey (which exclude top executive salaries, the subject of recent publicity about higher increases) over the years since 1979, the lowest decile adult male full-time workers have obtained a real increase of about 1 per cent a year, compared with an increase in average male earnings of over 2½ per cent and an increase in highest decile male earnings of nearly 3½ per cent. Lowest decile full-time male earnings as a percentage of the corresponding highest decile rose from 40.7 per cent in 1970 to 42 per cent in 1979 and thereafter declined to 34 per cent by 1988. These trends towards ever greater inequality, which have been consistent over the 1980s, show every sign of continuing. Historical figures of lowest decile earnings show a long-term relative stability in the British earnings structure which seems to have obtained over the past 100 years. New Earnings Survey figures show a clear narrowing of the spread between low and median earnings over the 1970s, presumably under the influence of policies specifically designed to help the lower-paid and women, including equal pay legislation.

Low Pay in Europe

Most European Community countries have adopted some form of minimum wage legislation (see Appendix 1). The main reasons for this include providing a 'decent wage', combating poverty, reducing inequality and discrimination and eliminating competition based on low wages. Generally, other countries in Europe rely upon either a statutory minimum wage – as in the case of France and Spain – or extensive coverage of the labour market by collective agreements and a solidaristic labour policy: the UK does neither. According to work by the Low Pay Unit (Minford, 1989) in the 'league' of minimum agreed rates the UK minimum – which covers just 11 per cent of the workforce – ranks with that of Greece, Spain and Portugal.

As Britain moves towards 1992 debate continues – in government circles at least – on the issue of the rights of workers. In the long term the provisions of the 'Social Charter' and the notion of a European 'rate for the job' may offer the best hope for Britain's marginal workers.

Empirically, there is little to suggest that countries that do undertake widespread protection of their low-paid workers are less competitive or less prosperous than the UK. The macro-economic consequences of low pay are indeed far more complex and the relationship between pay, employment and economic performance is examined in more detail in section 2.

2 LOW PAY, GROWTH AND EMPLOYMENT

Low Pay and Economic Performance

Low pay is often and rightly discussed in terms of its social implications. However, low pay has an equally important macro-economic dimension. The TUC has consistently argued that low pay is a cause of under-investment in human and physical capital, with implications for growth, industrial competitiveness and employment. The recent increases in productivity in British industry should not obscure the fact that these gains are mainly in manufacturing, and they still leave Britain far behind the level of productivity in the United States, Germany and other advanced industrialized countries. There are few examples of successful advanced industrialized countries based on a low pay/low productivity economy. Those European countries with the highest standards of living and the strongest economies are those which have moved down the path towards high pay – high productivity economies. The issue is a dynamic one. Countries that grow fast have higher pay levels and higher productivity rates. A virtuous circle is thus engendered with causal links working in both directions.

Government policies appear to equate greater labour flexibility with the creation of more low-paid and insecure jobs. Such policies are in fact more likely to increase labour market rigidity by on the one hand creating a climate of insecurity which resists change and on the other leaving workers ill-equipped to respond to the changes being demanded by the introduction of new technology. If real flexibility is their aim, they are counter-productive. Common characteristics of low-pay industries are the relatively labour intensive nature of production and an unwillingness or inability to increase productivity by capital investment or innovation or through improvements in human capital. Reliance on low-paid labour acts as a strong disincentive both to invest in expensive capital equipment or indeed to train workers, and is often seen as the only way of maintaining a competitive edge.

The argument about the substitution of labour and capital cannot be taken too far, however. The level of technology is just as important a determinant of employment as the relative price of labour and capital. For example, it is highly unlikely that motor car manufacturers would give up the advanced robotic technology being introduced into their factories and employ more workers even if wages were cut significantly. Instead, the introduction of new machines, technology and production methods is increasingly being accompanied by investment in human capital, and this is necessarily reflected in higher pay levels and improved employment conditions. The importance of this is only slowly being recognized. Recent comparative studies of the German and UK furniture and clothing industries, for example, by the National Institute for Economic and Social Research (NIESR) found factories using similar equipment but with big differences in efficiency (in favour of Germany) reflecting in part greater skill levels in both management and workers in the German industries (Steedman and Wagner, 1987 and 1989).

Low pay is not simply a symptom of Britain's low-productivity industrial structure but one of the fundamental barriers to transforming the economy. The weaknesses in the national economy – the under-investment in training, new technology and new capacity and the relatively inefficient way in which assets are used – are in part caused by too many people employed in low productivity sectors where investment in people and capital is deterred by low pay. In the public sector this relationship is less recognized because of the problem of measuring the productivity of workers in health, education, and social services. Yet the problem of pay is one factor in the development of shortages in teachers, social workers, and nurses, all of which will in turn hamper the long-run development of the economy. In short, failure to address the problem of low pay will in the long term endanger policies designed to transform Britain into a high-productivity economy.

Government policies have tried to reduce unemployment by promoting low paid jobs, for example by subsidies to the employer (e.g. Young Workers Scheme). The evidence to date suggests that subsidizing low-pay employment has been a costly failure with many firms simply replacing existing workers with cheaper subsidized labour. Equally, there is little evidence to back the view that benefits are too high relative to wages to allow unemployment to fall. The 1988 Labour Force Survey, for example, shows that out of over 600,000 'inactive' claimants (i.e. not counted as unemployed according to international definitions), only 40,000 were inactive because they did not want or need work – about 2 per cent of all claimants on the register. An analysis of the British labour market and unemployment by the National Economic Development Office in March 1987 concluded: 'the rational case for preferring State benefits to paid work has not become stronger, so that there has undoubtedly been a large involuntary element in the increase in British unemployment' (NEDC, 1987). The evidence shows little or no increase in the ratio between benefits and earnings in the 1980s compared with the 1960s and 1970s.

According to the 1988 Labour Force Survey, there were nearly 0.8 million unregistered unemployed, on Organisation for Economic Cooperation and Development/International Labour Office

(OECD/ILO) definitions; a further 0.2 million 'discouraged workers' who are available to start work, but who believe there are no jobs for them; and a further large group who would like a job but for various reasons are not actively looking for work and cannot take the sort of jobs on offer. However, the 1988 Labour Force Survey shows that domestic and childcare responsibilities are the major barrier to women taking up employment, with health related problems being the major barrier for men. Other obstacles can be inadequate transport, lack of information and employer hiring practices. As well as restricting access to work however, these barriers can restrict the low-paid to low pay – often part-time employment – and ensure they never receive the training, education and experience which would increase their opportunities to climb the jobs ladder.

Active labour market and other policies to, for example, provide adequate child-care, cheap and reliable public transport and sheltered employment are all vital in assisting workers with skills to move out of low-paid employment.

The TUC's recent statement, 'Skills 2000', sets out proposals for a new approach to training which would both help ensure economic growth and competitiveness, and also help individual workers realise their potential. Undertraining is in fact evident throughout the jobs ladder. However, one group which particularly suffer from lack of access to training opportunities are women, who also feature predominantly among low paid and 'marginal' workers. The TUC has called for a range of measures, including women-only provision, special assistance to companies putting on courses to allow women to move to traditional male occupations, and childcare provision on government training courses. However, equally important is the work of trade unions, both inside and outside the National Council for Vocational Qualifications framework, to ensure that particular jobs are not defined in terms which effectively allow firms to segregate lower-paid women workers from higher-paid male workers in order to avoid the equal pay provisions, and also to ensure that the skills required for many jobs currently classified as unskilled and paid accordingly are fully recognized and rewarded.

Low Pay and Tax and Benefits

The shortcomings of the tax-benefit system are already well researched and documented by other bodies including the Institute for Fiscal Studies, the Child Poverty Action Group and the Low Pay Unit. In all the work that has been done on the present system two conclusions consistently emerge: firstly, that means-tested benefits – as opposed to universal benefits – provide an effective barrier for those dependent upon them to taking up employment opportunities; and secondly the present system of levying both employers' and employees' National Insurance contributions – the so-called 'hidden' tax – acts as a major disincentive to increased participation and better wage rates.

The issue of low pay cannot be divorced from the question of taxation and benefits. Low-paid workers in the past often received benefits in kind from employers, such as agricultural workers in tied accommodation: today such 'non-pecuniary' benefits are more common for higher-paid workers (e.g. company cars). Most low-paid workers receive income-related benefits from the state, and these can be a significant amount of household income. This obviously raises important policy issues concerning the impact of changes in tax, benefit, and earnings on low-income households, in terms of income distribution and labour force participation. Many of the government's 'supply side' measures depend on the incentive effects of reduced taxes but the evidence to support an incentive effect from tax cuts to date is hard to find. Recent work by Brown of the University of Stirling found no evidence that tax cuts for higher-income earners had any measurable impact (Brown, 1988). Cuts in basic rate tax (or raising tax thresholds) have relatively little impact on many low paid workers because often they have little or no taxable income. The tax which affects low-paid workers most is National Insurance, which unlike income tax is highly regressive and has a very high marginal rate for workers who just move over the threshold. When combined with the loss of means-tested benefits, the result is that household income can in extreme cases fall as a result of increased earnings (the 'poverty trap') and in any case the worker is subject to very high marginal tax rates.

The government has recognised the problem, and measures were introduced in the 1988 reforms of social security and the 1989 Budget reforms of National Insurance contributions. The changes fell far short of what was needed. Recent official estimates (given shortly before the April 1989 Budget) suggest that over ½ million 'heads of tax units' faced marginal tax rates of 70 per cent of more, and more recent work by A. B. Atkinson and H. Sutherland suggests the same is true for working married women, who are not usually heads of tax units (Atkinson and Sutherland, 1989). The practical effect is to deter low-paid and often part-time workers from taking on extra hours or seeking jobs which pay just above the National Insurance threshold. As the system by which employers have to pay contributions has not been reformed to improve its progressivity, the present system – notwithstanding the 1989 reforms – acts as an incentive for the creation of low-paid jobs just below the threshold. Work by the Institute of Fiscal Studies confirms that such a 'bunching' of earnings does in fact exist (Dilnot and Webb, 1989).

A number of reforms have been suggested by the Institute for Fiscal Studies and by A. B. Atkinson and others, and in 1989 the TUC argued along similar lines. The TUC argued in its 1989 Budget Submission for National Insurance contributions to be assessed only on earnings over the threshold; to introduce new banded rates; and to abolish the upper earnings limit. According to estimates by Atkinson, reform of National Insurance contributions alone could reduce the number of family heads facing marginal taxation rates of 70 per cent or more by a quarter and the number of married working women by nearly a half (Atkinson, 1988). Even after the 1989 Budget changes, reform of National Insurance contributions along these lines would still help reduce the unfair taxation of the low-paid, but it needs to be accompanied by an increase in non-means-tested benefits if the 'poverty trap' is to be eliminated. The TUC has actively campaigned for an immediate and significant increase in child benefit as one of the most effective ways of helping families with low-paid jobs. This would be of particular benefit to single parent families. Estimates by Atkinson and Sutherland published after the April 1989 Budget suggest that combining reform of national insurance with an increase in child benefit could reduce the number of family heads and wives facing very high marginal tax rates by 40 per cent (Atkinson and Sutherland, 1989).

These reforms, however, might increase the number of low-paid workers even though it reduced significantly the number of low-income households. Workers would have more incentive to take on extra hours of low-paid work, and employers would find it cheaper to employ more low-paid workers. A national minimum wage is therefore vital to offset these effects. Moreover, a national minimum wage *combined* with the tax and benefit reforms could significantly reduce dependency on means-tested benefits. A key factor which is more difficult to quantify is the impact of trade union bargaining strategies on the low-paid within the workplace.

3   TRADE UNIONS AND LOW PAY

The TUC has argued that the problem of low pay must be solved through a combination of long-term policies – the reform of taxes and benefits, active labour market policies and particularly training, and above all through the introduction of a statutory National Minimum Wage, a policy adopted by Congress in 1986. This change was brought about by the recognition that collective bargaining policies alone were not reducing the disparities and inequalities in pay, and that the growth of employment in areas outside the scope of traditional collective bargaining agreements was leaving increasing numbers of worker in highly vulnerable positions. The weakening, and now the potential abolition of Wages Councils, and the abolition of the Fair Wages Resolution and Schedule 11 all increased the perception of the growth of inequality in the 1980s, and this in turn provided the basis for a consensus within the trade union movement on an agreed approach to low pay. However, it would be wrong to give the impression that trade unions have proved ineffective. Trade unions do improve the pay of their members compared with non-members in similar occupations and industries. Overall, the union 'mark up' is estimated at 10 per cent, but 'sword of justice' effects have been identified for groups of workers often associated with low pay – notably women, the disabled, and ethnic minorities (Blanchflower and Oswald, 1988; Metcalf, 1989).

Social Justice

Interventions by the state have in part been based on a social consensus that there was a socially unacceptable level of pay below which no one should be asked to work. This was not simply in the interests of the workers: many employers in labour intensive industries recognized the value of enforceable agreements which prevented competitors undercutting them. Nonetheless, a sense of social justice has underpinned the statutory approach to low pay. An important distinction to make is between relative low pay and pay which in an absolute sense is too low. The TUC takes the view that issues of pay and income distribution need to be addressed in relative terms, in other words people should receive an income which allows a reasonable standard of living which is set with regard to the average prevailing in society at the time. This view has given rise to important concepts such as a 'living wage' and the 'poverty line'.

So far this analysis has concentrated on the economic issues surrounding the problem of low pay. Whilst the government may seek to justify low wages in economic terms, poverty is also a moral and social issue which trade unions have a legitimate and collective interest in reducing, and ultimately eliminating. The trade union movement is not just a wide social grouping but a mass movement with membership of over 9 million employees in all industries and occupations, with direct effects on the livelihood of many more millions in these members' families, and with indirect effects on the terms and conditions of workers generally. It can therefore, with much less pretence than many others, claim to be concerned about a 'common good' beyond its immediate needs and interests.

The trade union movement also has objectives of which the improvement in lives and livelihoods is paramount, and concepts such as 'fair pay for a fair day's work' or 'equal pay for work of equal value' or 'help for the low paid or most needy' are further expressions of this general social view. Principles obviously have to be applied with regard to the circumstances and cannot be pursued so singlemindedly as to exclude consideration of those very means – higher productivity, efficiency and competitiveness – on which attainment of the ends ultimately depends. Trade unions are not concerned about the position of the low-paid, or of workers generally, just from the standpoint of their pay. They are equally concerned about the standard and status of their jobs and about the waste of national resources implied by workers doing jobs well below their productive potential with no opportunities for advancement or development.

The Trade Union Response

There has been an extensive debate within the trade union movement about how best to approach the low-pay issue. One view is that statutory intervention undermines the role of collective bargaining and organizations, and trade unions can both raise the wages of low-paid workers and improve their relative position through negotiation. Other views however have pointed to the persistence of low pay and unequal income distribution, and the weak bargaining position of many low-paid workers in arguing in support of an interventionist approach. Yet another view has been that improving the relative position of low-paid workers in this way can be achieved only by worsening the relative position of better-paid workers – in effect squeezing differentials. The problem, it is argued, is essentially one of low income, not just low pay, and should be tackled through the tax and benefit system. Whilst to some degree this debate still continues within the trade union movement the adoption in 1986 of TUC policy on a Minimum Wage backed by legal force represents a major step forward. This reliance on statutory instruments, rather than collective bargaining procedures, was necessitated by the changing economic circumstances facing low-paid workers, not least the growth in inequality combined with a considerable reduction in their statutory protection. This and the development of related policies are dealt with in some detail below.

Solutions to the problem of low pay have to be seen in the context of objectives. For the trade union movement the fundamental objective is a decent income for all. This has led to the development of a fair wages strategy based on the twin pillars of collective bargaining and legislative support. Collective bargaining by itself will not be able to reach all those in poorly organized sectors where low pay so often prevails and that is why protective legislation will be needed to underpin a strategy for fair wages to eradicate low pay.

However, the government has been embarked on a programme of dismantling protective legislation, and, given the worsening problem of low pay, many of the trade unions with membership in low-pay sectors have been looking at ways of strengthening collective bargaining through better organization. For some unions the solution has been seen to be in mergers and amalgamations and a number of important initiatives have taken place in, for example, agriculture, textiles, and clothing. The TUC is also doing important new work in these areas under the auspices of the General Council's Special Review Body.

The problem of pay is complex and solutions have to be tailored accordingly. Some workers are low-paid because they lack skills. Some workers are low-paid because their skills are systematically undervalued. And many workers are low-paid because they lack the necessary trade union organization to resist unscrupulous employers. Where low pay is a product of lack of skill or the undervaluation of skills, collective bargaining should include the availability of training, uprating undervalued jobs and improvements in job content. Other measures can include the restructuring of pay to redistribute income, to improve basic pay and restructure grading scales. Because of labour market developments such as the growth of contracting out, part-time employment and the abolition of much protective legislation, it is now recognized by the trade union movement that an effective national minimum floor needs to be established below which no workers should fall. The TUC is therefore committed to the introduction of a National Minimum Wage backed by the force of law.

The TUC fully recognizes the practical implications of introducing a national minimum wage. Implementation via collective bargaining would help to ensure that the impact on costs was minimized to avoid a fall in employment. The TUC does not accept that there would be undue pressure on relativities and differentials. This is because low-paid groups tend to be concentrated in particular sectors and negotiators in higher-paid sectors do not in practice quote lower-paid groups in other sectors to which they are unrelated in occupation or pay structure. However, it could be argued that a general increase in the earnings of the low-paid, as envisaged with the introduction of a Minimum Wage, could affect the general level of pay settlements via perceptions of the going rate. With the introduction of a satisfactory Minimum Wage legislation unions will be expected to undertake not to quote in claims for higher-paid workers that element of general percentage increase in earnings relating to moves to attain the National Minimum Wage.

The TUC suggests that there is a lot to be learned from the example of Sweden where a 'solidaristic' wage policy emphasized the need for pay levels to be set across all industries. This represented a consensus view that the way to improve the industrial base was to make sure that the more efficient employers were not undercut by low-wage rivals, and instead had an incentive to improve productivity. Even if such a policy created short-term problems, the Swedish response was one of active labour market policies within a policy framework committed to full employment. By most standards, the Swedish approach has had some noticeable successes. Unemployment has remained very low, living standards and social benefits are high. The industrial strength of Sweden's export industries has also increased.

There are clearly important lessons to be learnt, concerning not only the importance of combining policies on minimum wages with labour market policies but also the central role of trade unions. A key element in the successful implementation of these policies was high union membership and a relatively centralised and concentrated trade union structure. Whilst the Swedish model might not provide a comprehensive blueprint for the UK, it is important to note that Swedish employers welcomed these policies to improve minimum wage levels since they prevented unfair competition based on wage undercutting, which in turn aided expansion and enabled employers to improve standards.

It must be stressed that action to tackle low pay and the introduction of a national minimum wage are part of a wider strategy to achieve fair wages throughout the wages structure. Key elements in legislation to achieve this would be:

- a national minimum wage;
- restored and strengthened powers for Wages Councils, and extended coverage by Wages Councils;
- reintroduction of Schedule 11-type arrangements;
- a restored Fair Wages Resolution of Parliament;
- an end to compulsory contracting out of public services and to privatization;
- comparability machinery for the public sector and consideration of the need to extend this to the private sector;
- a renewed debate about the distribution of incomes generally, including the highest paid.

The TUC is also undertaking work in considering ways to improve the lot of female workers. In 1985 there were an estimated 960,000 one-parent families in the UK most of which were headed by women. Concern grows about the increasing emergence of an underclass of mainly female, lone parents who are effectively forced out of the labour market by, on the one hand, low wage rates, and on the other, a tax–benefit system that entraps them into dependence. Whilst the reforms suggested elsewhere in this chapter would undoubtedly reduce the number of lone parents in this category, genuine access to the labour market will be ensured only if both government and employees adopt a much more positive stance. Whilst the TUC welcomes initiatives by employers to encourage women to enter and re-enter the labour market, this is no substitute for comprehensive public provision of childcare facilities. This would need to be combined with other benefits such as statutory maternity leave and favourable employment conditions including more flexible working hours, school term time contracts and equal rights for part-timers.

The Equal Pay Act came into force in 1975. Following a European Court ruling, the Act was amended with effect from January 1984 to incorporate provisions for 'equal pay for work of equal value'. At that time the TUC criticized the amended Act and asked the government to make more radical changes. Experience has shown the TUC's doubts about the amended Act to have been justified. In particular, the procedure for claiming equal pay for work of equal value is unnecessarily complex and lengthy. And after four years important aspects of interpretation of the law are still unclear.

The TUC is still pressing the government to change the law to make it easier for women to pursue equal pay cases. Meanwhile, however, unions can still use the Equal Pay Act in their attempts to win equal pay for their women members – either by taking up cases or, more importantly, through collective bargaining. In August 1988 the TUC issued guidelines for union negotiators to help them pursue claims under the Act.

The European Social Dimension

Of course full implementation of a fair wages strategy requires legislation. The present UK government is continuing to dismantle protective legislation. The outright abolition of Wages Councils, which set out statutory minimum rates for over 2 million workers is currently under consideration. This would leave the UK as virtually the only country is Europe without any form of minimum wage protection. In these circumstances it should be no surprise that the British trade union movement is looking to the European Community to bring us back into line with the rest of Europe and with ILO Conventions which the UK Government has renounced.

It is of course the Social Charter of basic rights which provides the focus. Proposals are at an early stage but the TUC is looking for European Directives to give legislative force to implement the calls in the draft Charter for workers rights to membership of a trade union to be covered by a collective agreement, and the right to a decent wage. At the request of the TUC the European Trade Union Institute is undertaking a survey of minimum wage protection in European countries, the effectiveness of this, and national trade union policies for tackling low pay. It is the TUC's hope that this work might form the basis for further developing European level policy on low pay via the European Trade Union Confederation.

4　CONCLUSIONS

The trade union perspective on low pay is clearly based on a sense of social justice – that in an advanced industrialized society there should be a consensus about acceptable pay levels and minimum incomes. Were that the sum total of the trade union perspective, however, it would be an honourable but limited one. There are sound economic arguments for tackling low pay. The trade union perspective is that low pay is not only unjust, it is a major handicap to future economic progress.

The problem of low pay is a complex one and there are no easy or simplistic solutions. Low pay cannot be solved by the tax and benefit system alone, nor simply through a statutory Minimum Wage, nor by trade union bargaining. A combination of all three, however, combined with active labour market policies designed to improve both the supply of, and access to, better paid employment opportunities for the low-paid and those trapped in a choice between low-paid work and unemployment will allow significant progress to be made.

The main points from the above arguments are set out below:

1. Low pay is not confined to the traditional 'sweatshop' industries but is also common in parts of the public sector: TUC definitions suggest that up to a quarter of the workforce is low paid, and most of these are women.

2. Low pay is a major cause of under-investment in both human and physical capital, and hence of low growth, low productivity and reduced competitiveness in the economy as a whole.

3. For Britain to succeed in the 1990s, resources must be moved from low-productivity to high-productivity sectors: tackling low pay must be combined with policies directed towards investment, training, and research and development and innovation if this strategy is to succeed.

4. Low pay cannot be tackled by free collective bargaining procedures alone: many low-paid workers are outside the scope of traditional agreements, others have reduced bargaining power.

5. Action is needed in three key areas to tackle low pay and the associated problems of poverty as part of a long-term and combined approach: tax and benefit reform, active labour market policies, and a National Minimum Wage.

6. On taxes and benefits, priority should be given to reforming National Insurance contributions and boosting non-means-tested benefits.

7. Active labour market policies are needed – on training and education, on childcare provision, on accessible public transport, on sheltered employment provision – to allow workers to move up the 'jobs ladder'.

8. A national minimum wage should be introduced. The initial level would depend on discussions with government about what would be an appropriate level under the circumstances of the time. The Labour Party, for example, has recently recommended an initial level of half median male manual earnings.

Appendix 1: Minimum Wage Systems in Europe[2]

Country	System	Age	Details
Belgium	Salaire minimum interprofessionel garanti	21.5	– Nationally agreed at annual tripartite negotiations – Index-linked – Workers between 16 and 21.5 entitled to a per cent of minimum – Part time workers covered on pro rata basis
Denmark	Minimallon	18.0	– Supplemented by 'normallon' which sets basic rates by collective agreement – Covers most of the workforce
France	Salaire minimum interprofessionel de croissance	18.0	– Statutory minimum – Index-linked – Workers between 16 and 18 entitled to per cent of minimum – Covers all workers
Spain	Salario minimo interprofessionnel		– Nationally agreed at annual tripartite negotiations – Index-linked – Workers between 16 and 18 covered by graduated system
West Germany		18.0	– 90 per cent of workforce covered by legally binding collective agreements
Greece		18.0	– Laid down by national collective agreement (19 for white collar workers) – Workers in training and under 18/19 entitled to a per cent of the minimum

Country	System	Age	Details
Ireland		20.0	– Similar to UK with Joint Labour Committees covering certain sectors – Over 50 agreements setting a legal minimum rate for an industry
Luxemburg	Salaire social minimum	18.0	– Statutory minimum – Index-linked – Covers full-time and part-time workers – Workers between 15 and 18 entitled to a per cent of minimum
Netherlands	Wet minimumloon	23.0	– Statutory minimum wage – Workers between 15 and 22 entitled to a per cent of minimum
Portugal	Salario minimo nacional	20.0	– Statutory minimum wage – Covers full- and part-time workers – Workers between 18 and 20 entitled to a per cent of minimum

Notes

1. Produced by the Economic Department of the TUC, September 1989.
2. Adapted from Minford (1989).

References

Atkinson, A. B. (1988) 'Restructuring National Insurance Contributions', *Fabian Society Taxation Background Paper*, 2 (December) (London: Fabian Society).
Atkinson, A. B. and Sutherland, H. (1989) 'Taxation the Poverty Trap, and the 1989 Budget', *Fabian Society Taxation Background Paper*, 4 (April) (London: Fabian Society).
Blanchflower, D. and Oswald, A. (1988) *'The Economic Effects of Britain's Trade Unions'* (London: Employment Institute).
Brown, Chuck (1988) 'Will the 1988 income tax cuts either increase work incentives or raise more revenue?', *Fiscal Studies* 9 (4) (November).
Dilnot, A. and Webb, S. (1989) 'Reforming NICs' *Fiscal Studies* 10 (2) (May).
Metcalf, D. (1989) *'Can Unions Survive in the Private Sector?'* (London: Employment Institute).
Minford, M. (1989) 'Minimum Wage in Europe – is Britain out of line', *Low Pay Review* 37 (Summer): 20–37.
National Economic Development Council (NEDC) (1987) *'The British Labour Market and Unemployment'*, NEDC (87) 16 (London: NEDC).
National Economic Development Office (NEDO) (1988) *Young People and the Labour Market – A Challenge for the 1990s* (London: NEDO).
Steedman, H. and Wagner, K. (1987) 'A second look at productivity, machinery and skills in Britain and Germany', *NIESR Review* (November).
Steedman, H. and Wagner, K. (1989) 'Productivity machinery and skills: clothing manufacture in Britain and Germany', *NIESR Review* (May).

9 Incentives for the Low-Paid: The Issues for Public Policy

Alex Bowen and Ken Mayhew

1 INTRODUCTION

The general theme of the first National Economic Development Office Policy Seminar was to consider ways of bringing those who are low-paid into more effective competition in the labour market. It considered not only those who earn little from employment, but those of the unemployed or the economically inactive who would probably be low-earners if they got jobs. Improving incentives and removing obstacles to obtaining employment and to working harder or better or for longer hours could be one way of utilizing more effectively the nation's human capital and thus improving the supply side performance of the British economy. This concluding chapter seeks to draw attention to some of the most powerful arguments raised by the contributors, paying particular attention to the major policy issues. The comments of the authors and other participants at the seminar were very helpful in identifying these issues.

The papers presented at the seminar identified several intertwined strands of thought concerning incentives for the low-paid. First, there is analysis of the factors determining a person's decision to participate in labour market activities. Second, many of the same factors influence that person's preferred choice of hours and level of work intensity. These individual supply side decisions are made within a structure of financial incentives built by the processes of pay determination and by the government's tax and benefit systems. The National Economic Development Office's paper (Chapter 1 in this volume) provides a survey of the academic literature in this area. One of the most important themes of the seminar was the analysis of the consequences of taxes and benefits. Many of their effects are unintended and discourage labour market activity, but they can also provide levers for the public authorities to improve the utilization of the labour force. All the papers address this question, but it took centre stage in those by Tony Atkinson and Holly Sutherland, Hermione Parker and Patrick Minford (Chapters 2, 3 and 4). These authors consider in detail a number of radically different reforms with a range of implications for efficiency and equity, low net pay and poverty. However, concentration on such matters should not obscure the prior question of how pay and job offers are determined. The role of the demand side of the labour market and how demand and supply interact constitute a third strand of the issues unravelled at the seminar. The papers by the CBI and the TUC (Chapters 7 and 8) are particularly relevant here, reflecting the central importance of pay and employment questions for these organizations. The final strand is about how people do and should be able to improve their productive potential. The papers by Ewart Keep and Paul Ryan (Chapters 5 and 6) focus on this, developing the notion that Britain is in danger of being trapped in a low-skills–low-quality equilibrium. The TUC and CBI both stress that practical measures are needed to improve training, although they disagree about the merits of a National Minimum Wage. This final chapter draws out the main areas of agreement and disagreement concerning all these strands of thought. The implications for public policy are discussed.

2 HOW RESPONSIVE ARE PEOPLE TO INCENTIVES?

The standard economic analysis of the labour supply decision focuses on the responsiveness of individuals to changes in their rates of (post-tax) pay and in the income they receive if they do not work.

For most men, the decision as to whether to seek a full-time job at all is determined largely by age (and the answer to the question of whether study or retirement is an attractive alternative) and state of health. When discussing labour supply responsiveness for those actually in the labour force it is necessary to distinguish between the substitution effect of a change in the net wage and the income effect. An increase in a man's net wage rate tilts the trade-off he faces between work and leisure in favour of work – the substitution effect. For men, the average estimate of the responsiveness of labour supply from this source to changes in the net wage implies that an increase in a man's net wage of 10 per cent might increase the number of hours he would like to supply by around 1½ per cent (the National Economic Development Office's Chapter 1 reviews the sometimes conflicting evidence). On the other hand, the increase in total income received for any given amount of work which is made possible by the increase in the wage rate encourages him to take more leisure, and, in some circumstances, this income effect can outweigh the substitution effect. But if a tax or benefit reform is designed to remove upward steps in the schedule of marginal tax rates, the substitution effect can be expected to dominate. The evidence suggests that quite large positive labour supply responses might be obtained if the reduction in effective marginal tax rates is big enough (for instance, from around 90 per cent in the poverty trap to the 34 per cent facing standard rate taxpayers). However, estimates (which are themselves uncertain) of responsiveness to small changes in net income are probably an even more unreliable guide to responses when there are large changes in net income. Also, it should be borne in mind that hours of work are not very flexible for full-time workers, at least within a given job. They tend to be determined by collective bargaining arrangements or unilaterally by employers, but the empirical analysis of labour supply has yet to consider fully the implications of this.

Minford (Chapter 4) has found some evidence that both the unemployed and higher-earners may be more responsive than average; the latter finding in particular may be quantitatively important for output if high earnings are an indication of high productivity. Other researchers have noted that young men, too, may be more responsive. Alternative activities offering people a similar degree of satisfaction are readily available for some groups, such as potential students, potential retirees, and those unemployed who believe they can earn little more in work than they receive from unemployment and other state benefits. Incentives can be important to those at such margins of economic activity. The unemployment margin has been much studied and most of the evidence suggests that the aggregate unemployment rate is not strongly related to replacement rates (that is, the ratio of income received out of work to the income expected if employed, which necessarily differs according to personal circumstances). The other margins have been studied less closely in Britain, although some work has been done on the determinants of participation in education, for instance. The ageing of the labour force is an important issue (see, *inter alia*, the work of the National Economic Development Office and the Training Agency, 'Defusing the Demographic Time Bomb', the National Economic Development Office, 1989), as is its level of educational attainment, and so more investigation is desirable. What are the quantitative effects on labour force participation of different proposals for student loans and grants, training grants, the extension of higher education and youth/adult wage differentials? How do different types of pension arrangements affect the desire to retire? If greater flexibility in choice of retirement age were encouraged, what would be the consequences for the labour force?

The estimates of labour supply responsiveness for women are more varied than those for men, but are generally larger. Here again, the question is how people behave at one of the margins of economic activity. Mothers with young children show a lower degree of responsiveness then those whose children have grown up, because the advantages are less finely balanced for them; the family role is more dominant. But several participants at the seminar drew attention to the fact that the balance can be altered by public policy, in particular by the provision of child care assistance – crèches, child tax allowances – which reduces the financial costs of entering the labour force. The different measures are likely to have different consequences for families at different levels of income. Factors such as these are often not taken into account when responsiveness estimates are made.

One may conclude that financial incentives can affect the supply of labour, but much more so with some groups in society than with others. Many of the groups most likely to respond are actually or potentially low-paid. The design of tax and benefit changes to provide the correct financial incentives must take into account the fact that giving people a higher income without making the trade-off between work and leisure more favourable to work is likely to encourage people to want to work fewer hours (this is less important if people are still working fewer hours than they would like). However, given the very large changes in tax and benefit withdrawal rates which are sometimes proposed for people caught in the poverty trap, potential labour supply responses can be large, despite low labour supply elasticities. Neither should it be forgotten that there are non-financial incentives which can be used to make work more attractive, such as changes in the scope of employment protection legislation.

3 HOW MANY PEOPLE ARE AFFECTED?

How many people are at each of the relevant margins of economic activity? This is not an easy question to answer since it depends in a complex way on each individual's age, experience, education, sources of non-work income (e.g. social security benefits) and family responsibilities, as well as how well he or she understands the constraints and opportunities prevailing. The usual procedure is to try to estimate how many people are caught in the 'poverty trap', where working longer hours or in a more highly-paid job hardly increases post-tax family income, and in the 'unemployment trap', where finding a job similarly does not help boost net income much. Parker reminds us about the existence of other traps such as the 'disability trap' (invalidity benefits being clawed back) and the 'savings trap' (where savings reduce benefits paid). There are many circumstances in which someone who works harder or longer, or acquires new skills, does not receive a net return which approaches the return to society. When people do not claim the benefits to which they are entitled in the first place, they are less likely to be caught in an incentive trap, but at the cost of being worse off. Take-up rates as low as 50 per cent are not unknown with means-tested benefits.

Atkinson and Sutherland (Chapter 2) concentrate on the 'poverty trap', which they characterize in terms of the 'poverty mountain' which the low-paid have to climb. They review the evidence on the number of people affected (the precise figure depends on assumptions about benefit take-up rates and the definition of a 'marginal' increase in income). Perhaps around 400 000 workers who are heads of families face marginal tax and benefit withdrawal rates of 70 per cent or more (to which should be added other working members of these families). So only a small proportion of workers is caught in the conventionally defined poverty trap. However, a number of workers may have adjusted their labour supply so that their incomes fall below the poverty trap range. Their spouses may have decided on non-participation as well. Here it is worth noting that international comparisons suggest that there is still scope for more women and more over-55s to participate in the labour market in Britain. Bringing participation rates up to American levels, for example, would increase the British labour force by around 1 million women and 200 000 over-55s (with overlap of the two groups, of course). These figures provide a guide to the potential for increasing labour supply (in the form of full-time or part-time work) by improving incentives. In addition, there are still demand constraints stopping many people, including the involuntarily unemployed, working as many hours as they want at prevailing wage rates.

The CBI's paper (Chaper 7) looks in some detail at who are the lower-paid in employment. Young workers tend to be low-paid, but in general this is simply because they are to be found at the foot of job ladders. People with few skills, poor health, and broken employment histories are also at the higher risk of receiving low pay and thus women are more at risk than men. Part-timers tend to be paid less per hour as well as in total. The CBI emphasize that low pay is not to be equated with poverty; many of the low-paid (particularly amongst young people and part-timers) are secondary earners in families where the income per head is not low. However, lack of access to any paid employment is a major contributory cause of poverty and the overlap between the people at the margins of economic activity and the poor is considerable. It is when efforts to relieve poverty interact with labour market prospects that labour supply disincentives tend to be a problem.

4   REFORMS TO THE TAX AND BENEFIT SYSTEMS

Powerful disincentives arise in the tax and benefit systems, in the form of high marginal tax and benefit withdrawal rates. One source of the problem is that many benefits are subject to a means test, so that if earned income increases, benefits are reduced. This is a characteristic of any system which attempts to aim individual benefits at the poor or low-paid. The problem has been exacerbated by low tax thresholds brought about by the failure to index fully income taxes to real income growth over the post-war period as a whole, though this has not been a feature of the last ten years. The alternative approach of paying benefits at a fixed rate and clawing them back from the better off (including many recipients of those very benefits) through the tax system implies a much larger role for the government in the distribution of income and higher income tax rates to finance the payments (reducing disincentives considerably for a few but increasing them somewhat for many more). The greater the degree of redistribution attempted, the more acute are the difficulties of both approaches. Many of the contributions in this book have been concerned with locating the best trade-off between them.

Minford (Chapter 4) considers various reforms which have been proposed to release the unemployment trap and the poverty trap. To deal with the former, he favours a stiffer test of the involuntary nature of an unemployment spell and some move towards 'workfare', where receipt of state payments is conditional on willingness to accept employment or approved training. To deal with the poverty trap, he advocates maintaining the maximum benefit entitlements constant in real terms so that these will fall in relation to growing average earnings. This allows the rate of benefit withdrawal facing people in the poverty trap to be reduced. One way of doing this is to increase the earnings threshold at which benefits cease to be paid as the real economy grows in such a way as to keep the numbers in the trap constant. The lively discussion of the Minford chapter centred on the following issues:

1. Is it plausible to believe that the long run implication of the Minford plan, a substantial fall in the relative value of benefits, would be politically acceptable?
2. Can we avoid explicit value judgements about the implications of such schemes for the distribution of income? Minford appeals to the 'median voter' argument, that one should adopt the value judgements of the typical voter in one's analysis, as these determine the outcomes of political processes. Can one establish what those value judgements are, and is this an accurate representation of how decisions about taxes and benefits are actually taken?
3. Is it possible to work out the consequences of tax–benefit changes by looking at a 'typical' family, or is it necessary to investigate the impact of changes on a large range of family types? Atkinson and Sutherland believe that a representative sample of family types should be studied.
4. Can taxes and benefits be shifted on to employers by altering what gross wages are negotiated? The provision of generous child benefits, for instance, may reduce the pressure from employees in wage bargaining, so that the benefits end up partly as a hidden subsidy to employers. Thus the theory of tax incidence needs to be considered more carefully.

The chapter by Atkinson and Sutherland (Chapter 2) uses the London School of Economics tax–benefit model TAXMOD to investigate the 'poverty mountain', and considers the likely consequences of various reforms such as increasing the real value of child benefit, introducing a partial basic income, and restructuring National Insurance contributions. They discuss the issues of focusing benefits, the phenomenon of "churning", in which some households find they receive benefits which in effect are clawed back through a higher tax rate, and benefit take-up rates. Increasing child benefit is an attractive option in many respects. It has very high take-up rates and helps families; it is large families who are disproportionately at risk of being in poverty. At the same time, because it is not means tested, relieving poverty this way does not tip the trade-off between work and leisure towards leisure. On the contrary, by removing families from reliance on Family Credit, it can do the opposite. In the particular example which they investigate in detail, an increase in child benefit of £7.30, balanced by a reduction in Family Credit of the same amount and combined with a payment of £10 per week to all families with children, would reduce the number of Family Credit recipients by two thirds. This option would cost over £7 billion, implying a considerable increase in standard tax rates to finance it. Their approach is rather different from Minford's, being based on a much more detailed model, but one which some conference participants felt ignores the efficiency losses (from adverse labour supply responses) which are of central concern to Minford. Other participants stressed the possible importance of the total gross tax burden and raised the question of whether benefits cause the very sort of behaviour they are supposed to be directed against (particularly as monitoring the behaviour of recipients is difficult); in other words, the creation of a 'dependency culture'. As a practical matter, many argued that some set of agreed conventions is needed in presenting comparisons of potential reforms (for example, what does 'revenue neutral' mean and how should 'tax expenditures' be treated?).

Parker (Chapter 3) expounds the concept of Basic Income and her preferred version of the Basic Income Guarantee (BIG). Her disagreement with Minford about what BIG means illustrates the need to establish a consensus about how proposed tax–benefit reforms are described and compared. She advocates partial integration of the tax and benefit systems, but *not* a negative income tax; a negative income tax, centrally operated, does not permit benefits to be tailored sufficiently closely to particular family needs. These can change more rapidly than the tax system can respond. The transfer income which everyone would receive under BIG should be combined with cash help for job creation, training, and child care. The set of measures she recommends might be described as a 'family policy', and she draws attention to the disguised 'separation bonuses' which currently exist in the interaction of the tax and benefit systems. There is some danger in the view of some seminar participants that such schemes could turn into subsidies for employers (back to Speenhamland?).

Parker reminds us of the importance of non-quantifiable disincentives and the need to set tax and benefits systems in their social context. She argues:

> If people with low earnings potential are to be re-integrated into mainstream society, one of the first priorities is to consult those most affected. The existing tax and benefit systems are out of touch with the way people at the bottom actually live.

Part-time work, carried out predominantly by women, is another area where it is very easy to alter the balance of advantage facing people who have already shown by their choice of activity that they are at a margin of economic participation. Several chapters refer to the disparate tax and benefit treatment of part-time workers. There are several rights at work which are not available to those working fewer than 8 hours per week and which are obtained only after a longer qualifying period by those working between 8 and 16 hours per week. Some of these, such as guaranteed paid leave and maternity pay, affect the remuneration package. Workers face an 86p entrance charge to the National Insurance Contribution system if their gross earnings reach £43 per week, plus an effective marginal tax rate of 9 per cent in the form of National Insurance contributions up to the Upper Earnings Limit. This kink in the tax system is most likely to discourage extra work by part-timers. On grounds of economic efficiency, uniform treatment is desirable. At the moment, part-time work over a certain number of hours per week is discouraged. There may be more scope for part-time work as a transition stage between full-time participation and being entirely out of the labour force, for instance amongst young people also receiving training or general education, and amongst older people considering retirement.

5   THE ROLE OF TRAINING

So far as we have discussed the financial incentives or disincentives, as well as barriers like lack of child care provision, which might affect labour market decisions. Other chapters in the book consider how individuals might make themselves or be helped to make themselves more marketable. In particular the chapters by Keep and Ryan (Chapters 5 and 6) are concerned with the role of training. Whatever our vocational education and training system is failing to deliver for the low paid, this has to be placed in the context of its more general deficiencies. Concern has been voiced in several quarters including the National Economic Development Office that (according to some criteria) the UK appears to lag behind several of its major competitors in the area of vocational education and training (see, for instance, 'Competence and Competition', NEDO, 1984, and 'The Supply of Skills: Some Questions', NEDC Paper 88(12)). As Keep shows, this applies to aspects of the secondary and tertiary education system, to youth training and to adult training and development. During the last few years, commentators have turned increasingly to diagnosis of what is a long-standing and deep-seated problem. Unsurprisingly it has come to be characterized not simply as one of the insufficient supply of skills, but also as one of insufficient demand for them. There are a number of indicators of this, such as the sluggish response of skill differentials to skill shortages and evidence that employers fill vacancies by relaxing skill standards. Keep argues that much of British industry is trapped in what could be called in a low-skills low-quality equilibrium in which our producers rely on a competitive strategy based on low costs, thus occupying the low end of the market both in terms of products produced and skills required. If in the long term Britain's trading future relies on competing at the high end, then entire corporate strategies have to change and the UK's vocational education and training problem can be tackled effectively only as part of such a change. In the meantime there is an insufficient demand for skills. In a world where it is impossible for an employer to be sure of capturing all the returns to a training investment, purely private employer funding will not deliver as much training as the country needs. The question is where the extra funding should come from and to whom it should be directed.

Ryan considers the issue of training specifically for low-paid adults. He argues that the case for enhancing training opportunities for this group depends upon the answers to three questions:

1. Do they have fewer skills than other employees?
2. Can they benefit from more skills?
3. Do they themselves want more skills?

He shows that the low-paid are particularly deficient in those skills, certified by a formal qualification, which are most transferable. Any uncertified and informal skills, which they often possess in considerable quantities, tend to be in demand only in firms paying relatively low wages. Whether or not they will benefit from more training depends in part on the nature of the labour market. Labour economists distinguish between 'competitive' labour markets and 'segmented' ones. In the former, individuals who improve their skills can readily translate this into higher productivity and hence higher pay. In the latter, the low-paid can be trapped in dead-end jobs, where productivity is determined by the design of the job itself and is unlikely to be increased by the acquisition of further skills, unless they can move to a different employer. Nevertheless Ryan concludes from American and British evidence that training does benefit most of the low-paid who undertake it, but that (unlike others) the low-paid in fact often do have to change employers in order to realize the benefits.

Ryan finds that, although there may be some problems of low aspirations, the low paid actually do want to acquire more skills where there is a demonstrable link between skill acquisition and improved pay. Thus the issues become whether they can get it and at what cost. Low-paid men, he argues, receive less training than their better-paid counterparts, but the position is more equivocal for low-paid women. Poor provision by employers is the predominant reason for this, but the alternative route of 'self-sponsorship' has been of limited assistance because of problems of access, finance and motivation. The low paid are particularly badly placed to assess the merits of an investment, to cope with the risks involved and to find the necessary finance.

6   TRAINING AND THE STRUCTURE OF LABOUR MARKETS

Both Ryan and Keep relate their discussions of these issues to consideration of the nature of the labour markets in which the training might take place. Three types of market are distinguished: the 'occupational', the 'internal' and the 'secondary'. The occupational labour market is characterized by certified and transferable skills and is where individual sponsorship of training is most appropriate. The 'internal' labour market is where employers are often concerned with developing skills at least in part specific to their own enterprises. They may thus be suspicious of or unresponsive to outsiders with certified and general skills applying for jobs and of insiders who try to acquire such skills and who thus become more attractive to other employers. Secondary markets consist of workers with the sort of dead-end jobs mentioned earlier where, as a matter of policy, the employer makes little provision for training of any sort.

In the present environment, Ryan argues, self-sponsorship is the most viable route for the low-paid to acquire more skills. But it is a route which is costly and risky. It is risky because, having acquired skills, an individual may find it difficult to find a job vacancy with employers who operate internal labour markets, and because if the individual is already employed he may find himself in difficulties with his present employer. The latter risk, Ryan argues, could be mitigated by introducing statutory rights to training leave. Costs to firms and trainees could be reduced by an extension of the Career Development Loans Scheme and of other public subsidies (such as those to the Further Education system) but the cost to the public purse should not be forgotten. It is not estimated by Ryan.

Keep and the CBI also suggest more help to the individual. Keep mentions the possibilities of tax incentives to employees who pay for their own training, and advocates the extension of initiatives such as the Department of Education and Science's REPLAN. Keep goes on to argue that a better base of initial education and training is needed, not only to provide an adequate foundation for subsequent training, but also to provide the motivation for undertaking it. The CBI describe their 'Careership' proposals designed to achieve this end. These proposals are for all 16-year-olds entering the labour market to be given an education and training credit from the Government and an employment contract from the employer. Though there was general agreement that more needed to be done to encourage youth education and training, there was much disagreement as to precisely how this should be achieved. Some, for example, were worried that, unless the CBI's scheme was extended to those who remained in full-time education, there would be an undesirable distortion of the decision between entering school/college and work. More generally, there was disagreement about the necessary extent of public funding, and about the proportion which should go to individuals and the proportion which should go to companies. This disagreement was fuelled by uncertainty about the size of the costs involved.

A number of participants, echoing Ryan, were concerned that increasing training on its own would be relatively ineffective because substantial proportions of the low-paid were trapped in secondary labour markets, where employers design jobs to be unskilled and therefore not only have little interest in training their own workers but also have little incentive to hire those already trained. Though many participants rejected extreme segmentationist views, many more accepted the more moderate line that there was a systematic under-demand for skills: the low-quality–low-skill problem. They were sympathetic, therefore, to the view expressed by Keep that a major push to change employer attitudes is necessary. Keep suggests a number of possibilities which include:

1. encouraging key public sector employers to be exemplars of good training practice;
2. making the award of government contracts conditional on firms demonstrating high training standards;
3. exploiting supply chains so that good practice companies can influence others;
4. persuading more unions to make training a central issue in bargaining;
5. introducing statutory underpinning of training rights.

The TUC study (Chapter 8) contains a still more controversial proposal for breaking out of any low-quality/low-skills equilibrium: the introduction of a National Minimum Wage. Its proponents saw it as a way of moving to a high-pay/high-productivity economy; if people are paid more, it forces employers to adopt a strategy to make their workers more skilled and productive. Its opponents argued that this was putting the cart before the horse. High wages should follow high productivity, and not precede it. A minimum wage would cause either unemployment or, if more highly-paid workers acted to restore their differentials, inflation.

7 CONCLUSIONS

Discussion at the seminar was wide-ranging, including speculation about the form future reforms should take as well as differing appraisals of the present situation. Some participants gave a greater weight to achieving what they regarded as a more just society while others stressed the need for a more efficient economy. Although the National Economic Development Office organized the seminar in order to explore how to achieve greater efficiency, the two sets of considerations cannot be perfectly separated. Whatever an individual's set of values, there are likely to be courses of action which would increase efficiency but which he or she would not undertake because that would offend these values. Notwithstanding this, there were considerable areas of common ground.

- Though labour supply responsiveness in general is low, there are probably particular groups of people at various margins where the responsiveness is higher. The tax and benefit systems still contain high rates of effective marginal taxation for many of these groups, and thus potential disincentives. To a degree, this is the inevitable consequence of a means-tested benefit system. Whilst the commonly-studied poverty and unemployment traps remain important, stress was placed on the difficulties experienced by lone parents and the problems of married women wishing to return to work. Given the projected shortage of youth labour, a number of participants also talked of the need to increase the financial incentives for older workers to remain in their jobs or to return to employment.

- Training is one route to more effective competition for the low-paid. Opinion was varied as to whether, if more government funding was forthcoming, this should be directed mainly at the individual or the employer. However there was particular emphasis on direct funding of the individual, for adults as well as for young people. It was argued that, important though they were, specific measures to improve vocational education and training were bound to have only a limited impact. Such doubts stemmed from the nature of the jobs which the low paid did. Some models (segmentationist) of the labour market describe a secondary sector of jobs which are designed to be low-skilled and non-career. Even if this concept of segmentation is rejected, then there is a wider acceptance of the possibility of a low-skills/low-quality equilibrium. As long as this persists, the structure of jobs itself may militate against any improvement in the position of many of the low paid.

What types of policy change are implied by the areas of agreement mapped out above? Particular policy proposals are elaborated in more detail in the contributions to this volume, together with detailed discussions of their merits and pitfalls. Here it may be useful to focus on a small number of general proposals which found favour with many of the authors in this volume and the participants at the seminar:

1. *An increase in the real value of child benefit.* This was proposed by the CBI, the TUC and Parker and viewed favourably in Atkinson and Sutherland's article (see pp. 251–2, p. 271; p. 111; pp. 66–7). It is widely regarded as a well-aimed benefit (in the sense of reaching a large proportion of the target population), with desirable labour supply incentive effects for many (but not all) in the various benefit traps. It could be an important part of a new family policy along the lines proposed by Parker. However, its costs to the Exchequer would be considerable.

2. *An increase in earnings disregards (and other thresholds) when benefits of all sorts are calculated.* This too could improve incentives by reducing effective marginal tax rates for the low paid. The CBI and TUC stress this (see pp. 254; pp. 270–1). It would also strike a blow against the black economy, reducing the risk of eroding social cohesion to which NEDO's Director General draws attention in his foreword. The problem of the upward step in effective tax rates when the earnings disregard is exhausted would, however, remain, and increasing the disregards would raise the number of people in the poverty trap.

3. *Improved flexibility in the choice of hours.* Part-time employment has increased dramatically in the UK over recent years. However, as Atkinson and Sutherland demonstrate (see pp. 58–9), there are still aspects of the tax and benefit systems which discourage work over certain thresholds in the number of hours per week. There have been some reforms in this area recently, notably through changes in the National Insurance Contribution system. The extension of terms and conditions applicable to full-timers to part-timers would help.

4. *Reducing the barriers to labour force entry.* There is scope for more participation, probably part-time, by people in several demographic categories currently facing powerful financial and other disincentives. Women with young children, for instance, would find it easier to work if more child care facilities were provided. Parker and the TUC have specific proposals (see pp. 109–10; 279).

5. *An increased training effort, including greater government funding.* Many employers of the low-paid have little incentive at the moment to provide training, so, as Ryan argues, more government assistance is probably needed to help the low paid increase their earnings capacity. Cooperative arrangements among employers should be encouraged too. The new Training and Enterprise Councils have an important responsibility in this respect.

6.	*Adoption of a high-skills/high-quality product strategy by firms.*
	In the medium term this is necessary if firms are to be encouraged
	to train and generate a greater proportion of new jobs which are
	not low-paid. Keep reviews the relevant arguments (see pp. 148–
	50). This is also highly desirable for the sake of British productiv-
	ity growth and international competitiveness.

Index

Tables and graphs are shown in **bold** type.

299